LB2342.2.C3 P74 2005

Preparing for
  post-secondary education
     c2005.

D0648609

PREPARING FOR POST-SECONDARY EDUCATION

0134108024441

CHALLIS RESOURCE LIBRARY
CONFEDERATION COLLEGE

0000
72.00

JUN 1 2 2006

Preparing for
Post-Secondary Education

New Roles for Governments
and Families

Edited by
ROBERT SWEET
and
PAUL ANISEF

280101

DEC 8 2005

McGill-Queen's University Press
Montreal & Kingston · London · Ithaca

© McGill-Queen's University Press 2005
ISBN 0-7735-2963-2

Legal deposit fourth quarter 2005
Bibliothèque nationale du Québec

Printed in Canada on acid-free paper that is 100% ancient forest free (100% post-consumer recycled), processed chlorine free.

This book has been published thanks to a grant from Human Resources and Skills Development Canada (Canada Education Savings Program).

McGill-Queen's University Press acknowledges the support of the Canada Council for the Arts for our publishing program. We also acknowledge the financial support of the Government of Canada through the Book Publishing Industry Development Program (BPIDP) for our publishing activities.

The opinions expressed in this publication are those of the authors and do not necessarily reflect the policies or views of the Government of Canada.

Library and Archives Canada Cataloguing in Publication

Preparing for post-secondary education: new roles for governments and families / edited by Robert Sweet and Paul Anisef.
ISBN 0-7735-2963-2

1. Education, Higher – Canada – Finance. 2. Postsecondary education – Canada – Finance. 3. Education, Higher – Parent participation – Canada. 4. College students – Canada – Finance, Personal. 5. Education, Higher – Canada – Costs. 6. Higher education and state – Canada. 7. Education savings accounts – Canada. I. Sweet, Robert, 1943– II. Anisef, Paul, 1942–

LB2342.2.C3P74 2005   378.3'8'0971   C2005-902773-8

This book was typeset by Interscript in 10/12 Baskerville.

Contents

Tables and Figures   vii

Acknowledgments   xi

1   Changing Partnerships: Families, Schools, and Governments
    Robert Sweet and Paul Anisef   3

PART ONE
ACCESS TO PSE: PUBLIC AND PRIVATE COSTS

2   Access to Post-Secondary Education: An Analytical Framework
    and New Evidence on Background Effects
    Ross Finnie   17

3   Accessibility and Student Debt: The Shift from Public
    to Private Support in Canada
    Stephen Bell and Paul Anisef   55

4   Paying for a University Education: A Comparison of Public
    and Private Study Costs in Canada, Australia,
    and Selected European Countries
    Stephen Bell and Glen A. Jones   87

5   Financing Lifelong Learning: The Potential and Actual Role
    of Individual Learning Accounts
    Hans G. Schuetze   126

PART TWO
FAMILIES AND PSE PLANNING

6   A Revolution of Expectations? Three Key Trends in the SAEP Data
    Scott Davies   149

7   Distributing Scarce Resources: Parental Investment
    in Their Children's Post-Secondary Education
    Victor Thiessen and E. Dianne Looker   166

8   The Effects of Region and Gender on Educational Planning
    in Canadian Families
    Paul Anisef, George Frempong, and Robert Sweet   201

9   Family Structure, Child Well-being, and Post-Secondary Saving:
    The Effect of Social Capital on the Child's Acquisition
    of Human Capital
    James M. White, Sheila Marshall, and Jamie R. Wood   222

10 Parental Involvement in the Creation of Home-Learning
    Environments: Gender and Class Patterns
    Nancy Mandell and Robert Sweet   249

11 Exploring Limits to Parents' Involvement in Homework
    Robert Sweet and Nancy Mandell   273

12 Educational Planning in Families: Issues and Future
    Research Directions
    Paul Anisef and Robert Sweet   289

    Index   303

Tables and Figures

Table 2.1   Overall Participation Rates by Sex and Level   40

Table 2.2   Participation Rates by Family Type and Province   41

Table 2.3   Participation Rates by Parental Education Level   43

Figure 2.1   Supply and Demand for Post-Secondary Education   24

Figure 2.2   Response to an Increase in Demand for Education   26

Figure 2.3   Effect of Increase in Tuition – No Pass-On   30

Figure 2.4   Effect of Increase in Tuition – Revenue Passed On   33

Figure 2.5   An Expansion of Capacity   34

Figure 2.6   Recent Developments in Canada   37

Table 3.1   Average Undergraduate Arts Tuition by Province, 1993–94
             to 2003–04   59

Table 3.2   Monthly Student Living Allowances 2001–02   61

Table 3.3   Calculation of Parental Contribution   62

Table 3.4   Average Dollar Amount of Negotiated Canada Student Loans
             (CSL) – Full-Time Students Only   66

Table 3.5   Distribution of Full-Time Loans Negotiated, 1996–97
             to 2000–01 by Age Group, Institutional Type,
             and Gender   67

Table 3.6   Sample Monthly Repayment in $ of Canada Student Loan
             at 9.5 per cent   68

Table 3.7   Student Loan by Province (Trade Vocational School)   68

Table 3.8   Student Loan by Province (College)   69

Table 3.9   Student Loan by Province (University)   70

Table 3.10   Median Debt-to-Earnings Ratios   71

Table 3.11   Three-Year Default Rates (%) by Institution Type
                (based on dollars)   73
Table 3.12   Household Expenditures on PSE Tuition by Income Quintile,
                1992 and 1998   76
Table 3.13   Total Family Income and Highest Educational Attainment
                among Children 18–24, 1997   80
Figure 3.1   Total Number of Borrowers in Canada, 1980–99   65

Table 4.1   Tertiary Education Students per 100,000 Inhabitants
                for Selected Countries   92
Table 4.2   Gross Enrolment Ratio (%) for Selected Countries   92
Table 4.3   Percentage Change in Undergraduate Arts Tuition
                by Province   93
Table 4.4   Student Loan Levels and Difficulty Repaying Debt
                in Percentages   95
Table 4.5   Education Support for Students in Netherlands by Type
                of Grant and Living Arrangements, in Percentages
                (2001)   97
Table 4.6   Change in U.K. Distribution of Weighting Between
                the Maintenance Grant and the Student Loan,
                since 1990   102
Table 4.7   Loan Repayment Schedule (2002)   103
Table 4.8   Income Thresholds and Repayment Rates for Income Earned
                in 2000–01   107
Table 4.9   Grants and Loans for Students in Higher Education (DKK)
                1998   110

Table 5.1   Formal and Non-Formal Learning Activities and
                Their Financing   133
Table 5.2   Financing Models for Lifelong Learning and
                Their Coverage   135
Table 5.3   ILAs in Four Countries   143

Table 6.1   Expectations by Region and Rural-Urban Residence   151
Table 6.2   Expectations by Gender, Language, Ethnicity   153
Table 6.3   Expectations by Parental Income and Education   155
Table 6.4   Cultural and Social Capital: Child Engagement,
                Home Environment, Peers   156
Table 6.5   Student Quality   159

Table 7.1   Educational Savings Behaviour by Number
                of Children Aged 18 or Under   182

Table 7.2   Parental Educational Investments by Gender,
             Birth Order, and Amount of Leisure Time Spent with
             Child   185
Table 7.3   Parental Educational Investments by Indicators
             of Differential Sibling Merit   189
Table 7.4   Parental Educational Investments by Indicators
             of Differential Sibling Academic Effort   191
Table 7.5   Parental Educational Investments by Indicators
             of Differential Sibling Need   193

Table 8.1   A Profile of Rural and Urban Children Aged 9–18   210
Table 8.2   Distribution of Children by SESINDEX   214
Table 8.3   The Effects of Child School Characteristics
             and Parents' Financial and Other Educational Planning
             on University Expectation (Odds Ratio)   216
Figure 8.1   Variation in University Expectation by Region, Gender,
             and Socio-economic Status   214

Table 9.1   Means and Standard Deviations for Variables   236
Table 9.2   Standardized Regression Coefficients for Model Blocks
             for Effects on Social Engagement   237
Table 9.3   Standardized Regression Coefficients for Model Blocks
             for Effects on School Engagement   238
Table 9.4   Logistic Regression Coefficients for Model Blocks
             for Effects on Current Saving for Post-Secondary
             Education   239
Figure 9.1   Orienting Model   232
Figure 9.2   Research Model   235

Table 10.1   Structure and Process Antecedents of Parental
             Involvement   262
Figure 10.1 Parental Monitoring by Mother's Education and Child's
             Gender   264
Figure 10.2 Parental Encouragement by Mother's Education and Child's
             Gender   265

Table 11.1   Parental Involvement by Education Level and Work
             Status   282
Figure 11.1 Parents' Homework Involvement in Response
             to Children's School Performance   284

Acknowledgments

This book would not have been possible without the efforts of many organizations and individuals. Thanks are due to many people from the Canada Education Savings Program (CESP). The CESP staff provided us with valuable comments as well as sponsored a workshop in 2002 that helped shape the chapters comprising the present volume. Their efforts were very much appreciated.

Along the way, we lost a friend and colleague, Stephen Bell, who died in 2003. Stephen was involved in the project from its earliest stages and his scholarly skill, interest, and enthusiasm are apparent in two chapters in our book. We hope the book in its final form would have pleased him.

PREPARING FOR POST-SECONDARY EDUCATION

1

Changing Partnerships:
Families, Schools, and Governments

ROBERT SWEET AND PAUL ANISEF

Parents have always planned and prepared for their children's educational futures. Where their goals included post-secondary education, the requisite financial resources were set aside and time and energy were committed to the equally important matter of ensuring the child's successful progression through the school system. Both undertakings involved partnerships. The first was a financial partnership with government that acknowledged the state's obligations to meet at least a portion of the individual's post-secondary study costs. The second was that established by parents with their children's teacher and school. Parents continue to plan and prepare for their children's educational futures, but the conditions under which these essential partnerships operate today is very different. The purpose of this volume is to examine the nature of educational planning in Canadian families given the changing set of relations between home, school, and government.

For many years federal and provincial governments were able to fund the capital and operating expenses of universities, colleges, and technical institutes. This had the general effect of moderating institutional pressures to increase tuition fees. Governments also provided individuals with a generous system of grants and bursaries, as well as a very accessible Canada Student Loan Plan (CSLP). Institutional funding and direct assistance to students thus ensured post-secondary access to qualified individuals across the social spectrum.

In the early 1990s federal transfers of funds to the provinces were severely curtailed and universities and colleges reacted by raising tuition fees. Grants and bursaries largely disappeared and the CSLP became more selective. The immediate effect was to increase student debt levels and extend the time to graduation as students interrupted their programs to work. Overall, the change in government support policies did not dampen enrolments but did limit access to those who could afford the increased fees or were willing to assume significant debt. This situation reflected a general shift in policy among Western governments that saw public study costs reduced with a corresponding increase in private study costs.

While the level of financial support was reduced in Canada, the federal government did not entirely abandon its obligations. Rather, it called for a new partnership with post-secondary students and their parents, shifting the burden of payment for post-secondary education to families but retaining a supportive role for government. For example, Ottawa initiated various alternative schemes, the most prominent being the Millennium Scholarship Foundation. Operated in conjunction with provincial support schemes, the Millennium plan was intended to alleviate student debt levels and promote accessibility. A second major initiative, the Canadian Educational Savings Grant (CESG) program, was introduced in 1998 to augment existing registered educational savings plans (RESPs). Parents' RESPs would be augmented by government contributions to a maximum of $400 per year. A similar Individual Learning Accounts scheme was proposed to facilitate educational savings for adult learners. This program was not put into effect, although the importance of the lifelong learning concept to continued economic development was acknowledged in several government policy documents. The experiences of other countries with learning accounts indicates that some form of financial support for working adults is necessary to implement and sustain the lifelong learning model.

The Millennium Scholarship Foundation and the CESG may or may not have broadened the social base of post-secondary access. Research is equivocal on the relationship between family income and post-secondary participation (Corak, Lipps, and Zhao, 2003; Raymond and Rivard, 2003). Preliminary evidence suggests that post-secondary access for low-income families has suffered in the years of "fiscal restraint" (Barr-Telford, Cartwright, Prasil, and Shimmons, 2003). Student debt levels also have not moderated and the anticipation of significant debt and its consequences is a deterrent to many low-income families (Tomkowicz, Shipley, and Ouellette, 2003).

Initial critiques of the Millennium and CESG programs have been generally unfavourable. Participation in the CESG scheme by low-income families has been minimal. This appears to have been recognized by the government, as the 2004 Throne Speech proposed modifications that would augment the initial contributions of low-income families to an RESP. Particular criticism has been directed towards the Millennium Foundation, not only because it failed to stem the rising tide of student debt but most particularly because it appears to have argued that money is not the determining factor in the decision to participate (Junor and Usher, 2003; Canadian Federation of Students, 2003; Kirby, 2002). Financing a university degree or college diploma almost certainly represents a significant barrier for many Canadian families. However, it is not the only challenge parents face in preparing their children for post-secondary studies.

Building a foundation for post-secondary education and training is the result of extensive academic preparation and planning. In preparing their children for further learning, parents not only accumulate the necessary funds but also invest a great deal of time and energy in their children's learning. This takes many forms, including promoting children's engagement with community social, athletic, and cultural activities. Of particular consequence is parental contact with their children's school through communication between parent and teacher and involvement in the school's extra-curricular activities. A second, and related, dimension of the home-school relationship is the parents' involvement in their child's home learning. Parents (especially mothers) are recognized as one of "life's first teachers." While their involvement in the infant's and pre-school child's learning is acknowledged, the important continuing role parents play in their children's learning is less well recognized. Actively engaged parents are essential to building a home-learning environment for the school-age child that complements the work of the teacher. A quiet place to study as well as help and encouragement to initiate and complete homework assignments make a crucial contribution to the child's learning.

Parents' activities with the school and the derivative activity of homework represent the second partnership involving parents in their children's educational futures and, like the financial partnership with government, that with schools is undergoing considerable change. The public perception of schools as not only important but also competitive is seen in studies of parents' views conducted by Davies and colleagues (Davies, Aurini, and Quirke, 2002). Recent public debates on the subject of (too much) homework emphasize changing public perceptions of the value of school and the increasing pressure surrounding the preparation of children and youth for higher education.

Both the changing nature of post-secondary financing and the greater involvement of parents in their children's education reflect the economic demands of a knowledge economy as well as political and social realignments that emphasize the responsibilities of individuals in shaping their personal futures (Heinz, 1991). To the extent that individuals and their families are made increasingly responsible for their own well-being, realizing desired educational goals requires careful planning. Marshalling the necessary funds and ensuring that children acquire the academic prerequisites for post-secondary study are two basic dimensions of the educational planning process. How these are enacted in particular families and how parents' actions are shaped by the social structures of location, ethnicity, gender, or class are described in "parent involvement" literature, which is remarkably diverse in terms of content, methodology, and theoretical stance. Research dealing explicitly with educational planning in families includes analyses of investment savings strategies, aspirations and expectations, post-secondary institution and program choice, and parent involvement styles and strategies. Syntheses of this literature are available in several volumes and reports (Finnie and Schwartz, 1996; Daniel, Schwarz, and Teichler, 1999; Hoover-Dempsey and Sandler, 1997; Steinberg, 1996; Ryan, Adams, et al., 1995; Marjoribanks, 2003; Seginer, 1983; Hossler, Schmitt, and Vesper, 1999; Wentzel, 1998; Willms, 2002). The chapters in this collection add to the planning literature by reporting results from the 1999 *Survey of Approaches to Educational Planning* (SAEP), a national study of educational planning in Canadian families.

THE SAEP PROJECT

The financial resource accumulation and academic preparation dimensions of planning parallel the partnerships parents develop with governments and schools. The SAEP project was designed to examine in detail the strategies parents employed in negotiating the conditions of these partnerships. The SAEP was developed over a period of two years to gather information on these relationships as a basis for understanding the educational planning process as enacted in Canadian families. In 1999 data were collected through a survey of some 34,000 households conducted by Statistics Canada. This resulted in a sample of families with 18,000 children aged 0–18.

The SAEP project had two purposes: first, to inform policy-making by Human Resources Development Canada (HRDC)[1], who were charged with implementing the CESG, the federal government's initiative to encourage parents to save for their children's future education; second, to examine the nature and extent of parents' involvement in their children's schooling.

The questionnaire had three broad aims: first, to examine *parents' aspirations for their children* – questions were asked to determine what proportion of parents expected their children to go on to post-secondary education and what proportion of those children would attend a college or a university; second, to gauge *parents' awareness of the financial prerequisites and the scope and nature of their financial plans and intentions* – this involved examining their proposed sources of funding in relation to anticipated expenses, with particular attention to the various savings instruments available to and used by parents; third, to examine the pattern of *parents' involvement in their children's schooling* – this explored parents' efforts to increase the child's engagement in community and extra-curricular activities, establish contacts with their child's teacher, and establish an effective home-study environment.

Within the extensive literature on financial planning and parent involvement, few attempts are made to develop a general model of educational planning, reflecting perhaps the situated nature of the activity. Hossler's (Hossler, Schmitt, and Vesper, 1999) college choice model, for example, focuses on parents' ability to afford the fees charged by the preferred institution. While appropriate to the hierarchically arranged post-secondary system of the U.S., such a model has less applicability in Canada, where selection tends to be among programs rather than institutions (Davies, Aurini, and Quirke, 2002). Similarly, Connell's (2003) description of Australian middle- and working-class parents' educational aspirations and pattern of involvement in their children's schooling – which he terms parenting "projects" – appears strongly situated.

The conceptual scheme underlying the design of the SAEP questionnaire drew on the general financial planning and parent involvement literature to ensure that essential elements of Canadian parents' planning and involvement behaviours were included (Sweet, Anisef, and Lin, 2000). Within this framework, the questionnaire was intended to elicit from parents a detailed description of their educational planning intentions and behaviours. Parents' savings plans consist of specific financial commitments they are willing to undertake – e.g., savings or investments of various kinds. Such plans are motivated by parents' post-secondary aspirations for their children, differentiated by university, college, or some form of technical or trade training. These educational ambitions presumably are supported by parenting practices designed to transmit or activate the resources necessary to realizing their children's educational potential. Parental involvement is typically directed towards establishing links with the school, encouraging children's engagement in community and extra-curricular activities, and fostering home study. These processes result in children's acquisition of important forms of cultural and social capital that help to ensure their successful passage through the school system. Parents' investments of time and effort then are reflected in the children's school achievement and attitude towards learning. Both indicators of school performance are essential prerequisites to post-secondary participation and completion. The effectiveness of parental involvement and the extent and nature of parents' financial plans are qualified by structural factors such as ethnicity, region (rural-urban), gender, and socio-economic status.

ORGANIZATION OF THE BOOK

This book is organized into two sections. Part 1 describes the changing relationship between public and private study costs for post-secondary

education. Greater individual responsibility for financing higher education is not a phenomenon unique to Canada. Other countries and jurisdictions are undertaking similar reforms, although these are based on
different assumptions and practices. Part 1 deals with several central issues. Student indebtedness – a growing problem that threatens access to
higher education for many less-advantaged groups in society – is discussed. Increasing educational costs are examined in relation to demand
and the capacity of universities and colleges to supply the needed programs. This is especially important as interest in formal education and
training has increased among older, working adults as well as among the
youth who comprise the traditional post-secondary group. In the face of
limited government funding, rising demand, and limited capacity, innovations are needed in developing new financing policies. These are explored in relation to lifelong learning and the concept of an Individual
Learning Account, designed to accommodate the range and diversity of
working adults interested in furthering their education.

This overview and critique of policy provides a national and international context for the second section of the book, which details the responses of families to the task of planning and financing post-secondary
education for their children. The various analyses of educational planning
contained in Part 2 are conducted within the structure-process framework
previously described. While the full range of planning problems and issues
cannot be addressed in a single volume, some pivotal concepts and relationships are examined. Parents' aspirations for their children's future education influence their continued commitment and support, although
their antecedents remain uncertain and vary widely across groups defined
by social structures and situations. Family organization often limits aspirations: single-parent families face difficulties in accumulating necessary
resources, and families with three or four children must find ways of equi-
tably dispersing family resources. Similarly, parents' intentions to save and
the actual accumulation of funds for their children's post-secondary education are influenced by myriad situational and process factors. One of the
barriers to achieving educational goals is distance from the metropolitan
areas where most PSE institutions are located. Whether one's children will
have to leave home and find room and board or enter a university residence for their education is also consequential in the formation of parents' plans. The behaviours of family members are important elements in
educational plans. Children, for example, are agents in shaping their own
futures. Those who excel or exert particular effort in their studies are likely
to receive more willing support from their parents. And parenting styles
and strategies are key indicators of the possession and deployment of essential cultural and social capital. How parents become involved in their
children's schooling is an aspect of their more responsible roles and these

are explored in some detail. Together, the various chapters in this section begin to open up the terrain of educational planning within families.

PART 1: PUBLIC AND PRIVATE STUDY COSTS

CHAPTER 2

Ross Finnie proposes a model of demand and capacity that informs policy responses to the problem of increasing public interest in post-secondary education and a corresponding decrease in university and college capacity. Finnie's model provides a conceptual framework for identifying and separating the various factors that determine capacity and access, indicated by the total number of students accommodated and the composition of the student population. The model takes as its starting point a relatively simple supply-demand statement. The basic features of the demand for post-secondary education are presented – that is, the factors that determine who would like to participate in the system and who is able to do so in the sense of having the required financial resources. A stylized supply side is then described, which essentially reduces to the notion that institutions are willing and able to accept more students if and when they are given the incentives and financial means to do so. The effects of changes in the various determinants of equilibrium in the system are then analysed. These include tuition fees, the student financial aid system, and other factors, including family background. This is followed by a discussion of the sort of data that, in conjunction with the proposed model, might allow us to better understand access and efficiency issues associated with change in the post-secondary system.

CHAPTER 3

Stephen Bell and Paul Anisef note that the benefits accruing to young people who access and participate in Canadian higher education are well known and that sustaining access to post-secondary education has been important for a variety of reasons, including the human capital argument; the notion of providing equality of opportunity to social and cultural groups previously excluded from attending universities and colleges; and the increased importance of credentials in a globalized economy. Participation data provide ample proof that Canadians place enormous trust in their post-secondary institutions and the education they provide for enhancing their life-course destinations. At the same time, the study costs related to post-secondary education are increasingly being placed on the family. From a social inclusion perspective, this raises the question of whether particular segments of the Canadian population are experiencing difficulties in sustaining a presence in our post-secondary institutions. It suggests in particular that disadvantaged families now find it problematic to marshal the resources required if their children are to gain entry to our universities and colleges and, perhaps more importantly, complete their programs. These concerns form the basis for a re-examination of issues surrounding accessibility to post-secondary education.

CHAPTER 4
Stephen Bell and Glen Jones argue that while the state continues to be the major funder of university operating costs in most Western systems, the question of the appropriate balance between public (state) and private support for the costs of higher education has become an important public policy issue in many jurisdictions. They examine the financial relations established between students and higher education systems in Canada, Australia, and four European countries (Denmark, the Netherlands, Sweden, and the United Kingdom). This comparative analysis reveals the assumptions underlying the growing division between public and private costs in each jurisdiction and leads to a better understanding of the general inclination of governments towards increased private study costs.

CHAPTER 5
In the final chapter in this section, Hans Schuetze examines the Learning Accounts concept in relation to lifelong learning (LLL). LLL is seen as a possible skill-formation strategy for the new economy and, as such, has caused policy-makers to look for ways to implement and finance such a strategy. In addition to this problem, there are other concerns: the difficulty of estimating the approximate cost of lifelong learning; the principles by which these costs are to be distributed among the various stakeholders; and, finally, the problem of translating these principles into viable financing schemes. Schuetze traces the history of attempts to finance LLL, outlining their principles and practices to determine the extent to which they are applicable to the current debate on LLL and its contribution to economic growth. As a derivative of earlier approaches, the individual learning accounts concept has emerged as a potentially powerful means of involving government in a learning partnership that extends beyond children and adolescents to include adults. Various learning accounts models are described and their implementation in selected countries is examined. This analysis forms the basis for a critique of the Canadian government's recent, and unsuccessful, attempt to establish a learning accounts system.

PART 2: PARENTS AND PSE PLANNING

CHAPTER 6
Scott Davies begins by recounting the remarkable expansion in Canada of post-secondary education over the past half century. In that time, higher

education evolved from an elite system to a mass system, placing Canada among the world leaders in post-secondary enrolments. Some argue that rising skill demands in the labour market will force a further evolution to a universal post-secondary system. In this scenario, the vast majority of youth will be compelled by economic circumstance to attend post-secondary institutions. Davies poses three questions: First, are Canadians ready to accept this proclaimed stage of universal post-secondary education? Second, what implications does further expansion have for equality of access? Third, if post-secondary expectations continue to surge upwards should universities and colleges expect more weak and ill-prepared students, and will such students be distributed equally among these institutions? Davies concludes that in the era of the New Economy, higher expectations for post-secondary studies are emerging, but they are not likely to make the system more equitable. Rather, the future likely will be marked by greater institutional stratification, more competition among students to enter more highly valued fields of study, and perhaps more disappointment among students who are inadequately prepared.

CHAPTER 7
Victor Thiessen and Dianne Looker assess the basis for parents' decisions to distribute educational savings among their children. The difficult task families face in dividing scarce resources among the competing demands of everyday living is compounded by the fact that large nuclear families must provide for the educational costs of two, three, and sometimes four children. The authors address the question of whether or not educational savings are divided equally between siblings or reserved for children with academic potential or a particular gift or talent. The latter plan obviously lessens the post-secondary educational opportunities of those who do not possess these characteristics. In a very real sense, systematically disadvantaging siblings robs them of their entitlement to post-secondary education. Thiessen and Looker conclude that most parents attempt to apply principles of equity to their savings strategies and in the disposition of family resources.

CHAPTER 8
Paul Anisef, George Frempong, and Robert Sweet present an analysis of regional variations in educational plans made by parents. Their analysis is consistent with previous studies that have documented the greater likelihood of urban parents planning on a university education for their children. The analysis reveals that approximately 40 per cent of parents in rural and urban areas are actively saving, or intend saving at some future date, for their children's post-secondary education. In terms of total amount of savings, there is little to distinguish between rural and urban parents. When the use of RESPs is examined, the authors find that rural

parents are more likely to employ such savings for female rather than male children, a finding that is reversed in urban settings. When school performance and school attitudes were examined, rural females were found to achieve better results in school and possess more positive attitudes regarding schoolwork. In the next stage of their analysis, the authors investigate the influence of socio-economic status (SES) – based on an index composed of parental levels of formal education and income – on children's post-secondary expectations. Variations in university expectations by region, gender, and SES were examined. No differences in university expectations based on region and gender were found. However, in low and middle SES households, there was considerable variation, related for the most part to gender and region. The authors' analysis also suggests that a larger proportion of parents living in rural communities anticipate that their child will need to leave home to pursue post-secondary studies. This is especially true when the rural child opts for a university education. More than twice as many rural parents indicated that their children would move away from the community to study at a post-secondary institution. Within low SES rural families, the indication that children will leave home becomes an especially good marker of university expectations. However, the increased costs of higher education mean this decision by rural parents likely will disadvantage them economically in future years.

CHAPTER 9
James White, Sheila Marshall, and Jamie Wood explore the relationship between family structure, child outcomes, and saving for post-secondary education. Although they find support for a linkage between parental encouragement and child outcomes, the relationship between family structure and child outcomes is weaker and more tenuous. Thus, the authors argue that parental encouragement is a more useful measure of social capital than family structure and suggest that a critical "rethinking" of family structure as a measure of social capital is required. From a policy standpoint, the implication is that interventions should address parenting skill rather than family structure. There is very little evidence to suggest that family structure accounts for much other than a lack of resources.

CHAPTER 10
Nancy Mandell and Robert Sweet examine gender and class variations in parental involvement in children's schooling. In doing so, they assess the correspondence between heightened post-secondary aspirations (noted in Davies' chapter) and parents' ability to engage in the supportive behaviours needed to realize their educational ambitions. Mandell and Sweet focus on the influence of class and gender on elements of the parenting style employed by mothers and fathers in fostering their children's school performance. By focusing on parents' attempts to monitor children's study

behaviour and encourage their school efforts, a picture is drawn of the home-learning environment as constructed by parents. Within the limits of a classed and gendered society, the analysis of parents' style in guiding and directing children's learning in the home underscores parents' essential role in socializing their children to the role of student.

CHAPTER 11

Robert Sweet and Nancy Mandell assess the effects of time and resource constraints on parental involvement in their children's schooling. Viewing mothers rather than fathers as principally responsible for children's school adjustment and achievement, they assess the time limitations imposed on mothers by waged work. They also examine differences in involvement associated with personal resources, indicated by mothers' level of education. Mothers' employment status and their educational backgrounds are associated with complex patterns of involvement. Overall, however, they indicate the commitment of parents to their children's educational progress despite limited time and resources. Parents' ability to remain involved with vulnerable children during the middle school years is an important indicator of their willingness to assume the role of homework facilitator.

CHAPTER 12

In the concluding chapter, Paul Anisef and Robert Sweet outline some of the features of the changed context in which parents must plan and prepare for their children's post-secondary education. Taking into account this environment of shifting government policies and continual school reforms, they summarize and highlight the research conducted by the authors in Part 2. From this synthesis they identify the essential elements of a research program that would provide a better understanding of the educational planning process in Canadian families.

NOTE

1 HRDC's name was recently changed to Human Resources and Skill Development Canada (HRSDC).

REFERENCES

Barr-Telford, L., Cartwright, F., Prasil, S., and Shimmons, K. (2003). *Access, persistence and financing: First results from the Postsecondary Education Participation Survey (PEPS)*. Ottawa: Statistics Canada.

Canadian Federation of Students (2003). *2002 Submission to House of Commons Standing Committee on Finance*. Document retrieved August 2004 from www.cfs.ca.

Connell, R. (2003). "Working-class families and the new secondary education." *Australian Journal of Education, 47*(3), 235–50.

Corak, M., Lipps, G., and Zhao, J. (2003). *Family income and participation in post-secondary education.* Ottawa: Family and Labour Studies Division, Statistics Canada.

Daniel, H.-D., Schwarz, S., and Teichler, U. (1999). "Study costs, student income and public policy in Europe." *European Journal of Education, 34*, 7–22.

Davies, S., Aurini, J., and Quirke, L. (2002). "New markets for private education in Canada." *Education Canada, 42*(3), 36–9.

Finnie, R. and Schwartz, S. (1996). *Student loans in Canada: Past, present, and future.* Toronto: C.D. Howe Institute.

Heinz, W. (1991). "Status passages: Social risks and the life course: A conceptual framework." In W. Heinz, ed. *Theoretical advances in life course research*, vol. 1. Weinheim: Deutscher Studien Verlag. 9–22.

Hoover-Dempsey, K. and Sandler, H. (1997). "Why do parents become involved in their children's education?" *Review of Educational Research, 67*, 3–42.

Hossler, D., Schmitt, J., and Vesper, N. (1999). *How social, economic, and educational factors influence the decisions students make.* Baltimore: The Johns Hopkins Press.

Junor, S. and Usher, A. (2002). *The Price of Knowledge.* Montreal: Canada Millennium Scholarship Foundation.

Kirby, D. (2002). "Statistics and the Canada Millennium Scholarship Foundation." *Canadian Journal of Higher Education, 32*(3), 111–18.

Marjoribanks, K. (2003). *Family and school capital: Towards a context theory of students' school outcomes.* Dordrecht, Netherlands: Kluwer.

Raymond, M. and Rivard, M. (2003). *Have tuition fee hikes in the late 1990s undermined access to post-secondary education in Canada?* Ottawa: Economic Studies and Policy Analysis Branch, Department of Finance.

Ryan, B., Adams, G., Gullotta, T., Weissberg, R., and Hampton, R. (1995). *The family-school connection: Theory, research, and practice.* Thousand Oaks, CA: SAGE.

Seginer, M. 1983. "Parents' educational expectations and children's academic achievements: A literature review." *Merrill-Palmer Quarterly, 29*(1), 1–23.

Steinberg, L. (1996). *Beyond the classroom.* New York: Simon & Schuster.

Sweet, R., Anisef, P., and Lin, Z. (2000). *Exploring family antecedents of participation in post-secondary education.* Ottawa: Learning and Literacy Directorate, Human Resources Development Canada.

Tomkowicz, J., Shipley, L., and Ouelette, S. (2003). *Perception of barriers to education in a group of 18 to 20 year olds: For whom does money matter?* Ottawa: CTCES, Statistics Canada.

Wentzel, K. (1998). "Parents' aspirations for children's educational attainments: Relations to parental beliefs and social address variables." *Merrill-Palmer Quarterly, 44*, 20–37.

Willms, D. (2002). *Vulnerable children.* Edmonton: University of Alberta Press.

PART ONE

Access to PSE:
Public and Private Costs

Access to Post-Secondary Education: An Analytical Framework and New Evidence on Background Effects

ROSS FINNIE

Many important changes have occurred in the Canadian post-secondary education system over the last decade: substantial increases in tuition rates (Junor and Usher, 2002); shifts in the shares of student financial aid given in the form of grants and loans; increases and then stagnation in student borrowing limits; rising debt loads, the introduction and expansion of assistance in repayment and debt remission programs; the birth of the Canada Millennium Scholarship Foundation; and a widening of education-related tax credits.[1] On the other side of the coin, the financial support provided by provincial ministries to colleges and universities has generally been cut in real terms while institutions' costs have risen, resulting in hardship, cutbacks, and what most would call an overall deterioration in the quality of education offered (AUCC, 2002). But even as costs have risen for individuals and institutions have been pressed financially, the returns to post-secondary education have, if anything, risen as the "new knowledge economy" has placed an ever-increasing value on "highly qualified personnel" (Riddell and Sweetman, 2000).

The effects of these changes have been observed in the number of individuals going on to post-secondary education and in the make-up of the student body. The total number of students in the post-secondary system has risen slightly – albeit unevenly across jurisdictions and types of institutions – while overall participation rates (i.e., the share of the population of school-attending age enrolled) have increased more markedly. By family type, the limited evidence available suggests that participation rates have risen across all income levels, but that the increases have been greater for individuals from middle-income families than for those from wealthier families, and smaller among those from lower-income families, thus skewing the relative participation rates by family background (i.e., both smaller and greater differences in access – depending on the particular comparison made). Changes have also occurred in the percentage of students going part-time, in the amount of outside work during school, and in other characteristics and behaviour (Junor and Usher, 2002).

These changes – along with other factors – have fuelled a renewed interest in various questions regarding who goes on to post-secondary education in Canada, largely driven by fears that the opportunity of going to college or university has become increasingly related to family background rather than to the ability to do the work and the desire to succeed. Other concerns focus on whether we are keeping up with our competitors in terms of overall rates of college and university attendance. These two issues might be termed one of "capacity," or the *number* of places in our colleges and universities, and another of "access," or *who* fills the available places in the post-secondary system.[2]

The more specific questions include the following: What roles have family income and other socio-economic background influences, tuition levels, and the student financial aid system played in determining who goes on to post-secondary education? What changes should be made to the student financial aid system or tuition level policies to ensure that all qualified individuals have the opportunity to go to college or university without regard to family background? What needs to be done regarding the capacity of the system and what are the means of providing our colleges and universities with the resources required to provide the number of places that we think should be made available? These questions effectively embrace the twin issues of (a) equity, opportunity, and social justice, and (b) the nation's economic performance, thus presenting a powerful context for discussions of these and related policy issues.

These discussions have, however, been hamstrung by the lack of a general model that provides a conceptual framework for identifying and separating the various factors that determine capacity and access, i.e., the total number of students and the composition of the student population. As a specific example, what are we to make of the apparent "paradox" that although tuition rates rose dramatically through the 1990s, so too did enrolment rates, and more or less across the board, including individuals from all family backgrounds? Or what should we make of the effects of the various changes in the student financial aid system in a context where it would seem there is generally greater demand for places in the system than there are spots available and the ability to pay probably affects who gets those places more than the total number of students in the system? The policy implications of getting these things straight are extensive and important.

From an analytical standpoint, the problem is that various factors that affect the demand for post-secondary education have been changing while the overall supply of places in the system has been largely stagnant or has in some cases probably decreased as institutions have seen their core funding reduced. How can we disentangle these various influences to better understand what has been happening and, perhaps most importantly, predict what might be expected in the future as the factors affecting demand continue to alter and the supply of places in the system continues to fluctuate as a result of various government policies? From another perspective, how can we better understand what policy *should be* in terms of access and capacity?

This paper offers just such a general analytical model, which should be useful for clarifying these issues of post-secondary access and capacity. The model takes as its starting point a relatively simple supply-demand framework. Its development begins with an outline of the basic features of the demand for post-secondary education – the factors that determine who would *like* to participate in the system and who is *able* to do so in the sense of having the required financial resources. A stylised supply side is then described, which essentially reduces to the notion that institutions are willing and able to accept more students if and when they are given the incentives and financial means to do so. With these pieces in place, the general characteristics of the resulting "equilibrium" of the system are discussed.

The effects of changes in the various determinants of the system are then analysed. On the demand side, the effects of expanding the student financial assistance system are used as the primary illustrative example, but other factors, including changes in the returns to post-secondary education and family income levels, are also noted. One important implication of the model, especially in the current policy context, is that the number of post-secondary students will not necessarily change in the face of such demand-side shifts if there are capacity constraints – although the characteristics of who attends, especially with respect to ability and family background, will adjust. The effects of tuition increases are analysed in a similar manner, including the consideration of cases where the increased fees are not passed on to institutions and of those where they are. Supply-side influences related to changes in the capacity of the system are similarly analysed, with interesting sets of implications. The framework is then used to help cast light on the central developments in post-secondary education since the early 1990s in terms of tuition levels and the numbers and characteristics of those participating.

This is followed by a discussion of the data – some of which are already available, others about to be released – that might allow us to better understand the developments of the post-secondary system in terms of this conceptual framework. For example, it might be interesting to look at application data to measure how demand has changed in terms of students' characteristics (e.g., family background). That said, the best way to learn what has been happening to access is to look at data that provide information on who goes and who does not go, as well as information on as much of the overall structure of those processes as possible. In this way we can, for example, unravel the overall importance of family background on who goes to college and university, and where the various related influences appear to take effect and in what form – improved high school outcomes, management of the associated expenses, and so on.

The final part of the paper presents the results of a comparative analysis of patterns of participation in post-secondary education by family type using data from 1991 and from 2000, almost a decade later. The evidence is interesting and important, and fits with one of the principal themes of this book: the role of parents in ensuring that their children have the chance of pursuing post-secondary education, and the corresponding role of government in terms of creating equality of opportunity. The conceptual framework offered here provides a context for placing these discussions in the broader context of the demand for and supply of post-secondary education in Canada.

AN ANALYTICAL FRAMEWORK

The demand and supply concepts are first developed individually. They are then put together to represent the sort of "equilibrium" that is generated in terms of the number of students and the composition of the student body. The effects of changing various underlying factors, including student financial aid, tuition levels, and transfers to colleges and universities aimed at increasing the number of places, are then discussed in terms of how they might be expected to affect the number of students and their characteristics, especially with respect to ability and family background.

While the model is quite simple, the framework should be helpful for thinking about a number of important practical issues. For example, the framework makes it clear that we should not be surprised to see little relationship – or even a perverse positive relation – between tuition levels and enrolment rates, and that offering more student aid might not change the number of students but could have important effects on *who* pursues higher studies. The model is then used to put various developments in post-secondary education since the early 1990s in perspective. The section concludes with a discussion of a number of important measurement and data issues.

The Demand for Post-Secondary Education

The demand for post-secondary education may be defined as representing the number of individuals who would *like* to go to school and who are *able* to do so in terms of having the resources to pay the required tuition fees and overcome any other potential barriers, financial or otherwise, including meeting the required entrance criteria. This fundamental concept – simple as it is – is the basis of the discussions that follow.

The classic demand "curve" concept used by economists reflects the relationship between demand and price – in this case between the number of places sought at colleges and universities and tuition levels. The demand curve for post-secondary education – like virtually all demand curves – would be expected to be negatively sloped for the simple reason that at higher tuition fee levels, fewer individuals would want to go, or have the means to go, and vice versa.[3]

Given this general shape of the price-demand relationship, however, the particular position and form of the demand curve for post-secondary education will be affected by the various underlying factors that determine the demand at any given price. Having an appreciation for some of these factors is helpful for understanding various key aspects of "the market for post-secondary education," and the influences of various policies on access, including those related to family savings for their children's education, student financial aid, and other forms of preparation and support for post-secondary schooling.

Economists like to focus on education as an investment, and the degree to which post-secondary studies improve an individual's lifetime earnings or otherwise lead to improved job opportunities is an important determinant of the demand for higher education, especially in Canada, where these returns are estimated to be quite high (Vaillancourt, 1995; Vaillancourt and Bordeau-Primeau, 2002).

A related, shorter-run influence would be the availability of job opportunities for those who choose not to continue with their schooling. When unemployment rates rise, the demand for post-secondary schooling tends to increase, since the opportunity cost of going to school in terms of the alternative uses of the individual's time (i.e., making money) declines.[4]

Various other factors that affect the net returns to post-secondary education would also affect demand. For example, the distances to the post-secondary institutions individuals are interested in attending would have an influence, since needing to travel further to go to school would increase overall education costs (in terms of time and/or money), cut into the net returns to the education, and thus diminish demand (Frenette, 2002).

In short, any factor that affects the net benefits of a post-secondary education will enter the demand curve, and a change in any such factor will shift the curve.[5]

No demand for post-secondary schooling will, however, be effective – even for those for whom it might represent a good investment in terms of career opportunities – unless the individual is able to pay for it. Hence, family income levels, which are an important source of student financial support, have a significant effect on demand. So too does the availability of student financial aid. Any other factor that affects individuals' ability to pay for their studies – such as the availability of good summer or term-time jobs – will also affect demand for the same reason.

In summary, the demand for post-secondary education will depend on i) the net benefits of the schooling, and ii) the ability to pay for it. These different sets of considerations become important in the discussions that follow.

The Supply Side

It is difficult to characterise the supply of Canadian post-secondary education with too much precision because of the diversity of systems operating in the country, varying along provincial lines (post-secondary is a provincial jurisdiction) and with respect to the different types of institutions that exist, from small private vocational schools to our largest and greatest universities. However, a general stylization of the system that captures its essential elements can be constructed and will serve our purposes here in terms of constructing a conceptual framework that usefully captures the essence of the Canadian post-secondary education system.[6]

In this spirit, the post-secondary system in Canada may be considered to have a classical upwards-sloping supply curve, which indicates that as the price rises, more places will be offered. In short, higher tuition fees (the relevant price) – if passed on to institutions – make it feasible and worthwhile for institutions to expand their capacity. This is the basic concept used in the following discussions.[7]

Of course, to the degree that institutions do not receive the tuition fees their students pay, their supply curves will not be directly related to tuition levels in this exact manner. More generally, the capacity of institutions is often determined to at least some degree independently of tuition fees – dictated by other elements of the institutional funding formulas, education ministry directives, institutions' own strategic decisions, and other factors. Similarly, any increase in tuition fees that is received could be spent on improving the quality of the education offered, financial aid, or in other ways, instead of increasing the number of spaces. To the degree that any of these cases apply, the supply curve would be vertical – or "perfectly inelastic" –

with respect to tuition fees (i.e., capacity would not be related to tuition fees). Alternatively, in many cases institutions receive additional per-student grants on top of the tuition they collect, thus generating a supply curve that is essentially a mathematical transformation of the simple tuition-supply relationship hypothesized above.

Despite these and other complexities, the upward-sloping supply curve probably captures the essence of the Canadian situation as it concerns us here, in that the number of places in the system will grow if institutions are given the financial incentives and means to fund such increases – which higher tuition rates can do.[8] This basic paradigm can also be adapted to take other cases into account – including various forms of the "vertical supply curve" variant just discussed – some of which are discussed below.[9]

Equilibrium

Demand and supply can now be put together to consider a typical "market equilibrium" situation. Figure 2.1 shows the sort of upward sloping supply curve and downward sloping demand curve just discussed. It also shows tuition levels being exogenously given to the "market," as represented by the horizontal line at P, corresponding to the standard situation in Canada, where fees are set by provincial education ministries rather than determined by institutions themselves in response to market forces (i.e., supply and demand).[10] The number of places that institutions are willing to supply is represented by the point where the price intersects the supply curve, or N_S. The demand for places is represented by the point where the price intersects the demand curve, or N_D.

As drawn, the figure shows the typical situation in Canada, where, at given tuition levels, demand is greater than supply ($N_D > N_S$). That is, there are more individuals who would like to go to college or university (i.e., applicants and potential applicants) than there are places. In standard economics jargon, this is referred to as a situation of "excess demand."

Obviously the system can only accommodate as many students as the number of available places, so the number of participants is equal to the number of places available at the going price – N_S. Note that in such a situation (i.e., where demand is greater than supply), the number of students is "supply-constrained," that is, determined by the capacity of the system.

As to how well this model reflects the reality of the post-secondary sector in Canada, a number of arguments could be used to suggest it is a useful characterisation of the general situation. The logic of the demand curve is clear, the supply curve has been discussed above, and prices are clearly set more or less as described. As for the nature of the equilibrium that results, there are generally more applicants than places, while most institutions

Figure 2.1
Supply and Demand for Post-Secondary Education

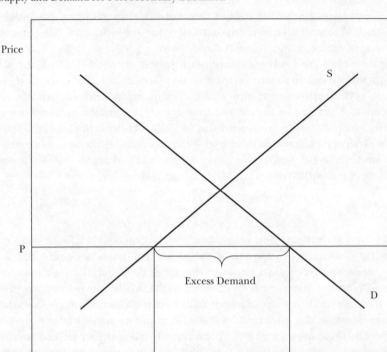

could be described as operating more or less at capacity – thus pointing to the excess demand/supply-constrained situation shown.[11, 12]

In any event, the ensuing discussions require only these basic tenets: that demand is greater than supply at prevailing tuition levels; and that the capacity of the system will grow (only) if it is given more resources either through an increase in tuition fees or in some other manner – and these would seem to represent a reasonable description of the current situation in Canada. The case where the system is not supply-constrained is also discussed, thus further extending the applicability of the model. In short, the model can be used to describe almost any situation, largely because it is so simple, so basic.

Given such a situation, the available places are rationed by entry requirements, or "ability." In such a system, it is not necessarily the best or most deserving students who get places, but rather the best and (perhaps) most deserving of *those who apply* – that is, who wish to go to school at tuition levels P *and* have the means to do so. In particular, some very good students from lower-income families who would like to go, and for whom post-secondary education would be a very good investment, may not have the money to do so; and others who possess the requisite raw talent may not have had the sort of high school (and earlier) educational opportunities that might have opened post-secondary opportunities for them when such choices were presented.

The wish to make post-secondary education accessible to all who merit the opportunity, rather than only to those who can pay for it, represents the underlying principle of the student financial aid system in Canada. Conventional "access" policies are focused on providing financial assistance to qualified individuals who would like to pursue their studies, but lack the financial means of doing so – that is, those at points on the demand curve beyond/below the point where it is intersected by P. Let us now consider what the effects of an increase in student financial aid would be, using this analytical framework.

The Effects of Increasing Student Financial Aid

The traditional policy instruments for student financial aid are grants, scholarships, bursaries, and loans, although since the mid-1990s debt remission programs have expanded substantially, while the tax credits provided to students and their families have become increasingly important. Here we focus on the effects of an increase in aid of any of these types on the demand for post-secondary education, on the number of students in the system, and on the characteristics of those who apply and are accepted in terms of ability and family background.[13]

First, an increase in student aid targeted to individuals from lower-income families will shift the demand curve for post-secondary education out – from D_0 to D_1 as shown in Figure 2.2.

More individuals who would like to participate will now be able to do so. The number of places sought at the prevailing tuition fee levels (assuming no change in fees at this point) thus increases to N_{D1}.[14]

However, supply will not change, but will remain at N_S, precisely because tuition fees have not changed, meaning that – in the absence of any other policy changes (as in the formulas that determine the funding going to institutions) – universities and colleges will not have the additional resources required to pay for such an expansion, and therefore will not do so. Since the number of places in the system remains unchanged, the number of students will be similarly invariant, remaining at N_S.

This is a simple but highly significant result: increasing student aid, and thus increasing the demand for post-secondary education, will not generally change the total number of students in the system. This is especially significant in the context of policies aimed at doing precisely this – increasing the number of "HQP," or highly qualified personnel.[15] The reason is

Figure 2.2
Response to an Increase in Demand for Education

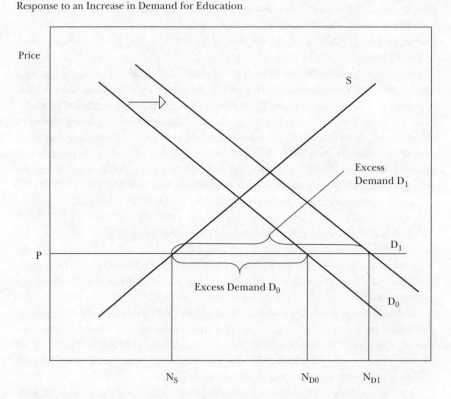

simple: if colleges and universities are already operating at capacity in terms of what is financially feasible at prevailing tuition fees (and other elements of the funding schedules they face), they will generally not create additional places in the face of an increase in demand. That would require either an increase in tuition fees or changes in other elements of the relevant funding formulas, such as being provided the money required for expansion directly from provincial ministries.[16]

An increase in student financial aid will, however, have other important effects. An increase in assistance – grants, scholarships, bursaries, loans, debt remission, tax credits – will, in particular, increase demand precisely among those who were previously unable to afford to pay for their schooling but are now able to do so thanks to the expanded financial support.[17] And those who pass the established eligibility requirements will find places in the post-secondary education system – whereas previously they did not participate. The number of applicants (i.e., those who actively express a demand for post-secondary education) and the actual student body will, therefore, have a greater proportion of individuals from lower-income families and fewer "stupid rich kids" (a term sometimes used to refer to the clientele of certain expensive American colleges and universities with low entrance requirements).

Therefore, overall participation rates would show no measurable change in response to an increase in student financial aid, but the characteristics of those participants would be altered. In particular, the measured relationship between participation and socio-economic status would become weaker, as a greater number of individuals from lower-income families were able to overcome the financial barriers to a college or university education. These effects would presumably be greater where financial barriers were higher, such as university relative to college, or for rural students relative to those living near a post-secondary institution. The framework applies equally, but the effects may vary in degree, which must be left to empirical analyses.[18]

A second significant effect is that entrance criteria are likely to rise in the face of the increased demand, as the same number of places will be allocated among a larger pool of applicants. The characteristics of the student body will thus change in terms of "quality" as well as socio-economic background.

More students from lower-income families will have the means of going to school, and will therefore apply, and this will change the composition of the student body to the degree this increased demand "crowds out" those who were previously able to go but no longer make the grade as standards are raised.

The improved access for capable young people from lower-income families is, of course, exactly the goal of student financial aid. The fact that, in the case of an increase in student financial aid but no action on the supply side (i.e., no increased capacity), these individuals will tend to take the places of others who might have gone in the absence of such aid is not necessarily a bad thing, but should be recognised. Depending on the costs and benefits of post-secondary schooling, along with the various equity concerns on which student financial aid systems are founded, this change in the characteristics of the student body with respect to family background and scholastic ability may or may not be the desired outcome – but the reality of the absence of any change in the overall numbers must be accepted.[19]

Finally, a change in demand stemming from an increase in the return to post-secondary education would have similar effects to an increase in student financial aid in terms of the quantity of graduates – that is, no change. This is again important from a policy perspective, because whereas other markets, including those for certain specific kinds of human capital, can generally be relied on to generate more of the sought-after kinds of workers through the normal workings of prices, supply, and demand, this is not likely to be the case for post-secondary graduates as a whole. If there were such an increased need for more "highly qualified personnel" – as is usually maintained – the model presented here suggests that governments would have to take supply-side measures to allow the system to respond to that shift in demand. Indications of such a situation would presumably include increased employment opportunities and salaries for graduates, greater numbers of applicants for the number of college and university places available, and increased entry standards. The challenge to governments is to respond to such signals with the appropriate adjustments on the supply side.

Increased Family Savings and Other Preparation – and Some Policy Implications

The effects of increased family savings – or other kinds of parental investments in their children's educational futures – would have similar effects to increases in student financial aid in terms of the overall numbers of students in the system, but different impacts with respect to who gains access to post-secondary education. In short, there would be a greater number, and share, of individuals from the types of families that undertook this greater preparation, by encouraging harder work during high school to meet entry requirements, increasing savings to make it more affordable (and worthwhile) for their children to go on to post-secondary education, or any other means. That is, the demand curve for post-secondary education among the children of these families would shift outward. But in the absence of any supply-side policies that expanded the capacity of the system, these individuals would tend to crowd individuals from other families out of the system. It is important to consider these implications in the context of government programs geared to helping parents prepare and pay for their children's education.

In particular, to the degree such policies increase the preparation for post-secondary education on the part of higher-income families, the children of those families will be more likely to go on to post-secondary education and – by the implications of the model presented here – take the place of others. Who, then, are the beneficiaries of recent government programs of this type, and who does not benefit? Or, in the context of this analysis, who is likely to crowd out whom as a result of these initiatives? It is important to consider such implications in terms of predicting the present and future effects of such government policies on access to the post-secondary system.

For example, the recent increases in the tax credits related to post-secondary education (e.g., the doubling of the basic tuition and education tax credits) will tend to result in higher participation rates of the children of the beneficiaries of those programs, offset by declines in the participation rates of non-recipients. The same could be said for the Canada Education Savings Grants and Registered Education Savings Program, which provide up to $500 per year for parents who save for their children's education and shelter the returns on these investments from taxes until the money is withdrawn, which can then be done in the name of the lower-taxed student rather than the parent.

The same logic applies to similar changes, including parents becoming more aware of the costs of post-secondary education and saving more for their children's education, beyond that which any government policy provides.

It is generally laudable to see increased preparedness on the part of parents for their children's education, and perhaps good for governments to contribute to this dynamic. But the full effects of these activities should be thought through. And the model provided here points to the risk of any resulting increased demand leading not to rises in the overall number of students but rather to a change in the characteristics of those students, with greater representation among those who engage in greater preparedness and fewer from those who do not. To the degree the system is supply-constrained, this is what has come to be known as a "zero sum game" – where "winners" are offset by "losers."

In the case of student financial aid programs, it has been suggested that this is not necessarily a bad thing, if the "winners" are individuals from lower-income families who are put on a more even footing in terms of getting into college or university relative to those from higher-income families. But it is probably safe to say that most recently adopted "pro-preparation" initiatives have disproportionately benefitted upper- and middle-income families, since lower-income families lack the financial means to save for their children's future education, do not benefit from the available tax credits, and so on.

Complementary policies could be adopted to match these newly gained advantages for the middle and upper classes to provide some sort of similar set of advantages – presumably of a different kind, such as increased direct need-based student financial aid in the form of grants, loans, and so forth – to lower-income families, but the importance of doing this to avoid the crowding out just described should be recognised. The failure to do so could result in the current policies that are intended to increase participation in the post-secondary education system creating (further) advantages for middle- and higher-income families, who benefit disproportionately from these programs, and leave lower-income families behind, in relative and absolute terms.

The alternative remedy to this thorny dynamic is an expansion of the capacity of the system to create the extra spaces required by the increased demand that is likely to derive from these pro-education government initiatives. The model presented here helps to illustrate all these issues and also points to the need to learn more about the actual magnitudes of the

Figure 2.3
Effect of Increase in Tuition – No Pass-On

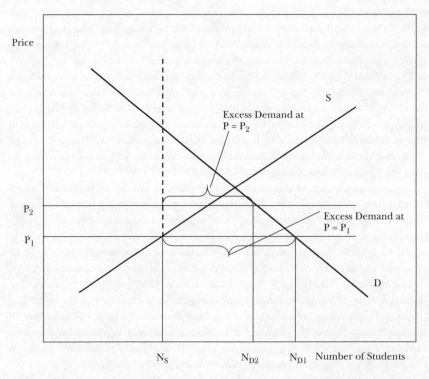

relevant effects – how the demand for post-secondary education has shifted in the past and is likely to shift further in the future as a result of each of the underlying changes being discussed, what the precise response of universities and colleges has been and is likely to be in the future in the face of these shifts in demand, and so on. The framework developed here should be useful for identifying the qualitative nature of these relationships in principle, but needs to be fleshed out with hard data for it to be more fully useful for policy formation.

Increases in Tuition With No Pass-On of the Revenues

This analytical framework can also be used to consider the effects of an increase in tuition fees. Suppose we undo the demand shift stemming from an increase in student financial aid and focus instead on such a price change. This is shown in Figure 2.3. The higher tuition fees – which in the Canadian context might again be assumed to be determined by provincial education ministries – are shown as the change from P_1 to P_2.

In the face of this price increase, the model predicts that demand will fall to N_{D2}. If we suppose that post-secondary institutions do not receive any of the increased funds (and there are no other policy changes affecting supply), the number of places at colleges and universities will not change, and will thus remain at N_S. This situation can be represented by the dashed line indicating a vertical supply curve at that point, which reflects that supply will not be affected by the change in price, precisely because institutions do not receive any of the increased revenue. Most importantly, there will again be no change in the number of students in the system, because although demand is still greater than supply, the number of places in the system is still supply-constrained, and there has been nothing to affect capacity.

At the same time, excess demand in the system will fall to N_{D2}-N_S, as some individuals are no longer able – or no longer willing – to pay for post-secondary schooling at the higher price. As a result, entrance criteria will be adjusted downward as institutions effectively dig deeper into the smaller pool of applicants to fill their places. The average "quality" of students will, therefore, decline. The nature of the student body will also change with re-spect to family background. In particular, fewer applicants are likely to come from lower-income families, as they are priced out of the market.

The ultimate effect on the mix of the student body is, however, more ambiguous, and will depend on the number who are no longer able to attend because they cannot afford the costs and the number who choose not to attend because post-secondary education is no longer a worthwhile investment at the higher fee levels – that is, the "affordability" and "rate of return" effects discussed earlier.

The overall effect on the number of applicants will depend on the relative strengths of each of these effects, and the correlation of the second effect, in particular, with family background (the first effect can, by definition, be assumed to be highly correlated with family background). In general, we might expect the price increase to cause a reduction in the share of students from lower-income families among applicants, but this is not guaranteed. If the price increase turns out to have relatively little effect on individuals' ability to pay ("affordability") and a strong effect related to schooling no longer being a worthwhile investment ("rate of return"), and if there is a strong correlation between the latter ("investment") effect and family income (i.e., those who "choose" to drop out come from higher-income families), the price change *could* actually result in an increased proportion of students from lower-income families in the new pool of applicants (although their absolute numbers would still decline). The final effects on the composition of the student body with respect to family background would then depend, additionally, on the admission criteria (i.e., "ability") and – again – the correlation of these with family background. These empirical questions can only be solved by an appeal to data.

Perhaps the most important aspect of this dynamic is that *opportunities* decline for those from lower-income families, while certain *optimal choices* might shift for those who still have the option of going in terms of having sufficient means. The former is a problem from both equity and efficiency perspectives: everyone with the ability and desire *should* have the opportunity to attend on fairness grounds *and* to ensure that the best students make it into the system to drive the economy forward.

Tuition increases are, therefore, an undesirable policy move in terms of the effects on the quality and characteristics of the post-secondary student body with respect to family background, while they will have no effect on quantity. The only benefit is that the government will receive the higher tuition fees.

Tuition Increases – Passing on the Revenue

Suppose now that post-secondary institutions – colleges and universities – receive the increased tuition fees postulated above. The demand effects remain as before, but there will now be an increase in supply in response to the higher price. This is shown as the change from N_{S1} to N_{S2} in Figure 2.4.

The result of the tuition increase is, therefore, an *increase* in the number of students in the system, because the system, as characterised here, is supply-constrained, meaning that any changes in overall numbers will be driven by changes in supply – that is, the capacity of the institutions. In this case, the change is precipitated by institutions' responses to the increase in tuition fees, which provides the means and incentives for them to grow.[20]

This dynamic implies, furthermore, that we will observe the "perverse" result that an increase in tuition results in an increase in the number of students in the system and higher overall post-secondary education participation rates (as conventionally measured). In contrast to common misperceptions, such an observation should not be taken to imply the absence of demand-side effects, but only that the number of students is (again) capacity-constrained, and increases only when institutions are given the incentives and means to grow. We are, then, measuring the supply-side response to an increase in price/funding – not the demand side at all. We should not look to observed relationships between tuition levels and the number of post-secondary students to tell us anything about the effects of tuition on access.[21]

However, demand-side effects will occur in response to the tuition increases. The number of applicants will change exactly as it did in the preceding case where the higher tuition fees were not passed on to institutions, because individuals will be responding to the same price change. Therefore, the "quality" of students will again change relative to the situation before the price change, as institutions again lower their entrance

Figure 2.4
Effect of Increase in Tuition – Revenue Passed On

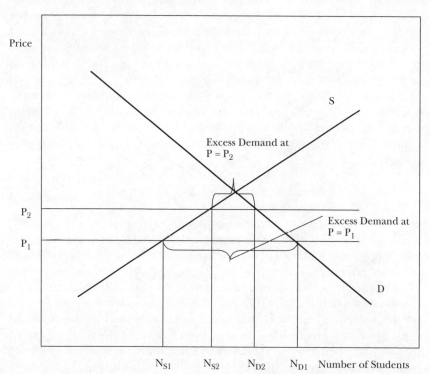

criteria to fill their places out of the smaller applicant pool that exists at the higher price. In addition, the increase in supply that results from the price increase means that there are even more places to fill, causing a further decline in entrance standards.

As for the changes in the composition of the student body with respect to family background, the effects are much the same as in the preceding case, except that more students get accepted. Probably most importantly, there will be an unambiguous decline in the number of applications from students from lower-income families, as such individuals are priced out of the market. There will also be a decline related to those who no longer see post-secondary education to be a worthwhile investment at the higher price. These are the same demand-side effects on applications as seen in the previous case where tuition was increased but institutions did not receive any of the increased revenue. The net effect on the *mix* of students applying to the system with respect to family background will again depend on the same relative strengths of these effects discussed above.

Figure 2.5
An Expansion of Capacity

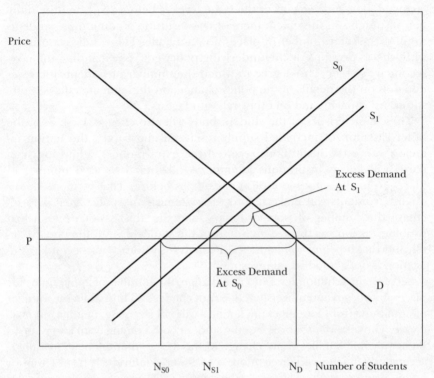

Furthermore, the "acceptance" effect described above will also occur, but will not be as strong as in the preceding case because acceptance rates are higher (for the reasons just described).[22]

Expanding Capacity

Another case to consider is where the capacity of the post-secondary system expands while tuition fees and other policies are left unchanged. This is perhaps an especially relevant policy consideration at a time when governments are committed to increasing the number of post-secondary graduates, but are at the same time reluctant to increase tuition levels for political reasons. In Figure 2.5, this scenario is represented by an outward shift of the supply curve from S_0 to S_1. Such an expansion could come in the form of more generous funding schedules or any other policy change that made it worthwhile for institutions to admit a greater number of students at any given level of tuition fees.

With such a shift in the supply curve, the quantity supplied at prevailing tuition fees (P) will increase from N_{So} to N_{S1}. Since tuition levels have not changed, demand remains at the same level as before (N_D), but the number of students in the system increases, as institutions admit more students to fill the greater number of places now available. This result is consistent with what is presumably the underlying policy goal of expanding the post-secondary system. The degree to which the number of students increases depends on the details of the policy change, on the ultimate effects on institutions' capacity, and on other relevant factors.

The characteristics of the student body will also change. First, as in the other situation of increased supply discussed above (i.e., the tuition increase where the institutions received the extra money), admission standards will fall as institutions attempt to fill their increased number of places from the same pool of applicants as before. That is, more "lower quality" students will make it into the system. If the policy goal is to increase the number of post-secondary students, this is not necessarily a problem, as long as the system does not dig so deeply into the pool of applicants that it begins to include individuals for whom a post-secondary education is not a good social investment.[23]

Second, since tuition levels do not change, the number of applications for places in colleges and universities does not change.[24] Thus, while the number of applicants from lower-income families will not decrease, neither will it increase. The relative proportion of the student body coming from lower- versus higher-income families could change to the degree that the new "marginal" acceptances include relatively more – or fewer – individuals from lower- or higher-income families. These are the same sort of "acceptance effects" as discussed above. However, this effect could run one way or the other.[25] The nature of the student body in terms of the share proportions of students coming from different family backgrounds may change as the institutions accept more applicants into the system – but the direction of this effect is difficult to predict, and a reasonable guess would be that no such change would occur.

WHAT HAS BEEN HAPPENING IN CANADA?

How can this analytical framework help us understand what has been happening to post-secondary education in Canada over the last decade? Although developments have varied significantly across provinces and over time, they can probably be broadly characterised by the following:

- Tuition rates have increased substantially;
- Returns to post-secondary education have risen, as labour market opportunities for those with lower levels of education have fallen sharply, whereas for those with college and university educations they have in

some cases improved (especially for women), in others remained stable, and in still others declined – but not nearly so precipitously;
- While the data are more sketchy, the number of applications for college and university appears to have climbed;
- The overall number of students in the post-secondary system has risen slightly – albeit unevenly across jurisdictions, institutions, and over time;
- Post-secondary education participation rates (e.g., as measured by the percentage of the 18 to 24-year-old population in school) have risen;
- Myriad changes have been made to the student financial aid system(s), although it is difficult to know what the overall effects have been in terms of providing money to needy students;
- Participation rates have risen across all family types; the increases have been greatest for those from higher-income families thus widening the differences in participation rates by family background.

These developments can be represented and interpreted using the analytical framework developed above. A broad characterisation is as shown in Figure 2.6. The tuition increases instituted in all provinces (although to varying degrees) are represented in the shift from P_0 to P_1. The substantial increases in the returns to post-secondary education are reflected in the outward shift in the demand curve (from D_0 to D_1). There has – roughly speaking – probably been a backward shift in the supply curve (e.g., to S_1).[26]

How do we know this? First, the tuition increases are obvious (Junor and Usher, 2002). Second, we should suspect that the demand curve has generally shifted outwards for a number of reasons. Labour market data indicate that the returns to post-secondary education have increased over this period (Riddell and Sweetman, 2000). Family incomes have generally risen, certainly since the middle of the last decade, and especially for the higher-income families among which participation rates are high, thus presumably driving demand outward still further (Frenette, Green, and Picot, 2004). Tempering this are the uneven changes in student financial assistance (Finnie, Schwarz, and Lascelles, 2003). We would thus predict a probable increase in demand based on the changes in some of the key underlying factors. Turning to the empirical evidence, despite the higher tuition levels, the available data seem to indicate that the number of applications has indeed risen – which would normally happen only in the presence in an outward shift in demand (Finnie and Usher, 2005).

The backward shift in the supply curve may be similarly deduced in two ways. First, there have been general reductions in the financial support provided to institutions by provincial governments, which are responsible for supporting post-secondary education in Canada (AUCC, 2002). In addition, costs have risen – largely because of an ageing, and therefore higher paid, staff of professors – meaning fewer classes can be offered, and fewer

Figure 2.6
Recent Developments in Canada

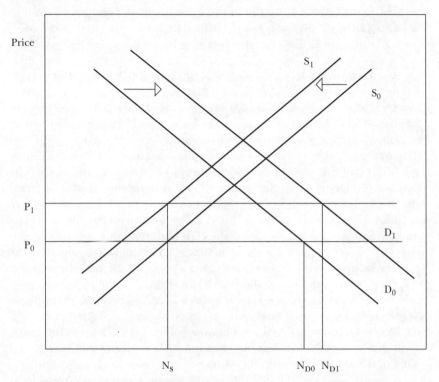

Number of Students

students taught, at any given level of support. In addition to apparent shifts in the underlying factors that affect supply, the empirical evidence indicates that the number of places that institutions offer has more or less held steady in the presence of higher tuition fees, rather than expanding, as would have been expected – thus suggesting the presence of a countervailing force, such as the postulated supply shift.

Changes in the demand for post-secondary education, and actual participation rates, for those from lower-income families, are more difficult to assess. The increases in the returns to post-secondary education noted above would presumably have shifted the demand for post-secondary education outward for all individuals, but changes in family income in the lower ranges and shifts in the student financial aid system are more difficult to assess in terms of their likely impacts. Again, we might look beyond these underlying factors to look at the actual data, and the scarce evidence that exists points to an increase in the number of applications and actual post-secondary participants at lower income levels despite the increases in tuition rates, and thus to an overall outward shift in demand – but perhaps less than in the case of middle- and higher-income families. While the tentative nature of any such conclusion must be emphasized, some new empirical evidence in this regard is presented.

NEW EVIDENCE ON PARTICIPATION BY FAMILY TYPE

How does access to the post-secondary education system vary with family background? This is an important issue for two main reasons. First is the question of fairness and equality of opportunity: to what degree do individuals gain the life chances associated with post-secondary education according to their abilities, desires, and willingness to do the work rather than to being born to families that deliver those opportunities as a matter of birthright. Second, and related, the nation's economic performance is largely determined by its human resources, and key to this is that the most talented individuals rise to the top of the skill hierarchy through having the chance to go on to post-secondary education rather than being stuck at some lesser point while those who are less apt but better placed slide through a system which treats them with privilege.

This section presents some recent empirical evidence on patterns of access to post-secondary education in 1991 in comparison to almost a decade later, in 2000, based on the School Leaver Survey (SLS – 1991) and Youth in Transition Survey (YITS – 2000), conducted by Statistics Canada.

One of the great changes in the post-secondary education system during the 1990s was the precipitous increases in tuition fees in most provinces. As a result, one might expect to find a general reduction in post-secondary and university attendance and a change in the composition of the student body away from those from lower-income families towards those better placed to meet these increases.

We find that, on the first point, the exact opposite has occurred: post-secondary education participation rates rose pretty much across the board over this period. On the second, the evidence is more mixed. In most cases, participation rates increased for those from lower parental-education families (a proxy for family income), but not as much as for those from higher-education families. These results suggest that participation rates are the outcome of many factors – on the demand side and on the supply side in terms of the framework developed here – of which tuition rates are but one.

Some interesting patterns by province are also reported, further illustrating how participation rates are determined by much more than tuition levels, since in some cases attendance increased most where tuition rates also climbed a great deal, and rose least where tuition increases were held lowest.

These results thus pose many questions. What has determined these patterns? What initiatives could be taken to make access more equal with respect to family background? What needs to be done about the total capacity of the system? The analytical framework proposed in this chapter should provide a useful starting point for beginning the search for the answers to these and related questions.[27]

DEFINITIONS AND OVERALL PARTICIPATION RATES

A significant literature exists on the links between participation in post-secondary education and family background, and generally finds that the two are significantly related, whether this be measured by family income, parental education, family type, or some other indicator.[28] But while much is known, the work reported here, based on two directly comparable data sources, shows for the first time how patterns changed from the beginning to the end of the turbulent 1990s.

The focus here is on participation rates for 18 to 20-year-olds, the age group that is overlapped in the two surveys used in the analysis. However, similar findings hold when we look at 20-year-olds alone, by which time participation rates are closer to reaching their peak as individuals move out of high school and into college or university – sometimes with a delay.

The specific measures of participation in post-secondary education employed are: i) having at some time been enrolled in post-secondary education of any type (trade-vocational, college, or university); ii) going to university. Analysing these two outcomes thus represents looking at successively higher levels of education.[29] The entire analysis is broken down by sex.

As shown in the top panel of Table 2.1, 39 per cent of male respondents and 49 per cent of female respondents aged 18–20 had participated in some form of post-secondary education in the earlier period (1991), according to the SLS data. These figures increase to 47 per cent and 59 per cent, respectively, in the later period (2000), according to the YITS. In comparison, 17 per cent of males and 23 per cent of females had attained some level of university education in the SLS (recall that this figure is for 18 to 20-year-olds combined – this aggregation necessitated by the relatively small sample sizes available), while the corresponding rates in the later period were 20 per cent and 28 per cent, respectively.

Post-secondary education participation rates thus generally grew significantly in the 1990s. The proportion of those *not* furthering their education beyond high school in the population of 18 to 20-year-olds included in our samples declined from 61 to 54 per cent for males, and from 51 to 41 per cent for females. Rates of attendance were proportionately up, with any post-secondary and university attendance increasing by 19–21 per cent in each case.

Table 2.1
Overall Participation Rates by Sex and Level

| | Rate | | | | % Change | |
| | Male | | Female | | Male | Female |
Variable	SLS	YITS	SLS	YITS		
Post-Secondary Access						
None	0.606	0.533	0.507	0.409	−12	−19
Any Post-Secondary	0.394	0.467	0.494	0.591	19	20
University	0.168	0.201	0.228	0.276	20	21

Note: % change refers to percentage change in descriptive statistics from the SLS to the YITS.

Although their increases were similar in relative terms, women started at higher participation rates than men (i.e., 49.4 versus 39.4 per cent for any post-secondary, and 22.8 versus 16.8 for university), so their increases were greater in absolute terms (9.7 versus 7.3 per cent for any post-secondary and .042 versus .033 for university). Thus, the gender gap(s) in post-secondary participation widened over this period. In the later period, female participation rates had risen to 59.1 per cent for any post-secondary and 27.6 per cent for university, while the male rates were 46.7 and 20.1, respectively.[30]

PARTICIPATION RATES BY FAMILY TYPE
AND PROVINCE

Family type has a large effect on the likelihood of post-secondary attendance, as shown in Table 2.2. In the SLS data (1991), 19 per cent of all males who lived in a two-parent family went to university, whereas the rates for those living in a single-parent household were significantly lower: 11 per cent in mother-only families; and 7 per cent for the relatively small numbers coming from father-only families. (The rate for the small number living in "other" arrangements is lower still, at just 5 per cent.) The YITS data (2000) reveal that male university participation rates rose for all family types through the 1990s, and more for those from single-mother families than for those in two-parent families (23 versus 18 per cent respectively). Despite these gains, participation rates continue to vary significantly with family type – hence something of a good news, bad news story.

Similar patterns hold for females, and at the any post-secondary education level participation rates are significantly higher for those coming from two-parent families than for those in single-parent situations, but

Table 2.2
Participation Rates by Family Type and Province

| | Participation Rate | | | | % Change | |
| | Male | | Female | | Male | Female |
Variable	SLS	YITS	SLS	YITS		
ANY POST-SECONDARY						
Family Type						
Live with two parents	0.423	0.492	0.532	0.615	17	16
Live with father	0.326	0.363	0.531	0.488	11	−8
Live with mother	0.282	0.382	0.341	0.532	36	56
Live other	0.185	0.368	0.305	0.437	100	43
Province						
Newfoundland	0.364	0.549	0.454	0.670	51	48
Prince Edward Island	0.318	0.489	0.420	0.585	54	39
Nova Scotia	0.307	0.478	0.399	0.687	56	72
New Brunswick	0.294	0.460	0.488	0.653	57	34
Quebec	0.590	0.616	0.728	0.772	4	6
Ontario	0.315	0.402	0.392	0.508	28	29
Manitoba	0.306	0.412	0.460	0.532	34	16
Saskatchewan	0.358	0.442	0.418	0.575	23	37
Alberta	0.377	0.387	0.480	0.468	3	−3
British Columbia	0.395	0.434	0.432	0.551	10	27
UNIVERSITY						
Family Type						
Live with two parents	0.187	0.220	0.251	0.304	18	21
Live with father	0.068	0.109	0.254	0.147	61	−42
Live with mother	0.106	0.131	0.143	0.178	23	24
Live other	0.053	0.159	0.102	0.214	201	110
Province						
Newfoundland	0.254	0.325	0.307	0.462	28	51
Prince Edward Island	0.266	0.326	0.301	0.389	23	29
Nova Scotia	0.212	0.336	0.312	0.513	59	64
New Brunswick	0.196	0.269	0.286	0.421	37	47
Quebec	0.080	0.084	0.134	0.130	5	−3
Ontario	0.175	0.209	0.238	0.280	20	18
Manitoba	0.211	0.263	0.362	0.368	24	2
Saskatchewan	0.230	0.294	0.308	0.405	28	31
Alberta	0.203	0.223	0.278	0.265	10	−5
British Columbia	0.206	0.268	0.205	0.367	30	79

Note: % change refers to percentage change in descriptive statistics from the SLS to the YITS.

rates rose across the board through the 1990s, and in every case more for those from single-mother families than for those from two-parent families, meaning the former did some catching up to the latter over this decade of change.

The participation rates by province, also depicted in Table 2.2, reveal significant differences in post-secondary and university attendance in this dimension as well. The any post-secondary education attendance rate in Quebec is especially high, at least partly because of the inclusion of their CEGEP system (Quebec's hybrid of high school and college) as a type of post-secondary institution, whereas their university attendance rates are lower for similar reasons. Ontario's lower numbers are at least partly because of grade 13, which delays the entry into tertiary education.

Perhaps most interesting, at least to the major themes developed in this chapter, is first, that most provinces had significant increases in the rates of any post-secondary and university attendance through the 1990s, in the order of 50 per cent for the eastern provinces and around 25 per cent for most others. Second, Alberta and Quebec saw little or no growth between the two surveys, in a context where Quebec, in particular, largely held its tuition rates constant over this period, while tuition fees rose sharply in most other provinces, including especially Nova Scotia, which registered among the greatest increases in participation rates.

The lesson pertaining to this chapter is that looking at the simple relationship between tuition levels and participation rates is not likely to show the effect of the former on the latter, because of all the other factors that determine who goes to school – including various demand-side influences and the supply side, as represented in the framework model.

PARTICIPATION RATES BY PARENTAL EDUCATION LEVEL

Finally, the results also show how parental education is very strongly correlated with participation in the post-secondary education system, as shown in Table 2.3.[31] Each additional level of parental education in two-parent families is associated with a higher rate of both any post-secondary and university attendance for male and female respondents in both time periods. The rate of going on to university is, in particular, much higher for the children of university-educated parents than for the children of parents with any other education level. For example, in every case, respondents are over three times as likely to go to university if their parents both have a university education as opposed to having less than high school completed. The patterns for any post-secondary attendance are in the same direction, but less extreme.[32]

Table 2.3
Participation Rates by Parental Education Level

	Participation Rate				% Change	
	2 Parents		Single Mother		2 Parents	Single Mother
Parent Education	SLS	YITS	SLS	YITS		
ANY POST-SECONDARY						
Male						
no HS	0.364	0.320	0.258	0.257	−12	0
	(.023)	(.031)	(.044)	(.044)		
HS	0.419	0.441	0.254	0.334	5	31
	(.032)	(.018)	(.048)	(.027)		
College	0.544	0.647	0.347	0.483	19	39
	(.070)	(.029)	(.092)	(.044)		
University	0.633	0.716	0.434	0.601	13	39
	(.038)	(.022)	(.085)	(.044)		
Female						
no HS	0.467	0.492	0.249	0.467	5	88
	(.022)	(.030)	(.038)	(.040)		
HS	0.517	0.547	0.434	0.487	6	12
	(.035)	(.017)	(.056)	(.031)		
College	0.584	0.727	0.299	0.576	24	93
	(.054)	(.028)	(.065)	(.038)		
University	0.675	0.792	0.463	0.756	17	63
	(.036)	(.020)	(.082)	(.037)		
UNIVERSITY						
Male						
no HS	0.092	0.098	0.119	0.071	7	−41
	(.014)	(.017)	(.033)	(.027)		
HS	0.199	0.166	0.083	0.091	−16	9
	(.026)	(.013)	(.031)	(.018)		
College	0.150	0.238	0.062	0.146	58	135
	(.051)	(.027)	(.046)	(.032)		
University	0.492	0.481	0.199	0.294	−2	48
	(.039)	(.025)	(.068)	(.047)		
Female						
no HS	0.147	0.145	0.072	0.132	−2	84
	(.016)	(.022)	(.023)	(.031)		
HS	0.219	0.245	0.917	0.145	12	−26
	(.029)	(.014)	(.045)	(.018)		
College	0.286	0.336	0.156	0.193	17	23
	(.050)	(.028)	(.052)	(.030)		
University	0.463	0.549	0.270	0.352	19	30
	(.039)	(.026)	(.073)	(.051)		

Note: Both parents have equal levels of education for two-parent families used in this table.

As for changes over time, participation rates generally increased the most for those with college-educated parents, those with university-educated parents came next, and those with completed high school and, especially, those with parents with less than high school completed experienced the smallest increases. The sample sizes begin to get small here, though, so the smaller differences should be regarded as not being statistically significant, and no fine-slicing should be attempted with these numbers.

HOW THESE FINDINGS PERTAIN TO THE THEMES OF THIS CHAPTER

These findings fit into the general topic of this chapter in a couple of ways. First, in showing that post-secondary education participation rates have generally risen through the 1990s, despite the sharp increases in tuition, they confirm that the number of students in the system is determined by much more than this one demand-side factor, and that it is impossible to identify the effects of tuition on demand using such simple two-way comparisons.[33]

Second, the results show how the various factors that affect the demand for post-secondary education have had differential effects by province and parental education level through the 1990s. Regarding the former, supply-side policies have presumably played at least a partial role – along with the various demand-side factors – in generating the differential increases in participation rates across jurisdictions over this period.

As for the changing relation between family background and access, the 1990s would appear to have been a period of some gains, and some losses, as single-parent families generally did some catching up to two-parent families, children with college-educated parents saw greater gains than those whose parents had university-level educations, but the increases in participation rates were smaller for those with parents lacking post-secondary education or not having finished high school, leaving them further behind than ever. Policy formation could presumably take advantage of these findings, even as they point to the need to know more about *why* these particular trends obtained.

SUMMARY AND CONCLUSION

This paper has developed an analytical framework for considering various questions pertaining to post-secondary education, including the determinants of the overall number of participants in the system, the characteristics of the student body in terms of scholastic ability and family background, and the effects of tuition fees on the supply of and demand for places in the post-secondary system.

One important aspect of this framework is how it draws attention to capacity issues – especially in a context where the system is probably supply-constrained to a significant degree. The framework shows how the number of college and university students can, in such a situation, be increased only if the capacity of the system is expanded. This is perhaps not a foreign concept to many observers of the post-secondary system, but coming at the issue with the benefit of a formal framework might be useful for thinking along these lines. This particular issue is, furthermore, especially important in a policy context where governments have been seeking to increase the number of post-secondary students, but have perhaps too often focused their attention on grants and bursaries and other demand-side issues, while largely neglecting the capacity issues that are at the core of the problem. The model also shows what might happen to the make-up of the student body in terms of family background and ability as various demand-side factors shift and governments take action, or not, on the supply side.

Probably the second most important aspect of the paper is its focus on access issues, especially those pertaining to the social basis of participation in the system. The framework developed here is useful for understanding what it means to improve access for those from lower-income families – by expanding student financial assistance, for example. It also shows what might be expected in terms of the effects on the total number of students in the system (perhaps no change), the average quality of students (it should rise), and the representation in the student body of families across the entire income spectrum (post-secondary participation rates should become more equal). The model also helps us to speculate on what might be the effects of the various government policies aimed at increasing participation through helping families save or otherwise prepare for their children's post-secondary studies. These are not always what was perhaps intended, especially where individuals from the higher-income families that are often able to take advantage of these programs may wind up crowding out those from lower-income families who cannot (or at least do not).

The third major contribution of the paper is to put tuition policies in the context of their effects on both supply and demand sides of the post-secondary equation. For example, raising tuition levels can – if institutions share in these revenues – lead to increases in the number of students, but it is important to understand that the composition of the student body will change in terms of both average "ability" (the model predicts it will decline) and family background (individuals from lower-income families will tend to be priced out of the system – although the effect on the mix of the actual student body is more ambiguous). The model also shows, in particular, that we should not be surprised to observe a positive relationship in tuition levels and the number of students across jurisdictions or over time – depending, that is, on the degree to which the money is ploughed back into the system, thus leading to increases in capacity.

Beyond treating each potential change in the post-secondary system separately, this framework also offers a way of understanding the effects of various combinations of policy measures – and of the real-world developments we have observed in the system. For example, the model shows how the system could be expanded by raising tuition fees and passing these additional revenues on to institutions so that they can grow, but indicates that the resulting negative impact on participation by those from lower-income families would need to be counteracted by compensatory increases in the financial aid available to students from lower-income families. Again, this is not an original idea, but presenting it in this formal framework clarifies the issues.

Data Issues

These discussions also provide a useful point of departure for thinking about what other data would help us better understand developments in the post-secondary system regarding access and capacity, and the magnitude of the various effects that have been sketched out in theoretical terms here – and otherwise contribute to our understanding of these and related issues.

What, then, to look for to better understand what has really been going on? Gaining access to application data would be very useful, as these could indicate what has been happening to the total demand in the system. Being able to break down application data, as well as actual participation data, by family background would also be particularly helpful, as this would allow us to better determine the net effects of the higher tuition fees, the increases in the returns to higher education, and the changes in the student financial aid system on access by family background.

One problem with such data is that they do not tell us about *non*-applicants, and so control groups have to be constructed, which is always a challenging task.[34] As usual, the perfect data for such investigations do not exist, and never will. Possibilities for investigating at least some of these questions will, however, improve with the release of two datasets currently under preparation by Statistics Canada. The first interview data of the Youth in Transition Survey (YITS), from which some preliminary results have been reported here, is one of these, as it includes extensive information, including participation in the post-secondary education system, on a large sample of 18 to 20-year-olds interviewed in 2000. Furthermore the data are similar enough in structure to those contained in the earlier School Leavers Survey, dating from a decade before, to permit the analysis of changes in participation rates and the underlying *structure* of those rates over that period.[35]

Second, the Post-Secondary Education Participation Survey (PEPS) builds on the standard Labour Force Survey to focus on various access questions, especially those pertaining to the role of the student loan system in facilitating participation in post-secondary education, as well as allowing another study of how post-secondary participation varies with family background.

Finally, there are many opportunities for administrative data, such as those in British Columbia that track individuals through high school into their post-secondary years. More such data, and combining these resources with other datasets, could be extremely useful for looking at issues of access to and participation in the post-secondary system in Canada.

THE FINAL WORD

The principal goal of this paper was to introduce a simple formal conceptual framework that would help us understand the determinants of the number of students in the post-secondary system, the make-up of the student body, and related issues, including various related policy issues. In first separating demand influences from those that operate on the supply side, and then drilling into each set of factors in some detail, this basic objective has perhaps been achieved.

While the model is perhaps overly simple, its careful use could be quite useful. For example, it could help us better understand – or at least formally represent – the importance of capacity constraints in determining the number and characteristics of students. Perhaps less dramatic, but more intriguing and ultimately more useful, is how it could help us think through the gamut of government policies in similar terms, especially those aimed at increasing access. It flags, for example, the possibility that many of the government's recent initiatives aimed at helping parents save for their children's education might have the positive effects desired for the targeted middle-income families – but perhaps at the cost of crowding out others, including those from lower-income families who tend to benefit less from such programs. Or do they benefit less? We need to find this out. The model helps us identify those places where most information is needed to understand the workings of the system – and develop better policy.

Finally, the paper also provides some new empirical evidence on post-secondary participation by family background and province, and on how these patterns changed through the 1990s, which saw such change in the system. These are interesting findings on their own, but are perhaps especially valuable here for how they tie into the themes of this chapter – and this book – by illustrating how complex the system is in terms of generating the size and composition of the student population.

It is hoped that this framework provides the basis for helping some observers understand the determinants of participation in post-secondary education and a point of departure for others doing research in the area.

NOTES

1 See Finnie, Schwartz, and Lascelles (2003) for details on these changes in student financial aid, estimates of federal and provincial government spending on the different kinds of aid, and some of the implications of these spending patterns for access to post-secondary education.

2 The definition of post-secondary education usually includes certain private colleges and trade-vocational schools, but the emphasis in this chapter is on the public system.

3 Tuition levels have two separate effects. First, being one important component of the total costs of going to school, tuition levels affect the rate of return to that activity: the benefits of doing so as compared to the full costs, including the opportunity costs of attending. Second, tuition levels affect the affordability of schooling, in the sense that some students for whom schooling is a worthwhile investment will be unable to go because they cannot come up with the cash to cover the associated costs, including not only direct costs such as tuition, books, and equipment but also their living costs. See Vaillancourt and Beaudry-Primeau (2002). These two effects can thus be thought of as: i) the rate-of-return effect; and ii) the affordability effect.

4 See Finnie (2004) for recent evidence showing that going to graduate school, in particular, appears to vary inversely with prevailing macro conditions: when the economy slows (and unemployment rates rise), attendance increases, and vice versa.

5 Education is, of course, more than just a money-driven investment, and the degree to which individuals gain other benefits from going to college or university – such as the pleasure of learning, the opening of career opportunities that are interesting and rewarding apart from any associated monetary benefits, and the chance to have an interesting social experience – will also affect the demand for post-secondary education. These factors are not focused on here, since they are less directly pertinent to the policy discussions at hand, but they could easily be incorporated into the discussions.

6 This stylisation may be somewhat better suited to the university sector than to the college sector, but taken in its entirety, the model may be judiciously applied and adapted to most situations.

7 This concept conforms to the standard micro-economic notion that firms – in this case post-secondary institutions – expand up to the point where marginal

cost is equal to the market price, or revenue received. Rising cost curves, as are considered to be the norm, generate the sort of upward-sloping supply curve described here.

8 Note that the author is not aware of any hard empirical evidence regarding the relationship between tuition levels and capacity. On the other hand, colleges and universities usually lobby for more money in one form or another – higher fees, larger cuts of the tuition fees their students already pay, or some other form – to expand, and it seems safe to assume that capacity is directly related to the funds universities have to operate to at least some degree. The ensuing discussions require no more than this, but – again – also treat the vertical supply curve case, where it is assumed capacity does not respond to tuition and is otherwise fixed or otherwise determined by factors outside the model.

9 Similarly, questions of fixed versus variable costs, in addition to corresponding issues regarding how funding is delivered to institutions (block grants, per-student transfers, etc.) would be relevant to any more detailed and specific characterisation of the system, but would not necessarily change the basic notion of an upward-sloping demand curve.

10 Some provinces allow some room for institutions to set their own fees, but usually within relatively narrow ranges. More general exceptions have emerged in recent years, but tend to apply only to specialised programs. For example, Ontario universities are now free to set fees as they like for most professional programs. The general thrust of the situation represented in this analysis therefore applies to most situations. Important exceptions are private colleges and trade-vocational schools, and the model developed here probably does not apply to them. This is, however, a relatively small component of the overall post-secondary system, and is in any event not within the realm of government policy in terms of determining the capacity of the post-secondary system.

11 Institutions could, of course, always increase enrolment with their given level of resources at the prevailing tuition levels, but in most cases only by reducing the quality of education they offer (e.g., bigger classes, less-qualified teachers). This is merely another way of thinking of the capacity situation as described.

12 The situation described here applies most directly to universities and more specialised college programs, where entry requirements serve this rationing function. Many vocational schools, a good number of college programs, and even some universities in at least some program areas have entry requirements that are so broad that almost anyone could enter and there is little in the way of excess demand. In such cases, the general analytical framework provided here still applies, but does not have the same equilibrium properties and will not change in the same way when the underlying demand and supply factors are adjusted. Such cases are, in addition, not characterised by the same problems as the bulk of the system that is meant to be characterised in this discussion (e.g., increasing demand will indeed lead to an increase in the number of students), and may simply be ignored for most of the purposes of this paper.

13 See Finnie, Schwartz, and Lascelles (2003) for a documentation of the amounts
   of the different kinds of student financial aid provided in this country and the
   implications for access. See also Bell and Anisef (chapter 3).

14 Preliminary work with the recently available PEPS (Post-Secondary Education
   Participation Survey) undertaken by the author indicates that approximately
   two-thirds of all government student loan recipients say they would not have
   been able to pursue their studies without that assistance. There is, though, surprisingly little hard empirical evidence on the degree to which other forms of
   aid have increased access, at least partly because it is a difficult thing to identify:
   it is difficult to know which recipients would not have gone in the absence of
   the assistance offered.

15 See, for example, the federal government's recent statement on this as found in
   HRDC (2002).

16 Of course this is not absolutely true in all cases; excess capacity in the system
   could lead to an increase in the number of students. Such situations are, however, likely to represent small numbers of places and generally be the exception
   rather than the rule, especially in the current circumstances where colleges,
   and especially universities, really do appear to be operating near to capacity in
   terms of both staff and physical plants. The case where the number of students
   is not supply-constrained is considered below.

17 See Finnie, Schwartz, and Lascelles (2003) for a discussion of the effects of each
   of these kinds of aid on access. For the purposes of the present discussion, it is
   only necessary to believe that increased aid has some effect on the demand for
   post-secondary education, which seems a safe assumption; see also footnote 20
   on the recent evidence on how most student loan recipients say they would not
   have been able to go to school without that assistance.

18 The effects of student financial assistance have been represented as a change
   over time, but the same logic would apply to comparing two provinces. For example, we would not necessarily expect to see a greater number of students,
   or higher overall participation rates, in a province that offered more generous
   student financial aid, but the composition of the student body would be
   different, with more students from lower-income families (other factors
   holding constant).

19 Most forms of student aid have two effects on post-secondary participation:
   i) it provides students with the money they need to pay the costs of their
   schooling – i.e., it makes schooling more affordable; and ii) to the degree the
   aid is provided in a non-repayable form (i.e., any non-loan program – although even aid in the form of government student loans is subsidized, as governments pay the interest on the loan while the student is in school, cover
   defaults, and so on), the assistance improves the rate of return to schooling
   because of the effective reduction in costs. The latter effects have various
   "efficiency" properties, and might cause some aid-receiving individuals to go
   to school even though the overall (social) rate of return is below that of other

non-aid receiving individuals. These important considerations are left aside in these discussions, which focus on access and capacity.

20 The actual formula by which the institutions receive the extra funding (e.g., directly or indirectly through changed funding measures) does not affect the essential features of the analysis. For example, complex agreements may relate the funds institutions receive to their number of students. As long as the higher tuition rates result in increased funding for the institutions and institutions increase their numbers of places as a result, the analysis holds.

21 In standard econometrics terms, this represents the well-known concept that in the presence of a supply-constrained system, price changes trace out or "identify" the supply curve.

22 Institutions may, of course, react in other ways to these changes, such as increasing the amount of aid to students from lower-income families. To the degree that such offsetting policies are adopted, the effects just described will be mitigated.

23 We are touching on efficiency issues here – which are again only mentioned in passing so as to focus on the relevant access issues. Determining the optimal number of students is a very difficult policy challenge, which lies at the heart of post-secondary education policy.

24 Over time, the number of applicants might change as more students are admitted to the system, since some students who previously perceived that they had little chance of being accepted now see that it might be worth applying. This is true in the other changes discussed above as well. Such dynamics do not, however, change the basic nature of the analysis, or its implications, in any essential way.

25 There is no strong reason to think that student ability, as represented by high school records and other factors that influence institutions' acceptance decision, is correlated with family income at the acceptance margin.

26 Supply has also been affected by the increased costs of the system, largely driven by the high costs of an aging professoriat, with its seniority-related pay scales. The same number of professors now costs more, meaning that fewer can be employed with the same amount of financing, and faculties have generally been shrinking as a result. This would be represented by a backward shift in the supply curve, as shown – in addition to the effects related to the real funding cuts that have been instituted in most jurisdictions over the last decade or so. We may think of the backward shift of the supply curve as being a function of a combination of decreased funding and higher costs. The result is that there is room for fewer students at any given tuition level, as shown.

27 The work reported here is extracted from a Statistics Canada Analytical Studies Branch Discussion Paper co-authored with Eric Lascelles.

28 Looker (2001) provides a recent overview of existing work in the area and presents policy recommendations. Other work includes Finnie, Lascelles, and Sweetman (2005), Butlin (1999), De Brouker & Lavallée (1998a, b), Finnie and Meng

(2002), Knighton (2002), Christofides, Cirello, and Hoy (2001), Foley (2001), Zhao and de Broucker (2002), Bouchard and Zhao (2000), and Frenette (2002).

29 The original analysis also uses additional breakdowns, but these two categories capture the essence of the findings.

30 Participation rates can be defined in many ways. Certain standard measures are based on the percentage of individuals of a certain age group (e.g., 18–24) at school, others on the education level of adults who are more likely to have completed their schooling. The rates reported here are simply those that apply to the samples and measures used in this analysis, and do not necessarily correspond to other published figures.

31 To simplify the analysis, two-parent families are only examined if both parents have equal levels of education (i.e., within the classifications shown). Finnie, Lascelles, and Sweetman (2003) also consider outcomes where, for two-parent families, the higher education level of the two parents is used; the results are very similar. Single-father families are not examined here because of their small sample size.

32 This finding contrasts to Bouchard and Zhao (2000), who find similar rates of any post-secondary education participation by parental income level, and significant differences only where university attendance is considered.

33 Junor and Usher (2002) show some very simple two-way regression results that further illustrate the lack of much association between tuition rates and participation rates.

34 We would like to be able to analyse who goes and who does not, in a modelling framework using simple cross-tab methods, with respect to family background and other individual and situational characteristics; but just looking at those who apply, or are admitted, does not permit this.

35 The author is ready, for example, to extend the simple tabular analysis presented here to estimate participation models using multivariable regression methods that will allow various extraneous factors to be controlled for and other variables of interest to be investigated.

REFERENCES

Andres, L. and Krahn, H. (1999). "Youth pathways in articulated post-secondary systems: enrolment and completion patterns of urban young women and men." *Canadian Journal of Higher Education, 29*(1), 47–82.

Andres, L. and Looker, D. (2001). "Rurality and capital: Educational expectations and attainment of rural and urban youth." *Canadian Journal of Higher Education, 31*(2), 1–46.

AUCC (2002). *Trends.* Ottawa: Association of Universities and Colleges of Canada.

Bouchard, B. and Zhao, J. (2000). "University education: Recent trends in participation, accessibility and returns." *Education Quarterly Review, 6*(4), 24–32.

Butlin, G. (1999). "Determinants of post-secondary participation." Ottawa: Statistics Canada. *Education Quarterly Review, 5*(3), 9–35.

Christofides, L., Cirello, J., and Hoy, M. (2001). "Family income and postsecondary education in Canada." *The Canadian Journal of Higher Education, 31*, 177–208.

De Broucker, P. and Lavallée, L. (1998a). "Getting ahead in life: Does your parents' education count?" *Education Quarterly Review, 5*(1), 22–8.

– (1998b). "Intergenerational aspects of education and literacy skills acquisition." In M. Corak, ed. *Labour markets, social institutions, and the future of Canada's children.* Ottawa: Statistics Canada. 129–44.

Finnie, R. (2004). "The school-to-work transition of Canadian post-secondary graduates: A dynamic analysis." *Journal of Higher Education and Policy Management, 26*(1), 35–58.

Finnie, R., Lascelles, E., and Laporte, C. (2004). *Family background and access to postsecondary education: What happened over the 1990's?* Analytical Studies Branch Research Paper No. 226. Ottawa: Statistics Canada. Retrieved August 2004, from http://www.statcan.ca/cgi- in/downpub/listpub.cgi?catno=11F0019MIE

Finnie, R., Lascelles, E., and Sweetman, A. (2005). *Who goes: Family background and access to post-secondary education.* Analytical Studies Branch Research Paper No. 226. Ottawa: Statistics Canada. Retrieved August 2005, from http://www.statcan.ca/cgi-bin/downpub/listpub.cgi?catno=11F0019MIE

Finnie, R. and Meng, R. (2002). *A recursive income model for Canadians: The direct and indirect effects of family background.* Queen's University, School of Policy Studies Discussion Paper No. 28. Retrieved August 2004, from http://www.queensu.ca/sps/working_papers/

Finnie, R., Schwartz, S., and Lascelles, E. (2003). "Smart money? Government spending on student financial aid in Canada." In B. Doern, ed. *How Ottawa spends 2003–2004: Regime change and policy shift.* New York: Oxford University Press. 155–86.

Finnie, R. and Usher, A. (2005). "The Canadian experiment in cost-sharing and its effects on access to higher education, 1990–2002." In A. Amaral, P. Teixeira and H. Vossensteyn, eds. *Cost-Sharing and Accessibility with Respect to Higher Education in Mature Economies.* Amsterdam: Kluewer.

Foley, K. (2001). *Why stop after high school? A descriptive analysis of the most important reasons that high school graduates do not continue to PSE.* Montreal: Canada Millennium Scholarship Foundation.

Frenette, M. (2002). *Too far to go? Distance to school and university participation.* Analytical Studies Research Paper No. 191. Ottawa: Statistics Canada. Retrieved August 2004, from http://www.statcan.ca/cgi-bin/downpub/listpub.cgi?catno=11F0019MIE

Frenette, M., Green, D., and Picot, G. (2004). *Rising income inequality in the 1990's: An exploration of three data sources.* Analytical Studies Branch Research Paper No. 226. Ottawa: Statistics Canada. Retrieved August 2005, from http://www.statcan.ca/cgi-bin/downpub/listpub.cgi?catno=11F0019MIE

Junor, S. and Usher, A. (2002). *The price of knowledge.* Montreal: Canada Millennium Scholarship Foundation.

Knighton, T. and Mirza, S. (2002). "Postsecondary participation: the effects of parents' education and household income." Ottawa: Statistics Canada. *Education Quarterly Review, 8*(3), 25–32.

Looker, D. (2001). *Why don't they go on? Factors affecting the decisions of Canadian youth not to pursue post-secondary education.* Montreal: Canada Millennium Scholarship Foundation.

Riddell, C. and Sweetman, A. (2000). "Human capital formation in a period of rapid change." In C. Riddell and F. St. Hillaire, eds. *Adapting Public Policy to a Labour Market in Transition.* Montreal: Institute for Research on Public Policy. 85–141.

Vaillancourt, F. (1995). "The private and total returns to education in Canada, 1985." *Canadian Journal of Economics, 28*(3), 532–53.

Vaillancourt, F. and Bourdeau-Primeau, S. (2002). "The returns to university education in Canada, 1990 and 1995." In D. Laidler, ed. *Renovating the ivory tower: Canadian universities and the knowledge economy.* Toronto: C.D. Howe Institute. 215–40.

Zhao, J. and de Broucker, P. (2002). "Participation in postsecondary education and family income." *The Daily,* January 9. Statistics Canada. Retrieved 22 August 2004, from http://www.statcan.ca

3

Accessibility and Student Debt: The Shift from Public to Private Support in Canada

STEPHEN BELL AND PAUL ANISEF

The benefits accruing to young people who access and participate in higher education are well known and consistently documented through studies conducted by the federal government (Lin, Sweet, Anisef, and Schuetze, 2001). Sustaining access to post-secondary education in Canada has been important for a variety of reasons, including the human capital argument; the notion of providing equality of opportunity to social and cultural groups previously locked out of universities and colleges; and the increased importance of credentials in a globalized economy. Thus, an increasing proportion of the primary university age group of 18 to 24-year-olds choose university over other activities. While the participation rate for full-time students fell slightly in the late 1970s it increased again by 1980. It then climbed significantly from approximately 12 per cent of the 18–24 age cohort after the 1982 recession and continued to grow throughout the rest of the decade until it reached nearly 20 per cent in 1993 (Junor and Usher, 2002). These data provide ample proof that Canadians place enormous trust in their post-secondary institutions and the education they provide for enhancing their life-course destinations. For many, the need to plan clearly for an uncertain future has been underscored by such factors as globalization, revolutionary developments in information technology, and rapidly changing modern economies. If anything, there is a greater sense, as we firmly enter the new millennium, that higher education will count more rather than less in our lives.

At the same time, the study costs related to post-secondary education are increasingly placed on the family. From a social inclusion perspective, this raises the question of whether particular segments of the Canadian population are experiencing social exclusion with respect to enrolling and maintaining their presence in post-secondary institutions. Are low-income families finding financial resources to permit their children to access post-secondary education? More children are growing up in poverty and some families are hard-pressed to provide resources for their children (Willms, 2002).

For these and other reasons that will become apparent in this chapter, it is important to re-examine the issues surrounding accessibility to post-secondary education; such issues have received only cursory analysis over the past decade or so (Andres and Krahn, 1999; Clift, Hawkey, and Vaughan, 1998). In a paper prepared for the Council of Ministers of Education, Anisef (1989) argued that: "Any treatment of accessibility to postsecondary education in Canada should be related to important historical and social trends. When this perspective is adopted, the result is the realization that 'accessibility' is a complex conceptual category that contains multiple meanings. Contributing greatly to the complexity and subtlety of this category have been the differences in historical development of the provinces along with the various perceptions of societal and educational needs."

However, as we moved into the late 1960s and early 1970s social scientists began to focus attention on the democratic and equity purposes of education, particularly higher education. Rather than examine participation rates at the national or provincial level alone, social scientists began to explore participation rates across different groups (e.g., socio-economic, ethnic, people with disabilities). This emphasis on variation in *group* participation rates subsequently led to an interest in equity groups and their treatment within higher education. Institutions were encouraged not only to improve equality of access to young adults but also to assume responsibility for offering programs that would respond to the needs, expectations, values, and cultures of diverse groups (Bell and Bischoping, 1998). More radical social scientists suggested that important forms of structural inequality remained invisible when researchers chose to focus their research on equality of access and equality of treatment. Rather, they argued an effort to address larger social inequalities should place more focus on equality of results or outcomes.

As we have indicated, the very meaning and understanding of accessibility requires that the concept be situated within the changing context of Canadian society. While issues pertaining to equality of access, equality of treatment, and equality of results or outcomes are still very much in evidence we contend that new issues are facing young people who aspire to enter our universities – issues that threaten to hinder their entry, negatively influence their experiences within the university, and affect their labour-market outcomes. The relatively recent shift from public to private support of the costs of higher education is of particular importance.

In Canada, post-secondary education has been a shared responsibility of the state through tax dollars and of students and parents through savings (Clark, 1998). Students typically provided 10–20 per cent of the direct costs. The notion that students should shoulder a greater burden of the costs of post-secondary education is rooted in studies that show that those who invest in post-secondary education receive greater benefits and higher financial compensation over a life cycle (Eicher and Chevallier, 1993; Volkswein et al., 1998; Little, 1997). Higher levels of education have been shown to relate to increased earnings over a life cycle and to low unemployment (HRDC, 1999). Such findings have been used to justify increasing personal responsibility for the cost of higher education. They are often used to support an ideological shift with respect to the role of the state in funding higher education. Magnusson (2000) argues that within the context of neo-liberal restructuring "responsibility for social welfare is shifted from the interventionist state to private individuals who pay for services that were once public" (117). Recent reforms to student funding policies emphasizing the responsibility of the individual student to pay a greater portion of the cost of post-secondary education are consistent with trends occurring elsewhere, including the restructuring of health care and other public services.

In this chapter, we consider whether students from disadvantaged backgrounds and their families are finding it more difficult to marshal the financial resources required to gain access to a university or community college education. We first review the structure and organization of governmental post-secondary funding, focusing on changes over the past seven years. Topics include: a review of student tuition increases; federal and provincial student assistance programs such as the Canada Student Loan Program (CSLP); the Millennium Scholarship Foundation; and loan programs available via the provinces and territories. By examining CSLP and provincial loan structures, the changes to these structures, and the consequences to borrowers, we may learn more about the financial capacity of families and governments to sustain accessibility and social inclusion. In addition, we discuss the role of the recently introduced Canadian Education Savings Grant (CESG) in increasing access to post-secondary education.

Next we examine participants in higher education and provide a general overview of student loan recipients in terms of consequences of transformations in student assistance programs. We then identify and review changes in the private financing of post-secondary study costs by students and their families that have occurred in recent years. Finally, we examine factors that influence access to post-secondary education and examines recent governmental initiatives such as the CESG, increased tax expenditures, loan forgiveness, and retroactive grants to determine their relative effectiveness in improving access to post-secondary education.

STRUCTURE AND ORGANIZATION
OF POST-SECONDARY FUNDING

In 1995 the federal government introduced the Canada Health and Social Transfer (CHST) program, which incorporated in a lump sum the transfer of resources for post-secondary education, social welfare, and health, and over the next three years resulted in a decline of federal funding to the provinces of $6.6 billion in cash and tax transfer points.[1] The provinces responded to federal funding reductions with higher tuition costs and reduced grants to universities, which significantly shifted the financial responsibility of education to students and their families (Little, 1997; Clift, Hawkey, and Vaughan, 1998; CAUT, 1999).

In 1998–99 student fees accounted for over 20 per cent of university revenues, which is the highest level since 1972–73 (Statistics Canada, 2002). The percentage of university fees attributed to students varies province by province; fees accounted for 28.5 per cent of university revenue in Nova Scotia, followed by Ontario with 25.3 per cent (Statistics Canada, 2003). The real revenue from student fees per full-time enrolment more than doubled from $1,584 to $3,271 between 1981 and 1998 (CAUT, 1999). Table 3.1 shows the average undergraduate tuition fee by province from 1993–94 to 2003–04. In 2003–04 the average tuition fee in Canada was $4,025; Nova Scotia had the highest average ($5,557) and Quebec the lowest ($1,862).

In terms of percentage change, average tuition has increased in Canada by 98.9 per cent between 1993–94 and 2003–04; Ontario has had the greatest increase (137.2 per cent) and Quebec the lowest (20.2 per cent). The low tuition fee in Quebec is the result of a tuition fee freeze instituted in 1995–96. Tuition freezes (and limited rollbacks) have been instituted in Newfoundland for the past five years and in Manitoba for the past four years. British Columbia has had a seven-year tuition fee freeze with a 5 per cent reduction in 2001–02. However, with the election of the Campbell government, tuition fees in 2002–03 were deregulated and most universities in BC are increasing their fees to the national average over the next three years. Ontario instituted a 2 per cent tuition increase for five years starting in 1999–2000; however, the McGuinty government subsequently instituted a two-year freeze in 2004. Alberta, Saskatchewan, Nova Scotia, New Brunswick, and PEI have had significant increases in the past four years.

Increases in tuition fees for professional programs have been particularly high in many provinces, thereby limiting student access to these programs. It is widely recognized that tuition fees for professional programs have been considerably higher than those in the arts; however, over the past seven years fees for medicine have increased significantly in most provinces, with a dramatic increase in Newfoundland in 1996 due to the

Table 3.1
Average Undergraduate Arts Tuition by Province, 1993–94 to 2003–04[1]

	1993–94	1998–99	2002–03	2003–04	1993–94 to 2003–04	1998–99 to 2003–04	2002–03 to 2003–04
	Current $				% change		
CANADA	2,023	3,064	3,749	4,025	98.9	31.4	7.4
Newfoundland and Labrador	2,000	3,216	2,729	2,606	30.3	−19.0	−4.5
Prince Edward Island	2,509	3,327	3,891	4,133	64.7	24.2	6.2
Nova Scotia	2,701	4,074	5,214	5,557	105.8	36.4	6.6
New Brunswick	2,385	3,225	4,186	4,457	86.9	38.2	6.5
Quebec[2]	1,550	1,803	1,851	1,862	20.2	3.2	0.6
Ontario	2,076	3,640	4,665	4,923	137.2	35.2	5.5
Manitoba	2,272	3,149	3,144	3,155	38.9	0.2	0.3
Saskatchewan	2,341	3,279	4,286	4,644	98.4	41.6	8.3
Alberta	2,209	3,519	4,165	4,487	103.1	27.5	7.7
British Columbia	2,240	2,525	3,176	4,140	84.9	64.0	30.4

Source: Statistics Canada, 2004

[1] Using the most current enrolment data available, average tuition fees have been weighted by the number of students enrolled by institution and field of study. Fees at both public and private institutions are included in the weighted average calculations.

[2] Both in and out-of-province students are included in the weighted average calculations.

tripling of fees at Memorial University. Manitoba, British Columbia, and Quebec did experience slight decreases in medicine tuition, though overall the cost has increased over time. The tuition freezes covering all disciplines in British Columbia and Quebec keep the national tuition fee averages for medicine, law, and dentistry low.

Despite the changes in federal spending on post-secondary education, the evidence is mixed regarding whether increasing tuition fees diminishes access to post-secondary education (Little, 1997; Junor and Usher, 2002). For example, although tuition fees increased 86 per cent from 1983 to 1995, enrolment rose 30 per cent. At first glance, these figures would seem to indicate that tuition fees remain affordable. On the other hand, some have suggested that the increased enrolment in the 1990s can be attributed to the recession and economic restructuring. Employees facing unemployment through downsizing in an uncertain economy began returning to post-secondary education. Little (1997) argues that a decrease in enrolments between 1994 and 1995 occurred because of an increase in tuition fees. He concludes that the impact of the recession may have post-poned the decline of enrolment rates at an earlier time. Other research in-dicates that the university participation rate for 18 to 24-year-olds from lower socio-economic backgrounds has increased very little in the last eight years in comparison to the rate for students from high socio-economic backgrounds, implying that higher costs of education have affected dis-advantaged families (Ministry of Advanced Education, 1999). Be that as it may, Corak (2001) indicates that there is very little direct evidence that ca-pable Canadian youth are limited in their access to post-secondary educa-tion by a lack of financial resources (10).

CANADA STUDENT LOANS PROGRAM (CSLP)

The CSLP was designed to provide Canadians with equal opportunity to pursue their studies beyond the secondary level; it offers student loans and non-repayable grants based on financial need to both full-time and part-time students. The program operates in conjunction with provincial stu-dent loan programs and the Canada Millennium Scholarship Foundation in all provinces and territories with the exception of Quebec, the North-west Territories, and Nunavut, which provide an integrated financial aid program (Bourgoin, 1995; Junor and Usher, 2002).

To be eligible for the CSLP, you must be a Canadian citizen or permanent resident, be enrolled in a program with a 60 per cent course load of twelve weeks duration, and attend a designated post-secondary institution. There is a separate program for part-time students. Program limits, lifetime limits, and debt limits are outlined in Junor and Usher 2002 (118–19).

The origins of and changes to the CSLP are detailed in Finnie and Schwartz (1996a). The CSLP changed very little from its inception in 1964 until 1994, when the government of Canada and participating jurisdic-tions increased the weekly loan limit from $105 per week to $165 per week or 60 per cent of a student's assessed need. Provincial governments pro-vide the remaining 40 per cent up to a loan maximum of $275 per week or $9,350 per academic year. According to Junor and Usher (2002) "in some provinces, assistance from the Millennium Scholarship Foundation (bursa-ries) can be added to the student loan maxima; in others, millennium bur-saries replace part of the student loan" (128). The maximum amount per week of study differs by province and the treatment of parental income and family contribution also differs by province (Junor and Usher, 2002).

Calculating Student Need

What level of financial resources do students need to complete a post-secondary program? This question has been debated and analysed by

Table 3.2
Monthly Student Living Allowances 2001–2002

Student Category	Province ($)											
	NF	PE	NS	NB	QC	ON	MB	SK	AB	BC	YT	NT/NU
Single student (At home)	341	365	360	356	388	386	383	359	369	386	400	429
Single student (Away)	740	727	773	741	805	914	801	747	777	935	905	1011
Married Student	1479	1455	1556	1488	1486	1777	1546	1451	1499	1865	1809	2047
Single Parent	990	941	1022	991	1016	1181	979	926	965	1192	1255	1438

Source: Junor and Usher, 2002, 122

Note: Further increments for each dependent child are provided married and single parents.

student aid officials and others over many years. Student need is calculated as follows: a student's category is identified; the costs of the post-secondary institution are assessed; and the student's available resources are determined. The need assessment is arrived at by subtracting available (or expected) resources from assessed costs. There are four student categories (see Table 3.2): single dependant – living at home; single dependant – living away from home; married; and single parent.

Assessed costs include both education and living costs for the entire academic year. Various dimensions of a student's resources are taken into consideration, such as pre-study and study-period income, living arrangements, and personal savings and assets. Most provinces adopt a similar approach, with some differences; for example, Quebec factors in a student's educational status in the previous year. The need assessment methodology takes into account the circumstances in different provinces (Junor and Usher, 2002).

Students complain that the CSLP and the provincial programs are restrictive and do not meet actual need. The federal, provincial, and territorial governments hold that the level of financial assistance is sufficient and that families should have an increased role in financing their children's education. A study commissioned by the CSLP identified problems in calculating student need. For example, assumptions, which differ markedly by province, are made that families of the same income and same size may be able or willing to contribute similar amounts to their children's education. Table 3.3 illustrates a province-by-province breakdown of the contribution that parents are expected to make toward their child's education, and outlines income exemption levels. However, the availability of resources may

Table 3.3
Calculation of Parental Contribution

Program	Parental income Exemption	Parental Contribution Rate	Treatment of Parental Assets
Canada Student Loans Program, plus all provinces except AB, BC, ON, and QC	The exemption varies by province, but below a minimum amount of after-tax income for a two-person family (between $26,100 in NB and $32,500 in BC, plus $5,000 per extra family member), no contribution is required	45% of the first $3,000 of after-tax income above the exemption level, 60% of the next $3,000 of after-tax income above the exemption level, and 75% of all income above that	At the discretion of each province, but generally assets are not considered as resources and so no contribution from assets is required
AB	Same as above	Same as above	5% of net worth of parental business assets over $250,000
BC	Same as above	Same as above	1% of personal assets (excluding RRSPs, vehicles, and principal residence) over $150,000
ON			No contribution from assets is required
QC	Below a pre-tax minimum income of $21,885 (if parents are living together) or $19,755 (if parents are living apart), plus an additional $2,105 if both parents work, plus $2,660 for the first child and $2,250 for each additional child, no contribution is required	The contribution is 23% of the first $36,000 of pre-tax income above the exemption level, 33% of the next $10,000 in income, 43% of the next $10,000 in income, and 53% of any income above that	Assets under $90,000 ($250,000 for farmers and fishers) are exempt; parents are required to make a contribution equal to 2% of their assets above this level
NT (repayable loans only)	N/A	No contribution required	None
YT and NU	N/A	N/A	N/A

Source: Junor and Usher, *The Price of Knowledge: Access and Student Finance in Canada*, 124

differ among those families and problems can occur when parents are not willing to contribute to educational costs. The study also found that even parents with a relatively high income may be unable to support their children because of other high financial obligations that are not considered in the policies (Goss, Gilroy Inc., 1997, 29).

Changes in the CSLP

Between 1964 and 1995 the CSLP provided a 100 per cent guarantee to financial institutions on all student loans that went into default. As a result, financial institutions had no incentive to follow up on outstanding loans. In 1995 the federal government negotiated financial arrangements with financial institutions based on the concept of "risk sharing," in which an annual "risk premium" of 5 per cent of the value of the total consolidated loan portfolio each year was assumed by these institutions. The idea was to reduce the level of student loan default while giving financial institutions an incentive to treat student loans much like other consumer loans (HRDC, 2000). Thus, as early as the mid-1990s the federal government recognized that the issue of student debt and ability to pay for post-secondary education was gaining increasing prominence as provinces replaced their former non-repayable grant programs with loans.

The "risk premium" idea had a very short life and was shelved in August 2000, when the federal government once again assumed the administration of the CSLP. Financial institutions found that the level of student debt had increased significantly and loan defaults continued to increase. The 5 per cent risk premium was not enough of an incentive to financial institutions and the federal government was unwilling to increase the amount of the risk premium. Thus, as of 1 August 2001 the government of Canada assumed responsibility for the direct administration of student loans.[2]

The 1997 federal budget introduced the Canada Opportunity Strategies (COS), which included a student debt reduction program. Loan remission was provided to students with repayment difficulties caused by high debt and low income over a specified time (HRDC, 1999; Plager and Chen, 1999; Bourgoin, 1995). The interest relief period was increased from eighteen months within the first five years after leaving the educational institution to thirty months (Plager and Chen, 1999). In addition, more students were deemed eligible for this program and increased opportunities were provided to reduce monthly payments and the overall amount owing (HRDC, 1999). Most provinces also have loan remission and loan forgiveness programs similar to the federal government's (Plager and Chen, 1999; Bourgoin, 1995).

The COS also introduced changes to bankruptcy regulations that had previously allowed students to declare bankruptcy and discharge their CSL two years after leaving their educational institution. The new regulation does not allow students to declare bankruptcy until ten years after completing their studies (Plager and Chen, 1999). Many student groups have argued that this measure has had a regressive impact on accessibility to education for poor and marginalized groups (Canadian Federation of Students, 2000).

Student Loan Administration: How It Works

Federal and provincial loans accumulate during the time of study while governments pay interest charges (Clift, 1998; HRDC, 1999; Plager and Chen, 1999). Repayments of student loans must be made six months after graduation or when a student withdraws. The repayment schedule is negotiated with the financial institution (students can pay off loans from 0 to 9.5 years) while the interest rate is set yearly by government and financial institutions (Clift, 1998; Plager and Chen, 1999).

A specific illustration of student loan administration can be gleaned from our home province – Ontario. In August 2000 the federal government and the province of Ontario agreed to harmonize student loans under the CSLP with student assistance provided by the province of Ontario via the Ontario Student Assistant Program (OSAP). The agreement creates a single loan and streamlines administration of loans (for example, only one set of documentation is required and students must adhere to a single repayment schedule instead of two). In addition, the two governments jointly agreed to fund interest payments on all loans during time of study, to maintain a thirty-month interest relief period, to extend interest relief for a further twenty-four months, and to increase debt reduction for borrowers facing financial hardship.[3]

Borrowers' Profile

Student loans are a major source of financing higher education for approximately half of the post-secondary student population. Figure 3.1 shows an overall increase in the number of borrowers in Canada from 1980 to 1999. Note, however, that the Quebec government and the CSLP both experienced a decrease in the number of borrowers in the 1987–88 academic year. The financial responsibility undertaken by families also varies depending on whether or not loans are received and what access students have to other resources such as bursaries, scholarships, parental resources, and part-time work. The financial responsibility undertaken by families in Canada is vastly higher than that in Denmark, Sweden, and Australia, but not higher than in the United States, Korea, or Japan (Daniel et al., 1999). The level of student aid depends on countries' social policies. Daniel et al. (1999) categorize these policies as follows:

Figure 3.1
Total Number of Borrowers in Canada, 1980–99[abc]

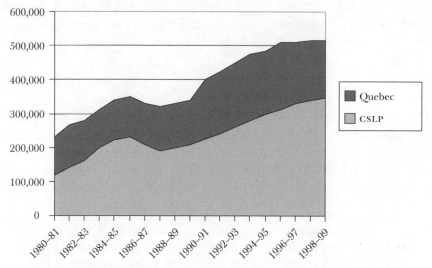

Source: CSLP research database and Aide financière aux études research database
Notes: [a] The total number of CSL borrowers for 1998–99 is a preliminary estimate.
  [b] The CSLP loan year runs from May 1 to April 30.
  [c] The totals for the CSLP include both part-time and full-time loans.
Quebec did not provide student assistance for part-time students during the period shown in the graph.

- Government gives full access to students regardless of parental resources;
- Government gives limited access to students and sees no need for financial support;
- Government gives variable access to students with a shared financing among state, students, and families;
- Government gives variable access to students who invest in their future and for whom student loan guarantees are established.

The debate about the issue of student loans and student debt does not usually recognize that 53–55 per cent of college and university students *do not* borrow to finance their post-secondary education. For those that borrow, the average dollar amount of negotiated Canada Student Loans increased significantly from 1990–91 to 2000–01, as shown in Table 3.4.

The data shown in Table 3.5 indicate that the distribution of full-time CSLP loans negotiated remained relatively stable from 1996–97 through 2000–01. Approximately two-thirds of borrowers are under 25, about half of all loans are negotiated by students attending university (with the proportion increasing from 48 to 53 per cent over the period), and over half of borrowers are women.

Table 3.4
Average Dollar Amount of Negotiated Canada
Student Loans – Full-Time Students Only

Loan Year	All Participating Provinces and Yukon
2000–01	4,554
1999–00	4,624
1998–99	4,630
1997–98	4,470
1996–97	4,615
1995–96	4,133
1994–95	3,847
1993–94	3,235
1992–93	3,010
1991–92	2,971
1990–91	2,767
1989–90	2,787

Source: http://www.hrdc-drhc.gc.ca/student_loans/
c/statistics/dollaramount.html

While Table 3.4 suggests an increase in unmet financial need among all full-time students in Canada, a recent study concludes that CSLP students who borrow the maximum loan limit are more likely to be students over 24 years of age, with dependants, who attend private vocational institutions. Also, students who move away from home to attend a four-year program of study can expect to pay up to $20,000 more than those who are able to remain at home while studying (Fred Hemingway Consulting, 2004; McMullen, 2004).

In the 1990s the distribution of student loans by type of institution changed. Loans to students at private vocational institutions increased from 12 per cent in 1992–93 to 21 per cent in 1996–97, while loans to students in universities decreased from 55 per cent to 48 per cent. The proportion of college students accessing student loans was stable (HRDC, 1999).

Loan Repayment

The increases in tuition fees and in the average amount borrowed have led to increased loan repayment difficulties. Loans are repayable at the time of consolidation and students can choose a floating rate of prime plus 2.5 per

Table 3.5
Distribution of Full-Time Loans Negotiated, 1996–97 to 2000–01 by Age Group, Institutional Type, and Gender

	Distribution of Full-Time Student Loans									
	Actual 1996–97	*%*	*Actual 1997–98*	*%*	*Actual 1998–99*	*%*	*Actual 1999–2000*	*%*	*Actual 2000–01*	*%*
Loans Negotiated by Age Group										
Under 25	230,128	67.05	238,260	68.00	232,513	69.13	234,413	69.95	243,942	71.00
25-29	59,201	17.25	58,351	17.00	53,114	15.79	51,981	15.51	51,525	15.00
30-34	24,964	7.27	24,354	7.00	22,894	6.81	22,188	6.62	21,789	6.34
35 & Over	28,931	8.43	29,809	8.00	27,821	8.27	26,521	7.92	26,332	7.66
Total	343,224	100.00	350,774	100.00	336,342	100.00	335,103	100.00	343,588	100.00
Loans Negotiated by Institution Type										
Universities	166,180	48.42	167,383	47.72	177,031	52.63	177,995	53.12	176,612	51.40
Colleges/ Institutes	117,233	34.16	125,435	35.76	110,083	32.73	113,338	33.82	121,344	35.32
Private	59,811	17.42	57,956	16.52	49,228	14.64	43,770	13.06	45,632	13.28
Total	343,224	100.00	350,774	100.00	336,342	100.00	335,103	100.00	343,588	100.00
Loans Negotiated by Gender										
Female	182,034	53.00	189,472	54.00	187,299	55.69	188,736	56.32	197,118	57.37
Male	161,190	47.00	161,302	46.00	149,043	44.31	146,367	43.68	146,470	42.63
Total	343,224	100.00	350,774	100.00	336,342	100.00	335,103	100.00	343,588	100.00

Source: http://www.hrsdc.gc.ca/asp/gateway.asp?hr=/en/hip/cslp/statistics/
09_st_Distribution.shtml&hs=cxp

cent, or a fixed rate of prime plus 5 per cent for loans made after 1995 (Junor and Usher, 2002, 139). In December 2002 the prime lending rate was 4.5 per cent. Table 3.6 gives examples of fixed loan payments at an interest rate of 9.5 per cent (4.5+5) with repayment amounts that vary from three to ten years.

A graduate who has a $25,000 debt will incur monthly payments of $323 for ten years. Indenturing students in this way will have an effect on the economy as newly graduated students will have fewer resources to buy cars, houses, and other consumer goods. More research is required to document the subsequent life-course consequences of increased debt. Furthermore, a large level of indebtedness may pose severe difficulties for students from disadvantaged backgrounds, who might be discouraged from participating in higher education (Clift et al., 1998; Mumper, 1996). An extensive literature

Table 3.6
Sample Monthly Repayment in $ of Canada Student Loan at 9.5 per cent

Principal Amount ($)	Repayment Period (Months)	Monthly Repayments ($)	Principal and Interest ($)	Interest Charges ($)
1,500	36	48.05	1,729.80	229.80
7,000	114	93.45	10,653.30	3,653.30
10,000	120	129.40	15,527.51	5,527.51
15,000	120	194.10	23,291.27	8,291.27
20,000	120	258.80	31,055.03	11,055.03
25,000	120	323.49	38,819.58	13,819.58
30,000	120	388.19	46,583.34	16,583.34

Source: Bernard Bourgoin, *Educational Quarterly Review,* 1995 and current OSAP Program

Table 3.7
Student Loan by Province (Trade Vocational School)

Loan	Student Loan			How much did you owe in 1995?			How much did you owe in 1997?			Any difficulties in repaying?		
	Yes	No	N	Mean	N	SD	Mean	N	SD	Yes	No	N
Newfoundland	24.1	75.9	2,223	$6,459	474	4,875	$6,405	340	6,116	46.3	53.7	270
PEI	36.1	63.9	415	$5,375	138	4,665	$4,221	100	3,976	47.5	52.5	101
Nova Scotia	26.8	73.2	2,961	$5,269	739	4,470	$5,276	565	6,014	45.4	54.6	471
New Brunswick	31.4	68.6	1,709	$5,605	505	4,201	$4,566	379	4,154	38.1	61.9	331
Quebec	21.6	78.4	31,040	$3,692	6560	3,628	$3,145	5,039	4,058	17.1	82.9	4,834
Ontario	19.1	80.9	7,552	$6,357	1303	4,579	$5,523	969	6,005	29.5	70.5	789
Manitoba	10.7	89.3	885	$5,067	77	4,958	$5,453	52	5,471	34.0	66.0	50
Saskatchewan	27.1	72.9	1,779	$5,896	428	4,146	$4,222	341	4,594	22.7	77.3	300
Alberta	30.3	69.7	2,125	$5,342	606	4,789	$4,200	467	4,726	29.5	70.5	414
BC	21.6	78.4	7,150	$5,904	1486	5,037	$5,390	1,178	5,390	36.2	63.8	984
Yukon	27.7	72.3	148	$3,883	41	3,313	$3,266	30	3,637	48.1	51.9	27
NWT	13.2	86.8	76	$3,993	10	4,109	$4,502	7	2,828	30.0	70.0	10
USA	75.0	25.0	4	$4,000	3	0	*	*	*	*	*	*
Canada	22.4	77.6	5,8297	$4,699	12434	$4,286	$4,096	9,531	4,861	25.2	74.8	8,600
Other countries	26.9	73.1	223	$4,175	60	1,243	$5,830	60	3,853	88.2	11.8	17

Source: Statistics Canada, 1997
Note: *Data are not available.

Table 3.8
Student Loan by Province (College)

	Student Loan			How much did you owe in 1995?			How much did you owe in 1997?			Any difficulties in repaying?		
	Yes	No	N	Mean	N	SD	Mean	N	SD	Yes	No	N
Newfoundland	52.0	48.0	883	$11,244	417	7,578	$10,061	369	7,997	42.7	57.3	300
PEI	39.5	60.5	347	4,647	126	3,755	4,415	97	4,450	32.9	67.1	79
Nova Scotia	46.5	53.5	1,795	9,286	809	6,324	8,635	632	7,107	45.1	54.9	477
New Brunswick	50.5	49.5	1,441	9,522	695	6,497	7,778	558	6,099	41.5	58.5	482
Quebec	57.1	42.9	1,7272	7,453	9,733	5,039	6,888	8,550	5,601	16.0	84.0	6,646
Ontario	45.7	54.3	36,278	9,909	14,917	6,296	8,170	12,475	7,893	28.2	71.8	9,783
Manitoba	28.7	71.3	2,659	7,654	706	5,058	6,421	535	5,497	24.8	75.2	487
Saskatchewan	50.3	49.7	1,984	12,512	904	10,276	9,797	797	10,147	20.7	79.3	653
Alberta	47.2	52.8	8,690	8,869	3,871	6,137	6,777	3,302	6,977	30.0	70.0	2,604
BC	30.9	69.1	9,035	10,489	2,692	9,307	9,593	2,369	9,213	34.9	65.1	1,835
Yukon	32.6	67.4	92	7,507	29	8,940	6,774	27	9,074	40.9	59.1	22
NWT	44.8	55.2	163	6,928	70	5,481	5,605	48	6,423	33.3	66.7	54
USA	62.0	38.0	71	7,448	37	5,661	2,736	29	4,120	0.0	100	22
Canada	46.3	53.1	8,1163	$9,126	35,147	$6,503	$7,760	29,901	$7,361	26.0	74.0	23,550
Other countries	32.1	67.9	498	5,107	139	3,695	3,674	112	4,247	37.0	63.0	108

Source: Statistics Canada, 1997

search in Canada found no research on this topic. Some research has been done in the United States (Baum and Schwartz, 1998).

Students who have a full-time job after graduation have fewer repayment difficulties than those who work part-time or do not have a job. The type of full-time job also affects repayment plans. Of the 48 per cent of students who had student loans at graduation between 1990 and 1995, 20 to 40 per cent repaid their loans two years after graduation. These students have, on average, small loans and less overall debt (Finnie and Garneau, 1996).

Tables 3.7, 3.8, and 3.9 contain the responses to several questions in the 1995 National Graduate Survey. Table 3.7 is for trade or vocational schools, Table 3.8 for community colleges, and Table 3.9 for universities. Each shows the number of students who borrowed, the average amount of the loan upon graduation, the average amount of the loan two years after graduation, and whether or not the students have had any difficulties in repaying the loan. Students who attended a trade or vocational school[4] have the lowest average loans ($4,699), but have the greatest problems in repaying loans two

Table 3.9
Student Loan by Province (University)

	Student Loan			How much did you owe in 1995?			How much did you owe in 1997?			Any difficulties in repaying?		
	Yes	No	N	Mean	N	SD	Mean	N	SD	Yes	No	N
Newfoundland	59.3	40.7	2,774	$1,3272	1,559	9,443	$14,284	1,264	11,563	36.1	63.9	987
PEI	56.1	43.9	799	11,053	419	8,202	10,515	334	6,999	32.2	67.8	214
Nova Scotia	55.3	44.7	5,373	12,635	2,810	9,608	12,956	2,335	10,671	32.0	68.0	1,724
New Brunswick	56.9	43.1	3,957	13,771	2,154	9,555	14,382	1,778	11,799	32.6	67.4	1,403
Quebec	50.9	49.1	48,076	10,162	24,146	7,263	10,075	20,057	8,058	17.0	83.0	15,845
Ontario	44.6	55.4	56,501	12,604	23,880	9,814	10,823	20,648	11,629	25.6	74.4	15,906
Manitoba	36.3	63.7	5,462	10,673	1,912	8,962	8,479	1,584	9,570	30.0	70.0	1,285
Saskatchewan	44.6	55.4	5,225	15,339	2,219	11,937	12,329	1,949	13,199	25.7	74.3	1,624
Alberta	54.7	45.3	11,467	13,878	6,047	9,606	11,040	5,272	10,540	24.9	75.1	4,377
BC	44.4	55.6	12,397	15,433	5,387	12,317	12,452	4,775	12,303	30.2	69.8	3,995
Yukon	23.4	76.6	94	14,649	22	7,293	13,023	21	9,006	50.0	50.0	12
NWT	76.6	23.4	175	43,881	134	32,266	43,989	121	35,618	39.0	61.0	41
USA	31.2	68.8	756	19,138	227	13,963	23,956	227	21,806	23.0	77.0	100
Canada	47.7	52.3	155,923	12,233	71,825	9,611	11,080	61,087	10,828	23.8	76.2	47,992
Other countries	33.0	67.0	2,840	10,615	904	7,309	10,370	716	8,577	21.7	78.3	480

Source: Statistics Canada, 1997

years after graduation (74.9 per cent); students who attended college and university have much higher average loans ($9,126 and $12,223 respectively). However, students from university had the least difficulty repaying loans, i.e., approximately 23 per cent compared to 26 per cent for college students. At the provincial university level, students in the Atlantic Provinces, Manitoba, and British Columbia had the greatest difficulty repaying loans; students in Quebec had the least difficulty.

Plager and Chen (1999) argue that students attending private post-secondary institutions have greater difficulties repaying their loans than do students attending community college and university. For example, 22.9 per cent of university students, 32.8 per cent of college students, and 47.2 per cent of students from private institutions experience repayment difficulties *within the first year after graduation*. This may suggest that students from private post-secondary institutions have greater difficulties in securing employment after graduation compared to college and university

Table 3.10
Median Debt-to-Earnings Ratios

Education Group	Sex	1982	1986	1990	1995
College/CEGEP	Male	0.13	0.19	0.20	0.28
	Female	0.15	0.23	0.26	0.41
Bachelor's	Male	0.14	0.24	0.28	0.38
	Female	0.17	0.29	0.32	0.51
Master's	Male	0.12	0.18	0.20	0.29
	Female	0.15	0.18	0.24	0.37
Doctorate	Male	0.08	0.12	0.14	0.25
	Female	0.09	0.11	0.15	0.22

Source: Finnie (2001), 106.

graduates. Loan recipients who made use of the Federal Interest Relief Program (FIRP) during the first year after graduation increased from 21.7 per cent in 1990–91 to 30.9 per cent in 1995–96 (Plager and Chen, 1999). Not only has the amount of debt reduction in repayment dollars increased exponentially from the 1998–99 academic year ($177,581) to 2000–01 ($2,958,661), the number of recipients has also increased significantly during this period (from 44 to 614).[5]

A recently released report by the Canada Millennium Scholarship Foundation indicates that six in ten college students expect to graduate with debt; one-quarter anticipate having debt over $10,000; and another quarter expect to have debt over $20,000 (R.A. Malatest & Associates, 2003). Approximately two-thirds of the 10,000 community college students surveyed expressed concern about having sufficient funds to complete their studies.

An analysis of borrowing patterns among male and female graduates (two years after graduation) indicates that women accumulate higher debt than men do. Even though borrowing seems to represent a greater burden for women, women pay back their loans at a similar or even higher rate than men, despite their lower earning levels (Finnie, 2000). Similarly, the debt-to-earnings ratios are generally higher for women than for men (see Table 3.10), but roughly follow the same pattern by discipline. Finnie (2001) offers the following reasons for female students' debt burden: "A good part of the female graduates' overall higher average debt burden – at least at the Bachelor's level – is, therefore due [to] their being over-represented in generally low earnings disciplines rather than having lower earnings (than men) in a given field of endeavor" (107). Additionally, Finnie hypothesizes that these gender differences may affect borrowing habits and access, including the decision to enroll in post-secondary education.

Loan Default

The average debt load of a CSLP borrower on graduation increased from $9,000 to $13,000 between 1990 and 1997, and the average of a federal and provincial student loan on consolidation increased to about $20,000 in 1999 (HRDC, 1999). More and more students face larger debts, with repayment scenarios that exceed their own annual income on graduation (CAUT, 2000). Debates continue about the increase of the weekly student loan to $165 and whether it supports students' access or discourages them from attending post-secondary institutions because higher loans usually imply higher debts after graduation (Usher, 1998). The debt load almost tripled from 1990 to 1998, whereas the income ratio remained relatively stable. This assumes a greater repayment burden for students (CAUT, 2000). With the increase of federal loan limits in 1994–95 and the reduction of grant programs, loan recipients are finding themselves with more accumulated debt than in the early 1990s (CAUT, 2000).

In 1989–90, 5 per cent of students holding a CSL accrued a loan of over $15,000, compared to 12 per cent in 1995–96 and 14 per cent in 1996–97. Of those students with $15,000 in accrued loans in their *final year of study*, the percentage increased from 16 per cent in 1995–96 to 18 per cent in 1996–97. On the other hand, loan recipients with less than $5,000 CSL decreased from 38 per cent in 1995–96 to 33 per cent in 1996–97. Additionally, defaulted loans and bankruptcy after one year of graduation increased from 17.6 in 1990–91 to 21.8 per cent in 1995–96 (Plager and Chen, 1999).

The literature provides several hypotheses for the increase of default rates, including low income and earnings after graduation, employment status (part-time as opposed to full-time), and the amount of debt burden (Finnie and Garneau, 1996; Plager and Chen, 1999). Finnie (2000) argues that high debt loads restrict the access to further education. His analysis of National Graduate Survey (NGS) data show that men are more likely to borrow than women and, as described above, are slightly less likely to pay back their loans.[6] Default rates differ by type of institution (see Table 3.11). In 1995–96 universities had a 3-year rate of 20.2 per cent, community colleges 31.9 per cent, and private vocational institutions 44.5 per cent (Plager and Chen, 1999).

The province of Ontario undertook measures to deal with student default rates in 1997–98. One measure involves a credit screening for new student loan applicants. Others are Ontario Opportunity Grants (OOG), which are intended to leave students with no more than $7,000 of debt per year of study, and the requirement that all provincially funded institutions inform their students of future employment opportunities in their chosen field of study. Furthermore, the province now requires institutions to share

Table 3.11
Three-Year Default Rates (%) by Institution Type
(based on dollars)

Cohort Year	University	College	Private
1990–91	16.6	23.5	36.1
1991–92	17.2	24.1	39.1
1992–93	18.0	25.2	38.7
1993–94	19.1	27.2	39.5
1994–95	23.0	34.1	48.5
1995–96	20.2	31.9	44.5
1996–97	18.2	29.8	45.5
1997–98	14.5	26.8	51.5
1998–99 P	12.6	26.2	45.6

Source: http://www.hrdc-drhc.gc.ca/student_loans/c/
statistics/institution.html
Note: A borrower's default is allocated to the last
institution they attended.
P: Preliminary

in the risk of OSL defaults. For these loans, institutions with a 1997 default rate 15 percentage points or more above the 1997 provincial average of 23.5 per cent were required to share the cost of defaults; for loans issued in 1999–2000, the policy applied to institutions with a 1997 default rate 10 percentage points or more above 23.5 per cent; for loans issued in 2000–01, the policy pertained to institutions with a 1999 default rate above 28.5 per cent; and for loans issued in 2001–02, the policy applied to institutions with a 2000 default rate above 25 per cent (OSAP, 2000).

Increases in the level of student debt can have a number of negative consequences. These include discouraging students from disadvantaged families from undertaking post-secondary education (Usher, 1998; Lowe, 1998; Angus Reid Group, 1998), thus limiting the role of students as consumers and the choice of jobs that a student will have available to them upon graduation. This implies that fear of debt creates a barrier to accessibility for students (Angus Reid Group, 1998).

According to the literature, loans represent a greater risk for financially disadvantaged students, implying that these students are less prepared for post-secondary education because they lack social capital. Moreover, studies indicate that students from low-income backgrounds are less likely to complete their academic program because they are ill-prepared for the demands of a post-secondary education. Those who do graduate are more likely to receive lower earnings, thus encountering more difficulty in repaying their loans. Although policies intend to remove price barriers by increasing loan limits, the literature argues that loans only delay payments. Given accumulated interest and the principal loan at the end of their studies, low-income student borrowers wind up paying disproportionately more for post-secondary education than high-income borrowers (Mumper, 1996).

Other studies mention that greater debt loads force students to find high-paying employment to pay back their student loans. However, one can assume that if students are unable to find such an employment, they will be forced to default on their loans (Angus Reid Group, 1998).

Debt Relief

Non-repayable grants for students attending post-secondary education in Canada were eliminated (except in very limited and special cases) in most provinces when the Canadian Health and Social Transfer (CHST) was introduced by the federal government in 1996. The availability of grants based on income would allow students to participate in education without amassing a huge debt. According to a CAUT study, non-repayable grants both decrease student debt loads, by reducing the amount borrowed, and lower the dropout rate (CAUT, 1999). Foley (2001) reports that 8.8 per cent of post-secondary school drop-outs cite lack of finances as their primary reason for leaving school. Several programs and policy amendments at both the federal and provincial levels have been introduced since the introduction of the CHST to deal with student debt as it is being amassed and after it has been amassed. Programs include special opportunity grants (such as the Ontario opportunity grant described above), deferred grants, remissions, and interest relief programs.

Canada is the only country that provides debt reduction as a means of student aid. The "end of period" debt reduction acts as a safeguard, protecting the government from giving out awards to students who leave their programs before completion. Debt reduction programs vary between provinces; they are, for the most part, portable. Newfoundland is the exception, providing debt relief only to students who attend a Newfoundland post-secondary institution; additionally, it offers debt reduction incentives for students who finish their programs in the allotted number of years (typically four).

Because of the "Canadian Brain Drain," debt relief incentives are also being offered to recruit or retain individuals with post-secondary educations. British Columbia, for example, has a loan remission program for students in nursing and medicine (because of the need for health care professionals), as well as for those entering childcare, a profession that typically does not pay well (Junor and Usher, 2002, 137).

These programs are not enough. If governments are serious about providing accessibility to post-secondary education, then the reintroduction of a financial student assistance model with grants and loans based on family income is necessary.

PRIVATE FINANCING
OF POST-SECONDARY EDUCATION

Students rely on more than government-funded loans to finance their education. These sources include parental contributions, summer or term employment, private loans, scholarships, grants, and personal savings. Trends in household spending show an increase of expenditures related to education, especially because of the increasing cost of post-secondary education. Average household spending on post-secondary tuition increased 60 per cent from 1992 to 1998. From 65 to 70 per cent of education expenditures are costs for post-secondary education (CAUT, 1999). The recent PEPS study indicates that, for full-time students 18–24, the source of funds most often used was employment earnings – earnings gained prior to and those gained since the beginning of the school year were used by 77 per cent and 64 per cent of students respectively (Barr-Telford et al., 2003, 13).

A 2001–02 student financial survey conducted by the Millennium Foundation reported that two out of three students work an average of nineteen hours a week during the school term. Part-time employment accounts for 40 per cent of the student's resources. Additionally, the report found that students aged 20 to 21 face an average monthly budget deficit of $142, not including accrued student debt, while the average student experiences a $56 monthly shortfall. The report concluded that monthly expenditures for students appear to be higher than the current assumptions as determined by government student aid programs (EKOS Research Associates, 2003).

Increases in household expenditures on education varied among the provinces because of different provincial policies. For example, expenses on all education items increased significantly between 1992 and 1998 in Nova Scotia (72.2 per cent), Alberta (66.7 per cent), Prince Edward Island (60.8 per cent), and British Columbia (60.8 per cent). For other provinces, increases in household expenditures for education remained rather moderate or insignificant (CAUT, 1999). However, studies indicate that average household expenditures on post-secondary tuition increased significantly in almost all provinces. The greatest increases were reported for Alberta (128.7 per cent), Newfoundland (97.1 per cent), Nova Scotia (94.8 per cent), and British Columbia (72.6 per cent). Despite the "tuition freeze" in British Columbia, the rise in household expenditures on

Table 3.12
Household Expenditures on PSE Tuition by Income Quintile, 1992 and 1998

	1992		1998		1992–1998
	Average expenditure ($1,998)	% of average after-tax income	Average expenditure ($1,998)	% of average after-tax income	% change in average expenditure
Lowest quintile	1,482	11.2	2,464	19.1	66.3
Second quintile	1,458	5.8	1,910	7.8	31.0
Middle quintile	1,045	2.9	1,751	4.8	67.6
Fourth quintile	1,358	2.8	2,112	4.2	55.5
Highest quintile	1,527	2.0	2,587	3.1	69.4
All households	1,387	3.5	2,221	5.3	60.1

Source: Calculations based on Statistics Canada, Family Expenditures in Canada, 1992, Cat. No. 62-555; Survey of Household Spending, 1998, unpublished data.

post-secondary education is assumed in the increase of full-time enrolment at public institutions and the increase of fees for private institutions in 1998 compared to 1992 (CAUT, 1999).

As tuition fees have increased, family incomes have declined. Undergraduate arts tuition fees changed compared to the after-tax income for families with children under 18 years old between 1989 and 1997 (CAUT, 1999): tuition fees increased by approximately 85 per cent and average family income for two-parent families with children under 18 declined by 5 per cent; for single-parent families income declined by 7 per cent. These results imply that the increasing costs for post-secondary education are affecting modest and middle-income families (CAUT, 2000).

Table 3.12 shows different income groups and their expenditures on post-secondary education in 1992 and 1998 and reveals that families of all income groups paid a larger portion on post-secondary education in 1998 than in 1992. While the ability to pay for their children's education has been impaired across all income levels, low-income families have felt the greatest impact of increasing tuition fees and decreasing disposable income.

A distinct generational effect is also evident. Parents who received financial support from their parents for their post-secondary education are more likely to contribute to their children's education (Steelman and Powell, 1991). This implies that access to post-secondary education is ensured through generations and is a powerful cultural and social phenomenon. Furthermore, parents' willingness to pay for their children's education increases with their socio-economic status (Steelman and Powell, 1991; Miller, 1997).

Students whose financial needs are not being met by parental contributions or government loans are increasingly borrowing funds from private institutions. An estimated 10 to 20 per cent of Canadian college and university students borrow funds from private sources (Junor and Usher, 2002). In a survey of over six thousand students graduating in 2000, the Canadian Undergraduate Survey Consortium (2000) found that almost 33 per cent owe money, averaging just over $8,000, to private sources. Students are more likely to have private debt when they are not receiving family support.

The Canada Education Savings Grant Program

For many years Registered Educational Savings Plans (RESPs) have been available to support families in saving for their children's education. The RESP is a tax-sheltered investment vehicle as opposed to a tax-deduction investment vehicle. Money allocated to an RESP grows tax-free until a child enrols in a post-secondary program. Until 1998 RESP programs were mostly used by upper-income families. In 1998 the federal government introduced the Canada Education Savings Grant (CESG) to make RESPs more attractive. For $2,000 saved by parents each year, a maximum of $400 is added by the CESG. The maximum annual contribution limit to an RESP has been raised to $4,000. At the same time, the number of RESP contracts has grown from 1 million contracts representing an average of $3,900 in 1998 to 1,700,000 contracts representing an average of $4,236 in 2000 (Junor and Usher, 2002).

A CAUT study hypothesized that because of income *availability* among socio-economic groups, CESG will primarily help financially *advantaged* families (CAUT, 1999). The early results of the CESG program show that is precisely the case. Data released by Statistics Canada in April 2001 on the Survey of Approaches to Educational Planning[7] show that 87.1 per cent of parents hope that their children will have a post-secondary education but only 40.7 per cent are saving for this education. Only 18.7 per cent of parents from low-income backgrounds ($30,000) are presently saving for their children's post-secondary education compared to 62.5 per cent of those with incomes of $80,000 or more. The higher the household income, the greater the hope that their children will attend university. Parents have rising post-secondary aspirations for their children regardless of their household income (see Davies, this volume).

Students' Contribution to Financing Post-Secondary Education

Living with parents or guardians while attending a post-secondary institution has a substantial impact on non-educational expenditures at all levels of education. According to Barr-Telford et al. (2003, 12), the median annual non-educational expenditure of full-time students living with their parents was $3,500, compared with just over $8,000 for those who did not live with their parents; over one-third of current students in the PEPS survey did not live with their parents. Differences also exist between ages and genders when considering the parental funding of post-secondary education. More men than women expect funding from their parents (6 per cent spread). Additionally, the Junor and Usher poll shows that as students age, their expectations for parental support decreases. At the ages of 18–19, 64 per cent of the student population expect that financial support will be supplied by their parents; by the time students reach 25 and older, only 21 per cent expect parental contributions. These results can possibly be explained by the RESP's constraint related to the age of the beneficiary.

A study of full-time undergraduate students at York University examined how students finance their education and compared students who do not receive financial assistance with students who rely on financial assistance through the Ontario Student Assistance Program (OSAP). The study found that students with OSAP depend on loans for 55 per cent of their financial resources, on employment for 23 per cent (14 per cent during academic year, 9 per cent summer employment), and on family support for 9 per cent. For non-OSAP students, 43 per cent relied on employment (summer and academic year included), and 33 per cent on resources from families (Hobson, Wallace, and Verilli, 1999). Clearly, paid employment is important to students whether or not they have student loans and is a factor in allowing students to attend post-secondary institutions. Furthermore, 59 per cent of OSAP students compared to 55 per cent of non-OSAP students rely on employment to *continue* their studies.

The introduction of on-campus work-study programs supports student loan recipients as well as those who do not have loans but demonstrate financial need. The government provides a wage subsidy up to a specified fixed amount. On campus work-study programs have grown significantly in the past few years, particularly in provinces where tuition fees have increased substantially. The program, however, offers low-income wages (usually just above minimum wage), which help pay for current educational expenses but do not offer a chance to reduce student debt load.

A study by the Angus Reid Group that also examined how students finance their education found that students from low-income families access less financial support from family savings (40 per cent) than do students from middle- (56 per cent) or high-income (75 per cent) households. The study concludes that students from modest family backgrounds rely more significantly on loans and employment to finance their education because of less available funds from parents (Angus Reid Group, 1998).

FACTORS INFLUENCING ACCESS
TO POST-SECONDARY EDUCATION

A large number of variables, including sociological, psychological, cultural, and financial factors, affect participation in post-secondary education. Individual characteristics that affect participation include educational achievement, family background, aspirations, and academic performance. These combined with the psycho-social and financial characteristics can create barriers that may discourage students from low-income families from considering participation in higher education.

Persistence of Social Advantage

The shift in financial responsibility from governments to individual students (and their families) underscores the fact that access to university remains dependent on one's social origins. The relationship between university accessibility and social class has altered little in thirty years. Participation rates by socio-economic class (SES) have increased substantially for the highest- and the middle-income quartiles compared to a small increase for low-income quartiles (Canadian Education Statistics Council, 2000; de Broucker and Underwood, 1998). Thus, students from low SES backgrounds continue to choose community colleges or private vocational colleges instead of university (Clift et al., 1998). This implies that students from low socio-economic backgrounds continue to lack the financial, social, or cultural capital to improve their social position through participation in the higher education system. And though Corak (2001) sees little evidence to support the assertion that children from low-income families are destined to become low-income adults, he agrees that the very well off virtually guarantee that their children will be among the most advantaged in the next generation (15).

Table 3.13, drawn from data from the 1997 Survey of Consumer Finance, illustrates the relationship between family income and the highest educational attainment obtained by children aged 18–24. Income was chosen as a marker of both socio-economic background and the financial capacity of families to marshal the resources required to support children's entry into post-secondary education. Table 3.13 clearly shows a positive relationship between total family income and the highest educational attainment of children. By way of illustration, for children achieving no more than a grade 8 education, the total (average) family income before taxes was $49,262, while for children achieving a university degree, the total (average) family income was $89,570.

In a recent study, Quirke investigates the effects of the rising costs of university attendance at the University of Guelph on low-income families; she

Table 3.13
Total Family Income and Highest Educational Attainment
among Children 18–24, 1997

Educational Attainment	Mean	N	Std. Deviation
No Schooling or Grade 8 or Lower	$49,262	20,887	$31,316
Grade 9–10	$58,602	76,060	$34,478
Grade 11–13 Not Graduate	$63,024	183,970	$43,961
Grade 11–13 Graduate	$70,782	273,694	$42,256
Some Post-Secondary, No Diploma, Degree, Certificate	$75,199	410,409	$46,832
Post-Secondary, Certificate or Diploma	$75,570	261,075	$42,547
University Degree	$89,570	67,030	$64,023
Total	$71,957	1,293,125	$45,444

Source: Sweet, Anisef, and Lin (2000)

identifies a negative relationship between students' socio-economic status and sensitivity to the cost of education (Quirke, 2000). Other studies show that participation in university is related to parents' socio-economic status and *their* educational attainment (Anisef et al., 1982; Guppy and Davis, 1998; Clift et al., 1998; Quirke, 2000). One such study is Statistics Canada's April 2001 Survey of Approaches to Educational Planning, which reveals that parents who have not completed high school hold significantly less "hope" (70.4 per cent) that their children will attend post-secondary school than parents who have earned a graduate degree (96.7 per cent). Educational attainment also indicates whether or not parents are saving for their children's post-secondary education. The level of education of fathers in particular is a significant determinant of students' participation; both the amount of parental contribution and the percentage of parents contributing increase as the father's education level (and most likely income level) increases (Fred Hemingway Consulting, 2004). Human capital theory argues that students engage in university education as long as the benefits after graduation compensate for the cost of education. This view assumes that potential students make informed and rational decisions about their university career in view of educational cost and future employment. However, students from disadvantaged family backgrounds do not have a detailed knowledge and understanding of prospective employment, financial gains, or loan repayment prospects (Angus Reid Group, 1998). Quirke concludes that, because of the increasing cost and debt loads of higher education, students from modest families may explore other pathways (Quirke, 2000; Angus Reid Group, 1998).

In his study of access to post-secondary education, Usher (1998) identifies direct and indirect income-related barriers that inhibit student access. Students affected by indirect barriers are not as likely to pursue higher education because of poor motivation from outside and low-income status, caused by their "at risk" status in society. Family conflicts at an early age and socio-economic difficulties can cause early withdrawal from mainstream education. Therefore, these students face not only direct barriers such as lack of income, but also indirect barriers that prevent them from *considering* planning for post-secondary education. Usher proposes options for governments to diminish these barriers, e.g., minimizing direct barriers by curbing tuition fee increases, increasing student assistance (grants), and introducing strategies for increasing overall family income. He proposes decreasing indirect barriers by increasing the overall level of education through tangible encouragement and incentives for young people to pursue post-secondary education.

Findings of the Angus Reid Group (1998) indicate that deciding to *continue* higher education depends on inter-dependent social, economic, academic, and personal aspects. Students' main reason for pursuing post-secondary education is driven by economic motivation, implying that students want to have successful and secure employment, future opportunities in the labour market, and a better lifestyle after graduation. Personal and academic improvement was second on the list for wishing to have a post-secondary education. Financial concerns about cost and debt loads of higher education are an important aspect for high school graduates, however, more so for the low-income cohort than for higher-income households (Angus Reid Group, 1998). The study clearly indicates that social inequality affects entrance to post-secondary education, implying that students from financially disadvantaged families face barriers in meeting the escalating costs of a post-secondary education. Parents and peers are also considered to have an impact on a student's decision to participate in higher education. Moreover, when parents are less motivated and less encouraging in seeking further education for their children this translates into less willingness to pursue post-secondary education (Angus and Reid, 1998). As a result, lower aspirations and lower educational attainment are underlying factors for the lack of cultural capital of low-income families.

Preliminary results from the Youth in Transition Survey indicate that among 18 to 20-year-olds, the most common barrier to a post-secondary education is financial. About two-thirds of those reporting facing barriers to attending school, as they would like to do, cited financial factors; the percentage doing so was similar for post-secondary leavers (71.4 per cent), high school graduates with no post-secondary education (70.7 per cent), post-secondary graduates (70.4 per cent), and post-secondary continuers (68.9 per cent) (Bowlby and McMullen, 2002, 59). Other studies analyse student loan programs as they relate to equity. The data reveal that students from low-income families are informed about their choices of financial support, but are more likely to be reluctant to take advantage of available loan programs and hesitant to borrow large amounts compared to students from higher-income families (Porter et al., 1973; Clift et al., 1998).

CONCLUSION

A recent study by Corak, Lipps, and Zhao (2003) explored the relationship between family income and post-secondary participation and found that, by the end of the 1990s, post-secondary education was no less the preserve of the relatively better off than it was in the 1980s. This, we would argue, is not a satisfactory state of affairs. As we indicate in chapter 1, parents are well aware of the changes that have occurred in Canadian society and are convinced that their children's success within a knowledge economy hinges on their post-secondary participation. At the same time the cost of gaining entry to universities and other post-secondary institutions has increased substantially and, for those students that rely on loans, indebtedness has risen to an all-time high, though it is important to understand that such costs vary by province. Escalating costs have made it more difficult for economically disadvantaged families to translate their children's university aspirations into reality, when compared with families from higher socio-economic backgrounds. Indeed, many of these families may decide that they simply cannot afford to support their children's pursuit of post-secondary studies. While the CESG is a well-intentioned federal initiative, it appears to primarily aid advantaged families. Perhaps it is time to consider the introduction of non-repayable grants for low-income students. If such strategies are not employed, then the persistence of social advantage will continue, or worsen, as the private study costs of post-secondary education continue to increase in Canada.

NOTES

1 Until 1995, the federal government transferred resources to the provinces *separately* for post-secondary education and health and welfare.

2 http://osap.gov.on.ca/eng/not_secure/new01.htm#Integrated Student Loans. For press release go to http://www.hrdc-drhc.gc.ca/common/news/youth/0101801.shtml

3 http://www.hrdc-drhc.gc.ca/common/news/hrib/99-44.shtml

4 The National Graduates Survey defines trade/vocational graduates as those who have completed skilled trades programs (excluding apprenticeships) that are three to twelve months long and do not necessarily require a high school diploma for admission.

5 Source: http://www.hrdc-drhc.gc.ca/student_loans/c/statistics/ Reduction.html

6 CSLP data show that women are more likely to negotiate loans than men and include all persons that enrol in universities, while the NGS includes only graduates from post-secondary institutions.

7 SAEP is the first Statistics Canada household survey to contain detailed information on how Canadians prepare for post-secondary education. The survey was conducted in October 1999 and data were collected concerning 20,353 children aged 18 years or under in 1999.

REFERENCES

Andres, L. and Krahn, H. (1999). "Youth pathways in articulated postsecondary systems: enrolment and completion patterns of urban young men and women." *Canadian Journal of Higher Education, 29*(1), 47–82.

Angus Reid Group (1998). "Canadians' perceptions surrounding saving for postsecondary education." Final report submitted to Human Resources Development Canada. Ottawa: Human Resources Development Canada.

Anisef, P. (1989). *Accessibility to postsecondary education in Canada: a review of trends and current issues (final report)*. Toronto: The Council of Ministers of Education Canada.

Anisef, P. and Okihiro, N. (1982). *Losers and winners: The pursuit of equality and social justice in higher education*. Toronto: Butterworth.

Barr-Telford, L.B, Cartwright, F., Prasil, S., and Shimmons, K. (2003). *Access, persistence, and financing: First results from the Postsecondary Education Participation Survey (PEPS)*. Education, Skills and Learning Research Papers. Ottawa: Human Resources Development Canada.

Baum, S. and Schwartz, S. (1998). *The impact of student loans on borrowers: Consumption patterns and attitudes towards repayment: Evidence from the New England Loan Survey*. Boston: Massachusetts Higher Education Assistance Corp and New England Loan Marketing Association.

Bell, S. and Bischoping, K. (1998). "Gender and contradictory definitions of university accessibility." *The Review of Higher Education. 21*(2), 179–94.

Bourgoin, B. (1995). "Financial assistance to postsecondary students." *Education Quarterly Review, 2*(1), 10–19.

Bowlby, J.W. and McMullen, K. (2002). *At a crossroads: First results for the 18-20-year-old cohort of the youth in transition survey*. Ottawa: Human Resources Development Canada.

Canadian Education Statistics Council (2000). *Education indicators in Canada. Report of the pan-Canadian education indicators program 1999.* Catalogue No. 81-582-XPE. Toronto, Ontario.

Canadian Federation of Students (September 2000). Submission to House of Commons Committee on Finance. Retrieved 21 August 2004 from http://www.cfs-fcee.ca/resource/20000901-fincomm.pdf

Canadian Undergraduate Survey Consortium (2000). *Graduating Student Survey.* Retrieved 18 August 2004 from http://www.edudata.educ.ubc.ca/Data_Pages/12-PSE/Undergrad.htm

CAUT (1999). "Not in the public interest: University finance in Canada: 1972–1998." *CAUT Education Review, 1*(3), 1–21. Retrieved 21 August 2004 from http://www.caut.ca/English/Publications/Review/9911_pubinterest/page1.htm

– (2000). "Out of reach: Trends in household spending on education in Canada." *CAUT Education Review, 2*(1), 1–7. Ottawa: Canadian Association of University Teachers.

Clark, W. (1998). "Paying off student loans." *Canadian Social Trends, 51,* 29.

Clift, R., Hawkey, C., and Vaughan, A.-M. (1998). *A background analysis of the relationships between tuition fees, financial aid, and student choice.* Paper presented at Canadian Society for the Study of Higher Education Conference, St. John's (June).

Corak, M. (2001). *Are the kids all right? Intergenerational mobility and child well-being in Canada.* (Paper prepared for Family and Labour Studies, No. 171). Ottawa: Statistics Canada.

Corak, M., Lipps, G., and Zhao, J. (2003). *Family income and participation in post-secondary education.* Family and Labour Studies Paper No. 210, Ottawa: Statistics Canada.

Daniel, H.-D., Schwarz, S., and Teichler, U. (1999). "Study costs, student income and public policy in Europe." *European Journal of Education, 34,* 7–22.

de Broucker, P. and Underwood, K. (1998). "Intergenerational educational mobility: An international comparison with a focus on postsecondary education." *Education Quarterly Review, 5*(2), 30–51. Ottawa: Statistics Canada.

Eicher, J.-C. and Chevaillier, T. (1993). "Rethinking the financing of post-compulsory education." *International Journal of Educational Research, 19,* 445–519.

EKOS Research Associates (2003). *Making ends meet: The 2001–2002 Student Financial Survey.* Toronto: Canada Millennium Scholarship Foundation.

Finnie, R. (2000). *Student loans: Is it getting harder? Borrowing, burdens, and repayment.* Ottawa: Canada Student Loan Program, Human Resources Development Canada.

– (2001). "Student loans: The empirical record." *Canadian Journal of Higher Education, 31,* 3.

Finnie, R., and Garneau, G. (1996). "Student borrowing for postsecondary education." *Education Quarterly Review, 3*(2),10–34. Ottawa: Statistics Canada.

Foley, K. (2001). *Why stop after high school? A descriptive analysis of the most important reasons that high school graduates do not continue to PSE.* Montreal: Canada Millennium Scholarship Foundation.

Fred Hemingway Consulting (2004). *Pressure points in student financial assistance: Exploring the Making Ends Meet database.* Montreal: The Canada Millennium Scholarship Foundation. Retrieved 4 August 2004 from http://www.millennium scholarships.ca/en/research/pressure_en.pdf

Guppy, N. and Davies, S. (1998). *Education in Canada: Recent trends and future challenges.* Catalogue #96-321-MPE No.3. Ottawa: Statistics Canada.

Hobson, D., Wallace, D., and Verilli, M. (1999). *How York undergraduates finance their university education.* Toronto: Office of the Vice-President, Enrolment and Student Services, York University.

Human Resources Development Canada (1999). *Ensuring opportunities: Access to post- secondary education.* Retrieved 21 August 2004 from http://www.hrdc-drhc.gc.ca/hrib/learnlit/cslp/ensure

Junor, S. and Usher, A. (2002). *The price of knowledge: Access and student finance in Canada.* Toronto: Canada Millennium Scholarship Foundation.

Lin, Z., Sweet, R., Anisef, P., and Schuetze, H. (2001). *Consequences and policy implications for university students who have chosen liberal or vocational education: Labour market outcomes and employability skills.* Unpublished Report. Ottawa: Applied Research Branch, Strategic Policy, Human Resources Development Canada.

Little, D. (1997). "Financing universities: Why students are paying more?" *Education Quarterly Review, 4*(2),10–26.

Lowe, G.S. (1998). *Postsecondary learner transitions and pathways.* Postsecondary Education Project, Learners, Pathways and Transitions. Toronto: Council of Ministers of Education, Canada.

Magnusson, J.-L. (2000). "Canadian higher education and citizenship in the context of state restructuring and globalization." *Encounters in Education, 1,* (Fall), 107–23. Winnipeg: Faculty of Education, University of Manitoba.

McMullen, K. (2004). *A family affair: The impact of paying for college or university.* Montreal: Canada Millennium Scholarship Foundation. Retrieved 4 August 2004 from <http://www.millenniumscholarships.ca/en/research/family_e.pdf>.

Miller, E. (1997). "Parents' views on the value of a college education and how they will pay for it." *Journal of Student Financial Aid, 27*(1), 7–20.

Ministry of Advanced Education, Training and Technology (December 1999). *Federal spending on post-secondary education: Transfers to provinces: Trends and consequences.* Retrieved 24 August 2004, from http://www.aett.gov.bc.ca/policy/chst.htm

Mumper, M. (1996). *Removing college price barriers.* New York: State University of New York Press.

Ontario Student Assistance Program (2000). *OSAP.* Toronto: Student Support Branch Ministry of Training, Colleges and Universities. Retrieved 1 July 2003 from http://osap.gov.on.ca

Plager, L. and Chen, E. (1999). "Student debt from 1990–91 to 1995–96: An analysis of Canada student loans data." *Education Quarterly Review, 4,* 10–35.

Porter, M. et al. (1973). *Does money matter? Prospects for higher education.* Toronto: York University Institute for Behavioral Research.

Quirke, L. (2000). *Accessibility and student finances: A two tiered effect at Ontario univer-sities?* mimeograph. Guelph: University of Guelph.

R. A. Malatest & Associates Ltd (2003). *Canadian college student finances.* Toronto: Canada Millennium Scholarship Foundation.

Statistics Canada (1997). *National Graduate Survey.* Ottawa: Statistics Canada.

– *Tuition and living accommodation costs for full-time students at Canadian degree grant-ing institutions.* Catalogue No. 81C0049. Ottawa: Culture, Tourism and the Centre for Education Statistics.

– (2003). "Average undergraduate tuition fees." *The Daily,* 12 August 2003.

– (2004). *Education in Canada.* Catalogue No. 81-229-XPB. Ottawa: Statistics Canada

Steelman, L.C. and Powell, B. (1991). "Sponsoring the next generation: Parental willingness to pay for higher education." *American Journal of Sociology,* 96(6), 1505–29.

Sweet, R., Anisef, P., and Lin, Z. (2000). *Exploring family antecedents of participation in post secondary education.* Unpublished report. Ottawa: Learning and Literacy Di-rectorate, Human Resources Development Canada.

Usher, A. (1998). *Income related barriers to post-secondary education.* Toronto: Council of Ministers of Education, Canada.

Volkswein, F. et al. (1998). "Factors associated with student loan default among dif-ferent racial and ethnic groups." *The Journal of Higher Education,* 69(2), 206–37.

Willms, J.D. (2002). *Vulnerable children: Findings from Canada's National Longitudinal Survey of Children and Youth.* Edmonton: The University of Alberta Press.

4

Paying for a University Education: A Comparison of Public and Private Study Costs in Canada, Australia, and Selected European Countries

STEPHEN BELL AND GLEN A. JONES

Who should pay for higher education? While the state continues to be the major funder of university operating costs in most Western systems, the question of the appropriate balance between public (state) and private support for the costs of higher education has become an important public policy issue in many jurisdictions. This question of balance emerges in every area of university activity, including research (government versus private sector sponsorship), service (public service versus fee-for-service arrangements), and teaching.

This chapter focuses on the balance between the public and private costs associated with studying at university. Our objective is to analyse the interface between the student and the higher education system in Canada, Australia, and four European countries (Denmark, the Netherlands, Sweden, and the United Kingdom) in order to understand the basic assumptions underscoring the division between public and private costs in each jurisdiction.

While private study costs are only one of a plethora of factors that affect access to higher education, there is little doubt that private costs and participation in higher education are directly related. In Canada, the topic of accessibility received increased attention in the 1990s when, under the guise of deficit reduction, federal government support of post-secondary education in terms of fiscal transfers to the provinces was significantly reduced. Most provinces responded by increasing or deregulating tuition fees, encouraging post-secondary institutions to become more entrepreneurial in raising corporate support from the private sector, and placing increasing responsibility on students and their families to fund post-secondary education. It had become clear in the late 1990s that patterns of access to post-secondary education may have started to shift as a result of high student fees, high student debt loads, and the inability of families of modest means to finance their children's education (Bell, Plickert, and Anisef, 2000). Are particular segments of the Canadian population experiencing social exclusion with respect to participation in post-secondary education? Are disadvantaged families finding it more difficult to marshal the resources required to permit their children to gain access to universities and colleges?

The extent to which study costs are handled through public mechanisms that deal with both the direct and indirect costs of post-secondary education (for example low or no tuition, grants, student loans) rather than private resources (individual or family) has become an important higher education policy issue in almost every jurisdiction. From the World Bank's controversial argument that tuition fees represent a democratizing force (Fischman and Stromquist, 2000), to recent policy changes in tuition and student financial support mechanisms in the United Kingdom, the Netherlands, and Australia, governments and international organizations have become increasingly interested in finding an appropriate balance between public and private study costs.

We begin by describing our approach and methodology for the study, then we briefly review trends in participation rates in the six jurisdictions. Next we present six case studies (beginning with Canada) conducted in 2001–02 to illuminate the private/public study costs dimensions in each jurisdiction. We conclude with a comparative analysis of the assumptions underscoring public/private study costs and review the Canadian case in the light of these assumptions.

METHODOLOGY

Relatively little comparative analysis of the public/private dimension of study costs can be found within the international literature of higher education. Publications such as the *UNESCO Statistical Yearbook* make no reference to direct student costs and funding; and publications by the OECD are similarly limited, often dealing with selected countries, and frequently omitting Canada. Recent World Bank studies acknowledge the importance of understanding direct and indirect, and public and private, study costs, but recommendations are frequently provided without supporting data (Girdwood, 2000; Task Force, 2000). The recent *Deutsches Studentenwerk* study is an exception in that it provides examples of direct costs and the funding of study costs in selected European Union countries. It also compares public and private costs, including various sources, principally the family. While it does refer to the role of parents in financing their children's post-secondary education, the *Deutsches Studentenwerk* report does not assess parents' monetary contributions in any detail, nor does it refer to other forms of family capital accumulation and transfer (1997).

One of the reasons for the limited analysis of this topic is the methodological complexity of comparing these macro-level dimensions in different jurisdictions. Quantitative analyses can be problematic because of the lack of data on both direct and indirect study costs in many jurisdictions, and the limited comparability of national data sets. Meaningful comparative quantitative analyses of these dimensions would also require a way of dealing with these costs in relation to broader economic factors. For example, meaningful comparisons of indirect costs would have to consider differences in cost of living, state social welfare programs, taxation, and a range of other complex variables.

Even in studies where some comparative quantitative data have been obtained, such as the *Deutsches Studentenwerk* study, researchers note the limitations of this form of analysis and conclusions generally take the form of defining broad categories of qualitative differences between jurisdictions. For example, in a recent analysis of government's role in financing postsecondary education in the European Union, Daniel, Schwarz, and Teichler (1999) noted the range of assumptions on which student support is based. Tuition and loans policies, for example, vary depending on the government's view of students' social role as:

1 A *learner and young citizen* for whom substantial (government) grants are provided regardless of parental financial resources.
2 A *child in a family-social system* for whom hardly any public support is provided for covering direct student expenditures.
3 A *child in a family-social system with a strong welfare component* for whom student aid depends on parental resources but (government) financial aid is provided to a large number of students.
4 An *investor* in his/her future for whom student loan guarantee arrangements are made.

These broad categories may assist in explaining the significant differences by system in terms of the share of direct private study costs in relation to system expenditures on higher education. In Canada, for example, post-secondary education has been a shared responsibility of the state through tax dollars and of students and parents through savings (Clark, 1998). Students typically provided 10–20 per cent of the total direct costs of post-secondary education. Despite evidence of a shift towards "individualism" and personal responsibility as determinants of post-secondary access amongst OECD countries, there does not seem to be a uniform or wholesale transfer of the financial burden of advanced education to families. In

Denmark and Sweden, for example, private contributions to study costs are negligible, while in the u.s. they are almost 40 per cent, and in Korea and Japan they exceed 50 per cent (Eurydice, 1999).[1] The reasons for this variability are not immediately obvious but relate in important ways to the values and assumptions that underlie relations between the individual and the state.

To further illuminate these assumptions we reviewed the direct and indirect cost arrangements and financial support mechanisms in Canada and five other jurisdictions in 2001–02. We included Australia and the United Kingdom because of the shared historical relationships and similar institutional forms, but we decided not to include the United States.[2] We selected Denmark, the Netherlands, and Sweden to include other developed European nations that are generally regarded as having different approaches to student financial support and different assumptions in terms of direct costs (for example, see Huisman, Kaiser, and Vossensteyn, 2000). In short, the six jurisdictions were selected because they are all developed Western nations but each has a quite different approach to the issue of public/private study costs.

Given that our objective was to analyse the definitions and assumptions underscoring public/private study costs by jurisdiction in qualitative terms, each case represents an attempt to provide an overview of these arrangements for undergraduate education in each jurisdiction. All of the case studies are based on a combination of primary and secondary source material, including recent government reports, scholarly articles, and, in some cases, correspondence with national scholars[3] to ensure that our understanding of a particular system was accurate. In the Canadian case, our analysis employs findings from a recent Canadian study (Bell, Plickert, and Anisef, 2000) that was one of a series of background papers informing a three-year study on educational planning in Canada, financed by the Government of Canada. It involved a synthesis of primary and secondary literature, university institutional research studies, government reports, and non-governmental association reports on student study costs and accessibility to post-secondary education in Canada. The study looked at whether or not students from disadvantaged backgrounds and their families are finding it more difficult to marshal the financial resources required to permit their children to gain access to universities and colleges. The authors examined loan programs available to students via the provinces and territories, assessed what changes had occurred over the past five years, and discussed the Canadian Education Savings Grant (CESG) that was recently introduced to increase student access in Canada.

We hope that through this selected comparison we can explicate the assumptions underscoring discussions of private/public study costs and the ways that study costs (in direct and/or broader indirect terms) are defined, and, by illuminating the diverse ways in which these concepts are understood and studied, contribute to the international comparative analysis of study costs in higher education.

PARTICIPATION IN HIGHER EDUCATION

Underlying the interest in public/private study costs is a concern for participation in higher education. Participation rates are calculated using a variety of indicators, but the two most common international indicators represent attempts to relate participation to the whole population of a given jurisdiction (the number of students enrolled in higher or "tertiary" education per 100,000 inhabitants) and to relate the total enrolment in post-secondary education to the population of individuals in the five-year age group following the traditional age of completing secondary school in the jurisdiction. UNESCO data for these two common participation rate indicators for the six countries included in this study are presented in Table 4.1 and Table 4.2.

Obviously levels of participation in higher education differ substantially by jurisdiction, with Canada having the highest participation rates of all of the countries included in this study. The common trend in all six jurisdictions is the increase in participation rates during the last two decades, and in some cases (such as Australia and the United Kingdom) these increases have been dramatic. In all six countries, policies concerning student financial assistance have been considered important mechanisms for increasing participation in higher education.

CANADA

Canadian studies have consistently shown that attending higher education pays off in terms of employment opportunities and potential earnings. Participation rates in universities have increased among the young (18 to 24 years of age), reaching 20 per cent in 1993, suggesting that Canadians continue to have confidence in the value of higher education and consider it a worthwhile investment. Unfortunately, participation rate studies also reveal systemic inequities in terms of accessibility to different parts of the higher education system. Likewise, inequities exist in terms of the potential long-term "pay off," thereby further affecting in a systemic way decisions about whether or not to access post-secondary education. Hence the systemic inequities that characterize the broader social structure of Canada appear to be reproduced with respect to accessibility to higher education and the potential pay off of participation. These inequities are generally conceptualized by equity theorists in terms of interlocking systems of oppression characterized by gender, race, class, sexual orientation, ablism, and ethnicity (Magnusson, 2000).

Table 4.1
Tertiary Education Students per 100,000 Inhabitants
for Selected Countries

	1980	1985	1990	1995
Australia	2,222	2,366	2,872	5,401
Canada	5,770	6,320	6,897	6,984
Denmark	2,074	2,275	2,782	3,272
Netherlands	2,546	2,794	3,203	3,485
Sweden	2,423	2,115	2,250	2,810
United Kingdom	1,468	1,824	2,186	3,126

Source: UNESCO (1997)

Table 4.2
Gross Enrolment Ratio (%) for Selected Countries

	1985	1990	1995
Australia	27.7	35.5	71.7
Canada	69.6	94.7	102.9
Denmark	29.1	36.5	45.0
Netherlands	31.8	39.8	48.9
Sweden	30.0	32.0	42.5
United Kingdom	21.7	30.2	48.3

Source: UNESCO (1997)
The Gross Enrolment Ratio is calculated as total
enrolment in tertiary education regardless of age,
expressed as a percentage of the population in the five-
year age group following from the secondary-school
leaving age.

As in other industrialized countries, Canada's economy has undergone re-structuring such that parts of the national economy have become parts of transnational economies. Canada's restructuring process has been charac-terized by neoliberal policies similar to those evident in the U.K. and U.S. Nevertheless the impact of this restructuring process on higher education is somewhat more complex than in the U.K., for example, primarily because jurisdiction for education is a provincial rather than a federal/national mat-ter. In some respects Canada has no single "system" of higher education, since the provinces play a central legislative and regulatory role and policy approaches and institutional arrangements differ significantly by province (Jones, 1997; 1998). However, since the Liberal government assumed power in 1993, restructuring of the federal transfer payments to the provinces and

Table 4.3
Percentage Change in Undergraduate Arts Tuition by Province

	1991–92 to 2001–02 % change	1996–97 to 2001–02 % change	2000–01 to 2001–02 % change
Canada	101.4	30.0	2.0
Newfoundland	92.4	11.2	−10.0
PEI	74.1	26.4	6.0
Nova Scotia	115.0	35.2	4.9
New Brunswick	87.0	36.7	7.4
Quebec	46.2	19.9	1.6
Ontario	127.6	38.4	2.3
Manitoba	61.1	12.1	0.1
Saskatchewan	111.4	44.2	8.2
Alberta	160.8	33.8	3.4
British Columbia	29.0	−6.6	−2.2

Source: Statistics Canada (2003)

provincial policy reforms have stimulated the restructuring of health and post-secondary systems in all provinces. Certain provinces, such as Ontario and Alberta, have experienced more intensively the fallout of neoliberal economic policies and their impact on the post-secondary system. These provinces have been under the control of populist right-wing provincial governments and are therefore further along in terms of neoliberal restructuring of public systems (Magnusson, 2000). Neoliberal policies of economic restructuring have involved shifting responsibility for funding higher education from the state onto private individuals. This has been a shift not only in economics and policy but also in the ideology and discourse constructing citizenship and notions of entitlement. Table 4.3 illustrates changes in average tuition fees by province over the last decade and demonstrate the differences in approach to tuition policy by province.

Student Assistance and Student Debt in Canada

Student assistance in Canada is a shared responsibility between the federal government and the provinces. A number of financial options exist, each reflecting a somewhat different view of the individual's responsibilities for direct and indirect costs. Among the more important forms of financial aid in this country are institutional (e.g., university) and government-sponsored plans, including a variety of scholarships, bursaries, awards, and loans. A recent federal government initiative is an educational savings plan designed to encourage families to invest in the future education of their children. Termed the Canadian Educational Savings Grant (CESG), this plan involves both parents and the government in an RRSP-like savings arrangement. It may be expected that generally similar "investment" plans have been contemplated or implemented in other countries with advanced capitalist economies but the extent or nature of such schemes and the manner in which they complement family policies is not known (Mora, 1998). This is partly because financial support policies are inherently complex, and those that involve the interplay of public and private (family) resources are even more difficult to research. Current Canadian research has focused on the structure and organization of the Canada Student Loan Plan (CSLP) or the difficulties that students encounter in assuming a large debt and in repaying their loans in an uncertain labour market (HRDC, 1998).

Social Advantage – Still

Before examining the shift in financial responsibility from governments to individual students (and their families) it is instructive to note that access to university continues to depend largely on one's social origins – the relationship between university accessibility and social class has altered little in thirty years. Participation rates by socio-economic class (SES) have increased for the highest and the middle-income quartiles compared to a small increase for low-income quartiles (Canadian Education Statistics Council, 2000; de Broucker and Underwood, 1998). Thus, students from low SES backgrounds continue to choose community colleges or private vocational colleges instead of university (Clift et al., 1998). The 1997 Survey of Consumer Finance illustrates the relationship between family income and the highest educational attainment obtained by children aged 18–24. Individuals who had obtained a university degree by 1997 came from families where the average total income was $89,570. In contrast, individuals of the same age who graduated from high school by 1997 came from families where the average total income was $70,782 (Sweet, Anisef, and Lin, 2000).

Government Devolution and Rising Student Debt

Non-repayable grants for students attending post-secondary education in Canada have been eliminated in most provincial student aid programs except in very limited and special cases.[4] This is in stark contrast to the European countries that we have selected for comparative analysis, where grants and loans co-exist. The marked increase in tuition fees combined with the elimination of grants has increased the average amount borrowed per person per year. This has led to increased loan re-payment difficulties upon graduation as shown in Table 4.4.

Table 4.4
Student Loan Levels and Difficulty Repaying Debt in Percentages

	Student Loan			How much did you owe in 1995?			How much did you owe in 1997?			Any difficulties in repaying?		
	Yes	No	N	Mean	N	SD	Mean	N	SD	Yes	No	N
Ontario	44.6	55.4	56501	12604	23880	9814	10823	20648	11629	25.6	74.4	15906
Canada	47.7	52.3	155923	12233	71825	9611	11080	61087	10828	23.8	76.2	47992

Source: NGS, Statistics Canada (1997)

Table 4.4 presents data from the National Graduate Survey (NGS) that illustrate how much students owed upon graduation in 1995, how much they owed in 1997, and whether they had any difficulty repaying the student loans. The average student debt in 1995 was approximately $12,200. The average debt has been reduced to approximately $11,000 two years later with 23.8 per cent indicating that they were having difficulties repaying the loans. Ontario data are presented for comparison.

Present government policies at both the federal and provincial levels have been designed to deal with student debt after it has been amassed. These programs include special opportunity grants, deferred grants, remissions, and interest relief programs. A new Government of Ontario policy indicates that students who accumulate more than $7,000 per year in post-secondary debt will be provided with some relief.

Family Capacity and Private Study Costs

As tuition fees have increased significantly, average family income for two-parent families with children under eighteen has declined by 5 per cent and for single-parent families by 7 per cent (CAUT, 1999). All families committed a larger portion of their incomes to post-secondary education in 1998 than in 1992. Low-income families in particular absorbed the greatest impact of increasing tuition fees and decreasing disposable income during this period, further impairing their financial capability to pay for their children's education (see Bell and Anisef, chapter 3).

Recent studies have looked at the personal financial circumstances of post-secondary students. Given the nature of Canadian student assistance arrangements, students rely heavily on financial support from their families and on employment income. Bowlby and McMullen (2002) found a very heavy reliance on employment income among post-secondary students and noted that post-secondary "leavers" are less likely to receive financial support from their families than those who continue with their studies. Baseline results from a major national study on the finances of post-secondary students reinforce this reliance on employment income, but these data reveal that the median level of summer earnings for students was $3,200 (the mean was $3,500). This was viewed as "startlingly low" and the study report notes that "with the rising cost of living, tuition, books and other necessities, it is virtually impossible to imagine how students can subsist on this level of income, without relying on either significant assistance, or generating significant debt" (Canada Millennium Scholarship Foundation, 2001, 2).

Summary

The Canadian approach assumes that the student is responsible for paying tuition and maintenance costs. The level of tuition varies considerably by province, program, and in some provinces, by institution. While the student is responsible for maintenance costs, a variety of student assistance mechanisms are available for financial support. The responsibility for student assistance is shared by the federal government and the provinces. There is a heavy reliance on student loans, and a number of new mechanisms have emerged to assist students with heavy debt loads. Families are encouraged to save for the post-secondary education of their children through a new federal program.

THE NETHERLANDS

The Netherlands has a long tradition of generous support for students in post-secondary education. Since 1986 the *Netherlands Educational Assistance Act* guarantees the student the *right* to financial assistance for full-time study. However, the system has been amended several times, in part because the initial scheme was viewed as overly generous and the government could not bear its costs: grant amounts were reduced, tuition fees increased, and a new emphasis on student loans was instituted. In 1993 academic achievement benchmarks were introduced. The reforms were considered to be "steering at a distance" (Vossensteyn, 2002) and were consistent with developments in other European countries in terms of increased emphasis on private responsibility for student support.

The present student support system for students has three components, based on monthly budgets: basic grant (HFL 454); maximum supplementary grant (HFL 471); and interest-bearing loan (HFL 504) for students not living at home. For students living at home the basic grant is lower (HFL 147); the supplementary grant is HFL 436 at maximum; and the interest-bearing loan is HFL 504.

Table 4.5
Education Support for Students in Netherlands by
Type of Grant and Living Arrangements,
in Percentages (2001)

	Basic	Supp.	Loan	Total
Independent				
Minimum	36	0	64	100
Maximum	36	33	31	100
At Home				
Minimum	15	0	85	100
Maximum	15	43	24	100

Source: Vossensteyn (2002)

The basic grant is *independent* of the level of parental and/or student income. The amount of the loan and the grants are adjusted yearly according to inflation. The basic grant includes a pass for the use of the bus and
rail systems (weekdays or weekends). Since a typical course of study at a
Dutch university can be completed in four years this is the maximum number of years that students can draw grants (Vossensteyn, 2002, 4).

The "performance-based" grant system has been in place since 1996.
The basic and supplementary grants are initially awarded as loans. Students may convert their loans to grants after their first year provided they
are in good academic standing, which is defined as 50 per cent or more of
the study credit points (Vossensteyn, 1998). For subsequent years of academic study the loans are converted to grants if the student graduates
within ten years. Students unable to complete their degree in ten years can
continue with the interest-bearing loans. Table 4.5 shows student support
by type of grant and living arrangements.

The large difference in the minimum and maximum level of the supplementary grant depends on a student's income as well as on parental income. Students with parental income of HFL 60,000 per annum or higher
receive no supplementary grants, while students with parental income of
HFL 25,000 or less receive full supplementary grants. A sliding scale is used
for parents with incomes between these levels, with parental income determined based on the three different levels of state tax tariffs. The number
of children under eighteen that a parent has to support is also taken into
account in the calculations. The maximum amount to be contributed by
parents is the total budget minus the basic grant.

Students may earn up to HFL 15,000 per year without influencing the
level of their grants. As income from employment increases beyond the

HFL 15,000 level, a student will be in eligible first for a loan, then the additional grant, and finally the basic grant. About 70 per cent of students have a job in which they work an average of 12 hours per week, but it is rare for a student to exceed HFL 15,000 per annum in wages (Vossensteyn, 2002, 24).

Student Expenditure

Student expenditures include tuition fees, study costs (books, equipment, and office supplies), maintenance (living) costs, and insurance costs (health). Tuition fees are very similar in most universities, about HFL 2,930 per annum. The Ministry of Education, Culture and Science budgets approximately HFL 1,085 per month for students who live at home and HFL 1,430 for students who live away from home. Students consider the monthly student budget determined by the state to be inadequate. Various studies (Vossensteyn, 2002) have shown that substantially higher monthly budgets are necessary. The state has agreed to fund further independent research on this topic.

Repayment of the Loan

The interest rate on student loans is the state loan rate. In 2000–01 this was about 5.2 per cent. Interest is charged on loans during the study period. Repayment begins after a "grace period" of two years following the completion of studies and must be completed within fifteen years. After fifteen years, any outstanding amounts are forgiven.

The minimum repayment is HFL 100 per month and repayment is income dependent. If taxable income is HFL 15,000 or less, no monthly payment is required. If taxable income is HFL 50,000 or more, HFL 560 per month is repayable. A sliding payment scale is used for incomes between HFL 15,000 and 50,000. The payments are collected and administered by an independent central office. If income fluctuates from year to year the repayment schedule does as well (Vossensteyn, 2002).

Other Financial Support for Students

Some companies provide grants to employees with children attending institutions of higher education. Several funds and organizations provide grants and loans for students in specific circumstances. Students belonging to a student association pay an annual fee – about HFL 25 – and receive a 10 per cent discount on materials such as books. Through "PC-privé projects," students can save approximately HFL 300 to HFL 500 on the purchase of a computer worth about HFL 3,000.

Level of Student Debt

The level of student debt has not been a problem in the Netherlands, as not many students actually take out loans. In the late 1980s and early 1990s a significant percentage of students took out loans and earned interest on the money in the bank. After 1992, when interest on student loans was introduced, the percentage of students taking a loan decreased significantly (Vossensteyn, 2002).

As a result of the low rate of student loans, the level of overall student debt is low. Default on student debt is not an issue, given the time-limited payback period of fifteen years.

The Issue of Access

The Student Finance Act of 1986 was designed to improve access by making students financially independent for a large part of their monthly budget. Participation rates for females attending university increased significantly from the mid-1980s. Student participation from lower SES backgrounds increased significantly in the HBO (non-university) sector. However, participation by lower SES backgrounds in the university sector did not increase, while the proportion of individuals from higher SES backgrounds did (Vossensteyn, 1999).

Considering the introduction of loans and the reduction of grants in the 1990s, de Jong (1996) postulated that students from lower SES backgrounds were afraid of risking a high student debt and therefore delayed participating in higher education to ensure that they were entering a program that was appropriate to their needs. Given that the opportunity to transfer between areas of study is restrictive and limited, they also entered HBO programs even though they were qualified for university, and chose relatively easy study paths so that they could complete their studies.[6] After a few years, however, this pattern of student activity began to shift, and a recent study concluded that financial incentives do not have a significant impact on student choice. Substantial tuition increases would not deter many potential students from entering higher education and considerable decreases in tuition fees in the engineering programs would hardly attract more students to these disciplines (Hans Vossensteyn, personal correspondence).

Summary

The Netherlands has a history of generous student financial assistance, though recent reforms have increased the importance of loans. Tuition fees are roughly similar across the country. Students are entitled to a student assistance package that is supplemented for those with low individual/parental income. The initial student assistance package is provided in the form of a loan that may include an entitlement component, a supplementary component based on income, and an additional component for students not living at home. The basic and supplementary component of the loan will be converted to a grant if the student meets modest academic objectives.

UNITED KINGDOM

In the late 1980s the Conservative government in the United Kingdom moved systematically to reduce public expenditures on higher education in response to budgetary constraints. As a result of a 1987 *White Paper,* in 1990 the government introduced student loans in addition to grants, and students' entitlement to social security allowances was abolished. Grant amounts were frozen at their nominal value. These changes were designed to handle increases in student populations, ease parents' financial burden, and increase access of disadvantaged groups to post-secondary education. Foremost, though, the changes were designed as a shift from total public funding for higher education by transferring part of the burden of student costs to students and away from parents and the state. The government argued that graduates benefitted more individually from higher education than did society as a whole and that the British system was still "elite." The government hoped that potential students and families would view higher education as a personal investment that would lead to greater income attainment. Finally, it became apparent that the United Kingdom was lagging behind other European nations in the number of post-secondary graduates and that this was adversely affecting economic performance (Eurydice, 1999, 179).

In 1994 grants were reduced a further 10 per cent and loans were increased proportionately to accelerate the financing reforms. The government also increased tuition fees and increased the re-imbursement of those fees to Local Education Authorities (LEAs). These changes further increased the number of student spaces and started to highlight in a stark way the role of the student as a consumer in higher education. The United Kingdom began to shift from an "elite" to a "mass" higher education system.

The move to mass higher education required modifications to higher education policy and further changes to the student assistance program. The Dearing Report provided a set of new recommendations in 1997. In terms of the discussion of public/private study costs, the Dearing Report recommended that post-secondary students pay for *all* their own study costs as well as tuition costs. According to Rowley (1997), the reforms were viewed as a means of rectifying the "chaotic" nature of student's financial support systems, which ranged from loans (public and private) to parental contributions and part-time work.

The Dearing Report was initiated by the Conservative government, but most of the reforms recommended concerning student assistance were implemented by the Labour government following the general election. In 1998–99 the new government introduced the *Teaching and Higher Education Bill*, which included more reforms. These reforms were designed to increase contributions from families who could pay and to further reduce students' dependence on the state.

Tuition Fees

The 1998 reforms introduced tuition fees that are paid by the student directly to the institution. Tuition fees were formerly paid by the state to the LEA and then allocated to the institutions. As the system changed and tuition fees started to become part of the loans system, the LEAs were bypassed and many English students now pay a tuition fee directly to the institution. The introduction of student tuition fees was quite controversial, and strongly opposed by student organization leaders. Under the current arrangements, the maximum tuition fee that is the responsibility of the student is £1,075 (2001–02 academic year). Students do not pay the fee if parental income is less than £20,000, and they pay only a component of the maximum fee if parental income is between £20,000 and £29,784. It is estimated that roughly half of all students will not pay tuition in 2001–02 (Department for Education and Skills, 2001). The Student Loan Company, a corporate entity wholly owned by the government, provides the institution with the difference between the assessed fee and the fee paid by the student.

Student Loan Statistics

The breakdown of grants and loans in the 1990s before the changes introduced in response to the Dearing Report is shown in Table 4.6.

In 1997–98, approximately 925,000 students were eligible for loans through the Student Loan Company. Of those eligible, just over 600,000 students (65 per cent) took out loans that year. The total value of the loans issued was £900 million, with the average value of each loan being just over £1,600. The percentage of eligible students receiving a loan has continued to increase, reaching 78 per cent in 2000–01. Approximately 759,000 students received a loan in 2000–01. The average value of an income-contingent loan received in that year was £3,100 (Student Loan Company).

The 1998 reforms abandoned maintenance grants, and loans became the primary mechanism for providing support for student living costs. All full-time students up to the age of 54 are eligible for loan support composed of a basic entitlement (75 per cent of the maximum loan) and an

Table 4.6
Change in U.K. Distribution of Weighting Between the
Maintenance Grant and the Student Loan, since 1990

Year	Maintenance Grant (£)	Student Loan (£)	Total (£)
1990–91	2,265		2,265
1991–92	2,265	580	2,845
1992–93	2,265	715	2,980
1993–94	2,265	800	3,065
1994–95	2,040	1,150	3,190
1995–96	1,885	1,385	3,270
1996–97	1,710	1,645	3,355

Source: Rowley (1997), 222

additional amount assessed on the basis of income (25 per cent of the
maximum loan). For students living with their parents, the maximum loan
for 2001–02 was £3,020 (£2,265 as an entitlement and up to £755 depending on income). For students living in London but not with their parents,
the maximum loan was £4,700, and for students living elsewhere it was
£3,815. Students who are financially independent of their parents can
earn income up to £7,500 without seeing a modification to their loan assessment, and all students can receive bursary or scholarship support from
other sources valued at up to £4,000 before student support is reduced
(Department for Education and Skills, 2001).

Other Forms of Funding for Students

Unlike before, students are not entitled to additional state assistance. The
British government offers no support to parents of students through the
taxation system and family allowances are awarded only until the child is
eighteen (Eurydice, 1999, 72–3; 79). Health benefits are the same for students as they are for the rest of the population. As for living expense discounts, meals are subsidized. Transportation discounts are provided, but
they are age based and independent of student status.

Access Funds are another form of grant that replaces the housing benefit that students were previously eligible to receive. Funds are based on
an institution's total student numbers and the cost of living in the area in
which the school is located. However, as Rowley (1997) (a critic of this
new loan system) points out, the British Treasury froze the amount of
funds available to the funding councils and thus the amount available to
the Access Fund did not keep pace with the increase in student numbers
and inflation.

Table 4.7
Loan Repayment Schedule (2002)

Annual Income (£)	Monthly Payment (£)	Repayment as % of Income
11,000	7	0.8
15,000	37	3.0
20,000	75	4.5

Source: Student Loan Company (2004)

Special grants are available for students who have one or more depen-dant children (the dependants' grant, the childcare grant, the loan par-ents' grant, the travel, books, and equipment grant, and the school meal grant) depending on student income and other circumstances, and for dis-abled students (disabled students' allowances). Other forms of financial support may be available from a student's college or university. In addition, the government has created a series of special programs designed to en-courage enrolment in specific fields.

Repayment of Student Loans in Britain

The government, through the Student Loan Company, underwrites loans. Interest rates are indexed to inflation and adjusted each year in line with a consumer price index. Repayment begins the April following the end of the study period. Payments are due monthly and it is expected that most loans will be paid back within five to seven years after graduation. Repay-ments are based on income and employers are responsible for the col-lection of payments from their employees. Payments are postponed until Gross Annual Income (GAI) exceeds £10,000 (Eurydice, 1997, 65), or earnings are 85 per cent of the national average (Rowley, 1997, 232–3). For students who have kept up their repayments, loan debts are cancelled once the student reaches the age of 65, or the student becomes perma-nently disabled or dies (Student Loan Company). Table 4.7 shows typical payments by income level.

Loans and Participation

Williams and Light (1999) hypothesize that the downloading of financial responsibility to students and their families may be the cause for a decline in the number of applications for full-time study by students over 23 years of age. Conversely they also think that another explanation for the re-duced enrolment may be that a high number of students enrolled *before* the September 1999 funding change.

Recent studies have focused on the participation of students from lower economic backgrounds in higher education and the possible impact of the loan-based student financial assistance program. Conner (2001) notes that while the major expansion of higher education in the U.K. led to an increase in the number of students from lower economic backgrounds, the participation rates of other social class groups have essentially increased in parallel. Participation rates continue to differ significantly by social class and "at the two ends of the social class spectrum, the gap is even greater, with an 80 per cent participation rate for young people from the highest social class (Group I: Professional) compared with just 14 per cent from the lowest (Group V: Unskilled)" (205).

The major expansion of higher education in the United Kingdom has had a positive impact on the participation rates of some groups. Participation rates for women and ethnic minorities have increased; "ethnic minorities as a whole in the 18–20 age group are now better represented in higher education than in the population at large" (Conner, 2001, 206).

The low participation rates in higher education for individuals from lower economic backgrounds has recently become a public issue, especially given the Blair government's public commitment to further expand participation rates to reach 50 per cent of the traditional cohort. The government commissioned a series of studies on this topic, and some preliminary findings suggest a relationship between the "perceived costs of undergraduate study, and the means of meeting them through loans, personal savings, family contributions or by working" and decisions to pursue (or not pursue) higher education, though this relationship is complex and multifaceted (Conner, 2001, 221). A number of interest groups, including student organizations and the Vice-Chancellors, have suggested that some form of student grants should be introduced to address the needs of students from poor families. While no specific reforms had been announced by the end of 2001, there are indications that the government is considering changes (Ryan, 2002).

Summary

The United Kingdom has shifted from an elite higher education system where students were not responsible for tuition fees and where they received maintenance grants to assist with living expenses, to a mass higher education system where students and their families are asked to assume a greater role in financing study costs. The current arrangements include the assessment of a maximum tuition fee established by the state, but where the fee component is forgiven or reduced depending on family income. Roughly half of all full-time students do not pay tuition. Financial assistance for student living costs is provided through a loan system where

75 per cent of the maximum loan is regarded as an entitlement and the remaining 25 per cent can be accessed by those with low incomes.

AUSTRALIA

Australian reforms in the area of public/private study costs preceded those in the United Kingdom, but both nations have adopted policies based on the notion that students should pay for a larger portion of the costs of their education. The Higher Education Contribution Scheme (HECS), established in 1989, shifted the balance of private/public costs. The Commonwealth would continue to pay the majority of the direct institutional costs of higher education, but students would assume responsibility for paying a fee through one of several mechanisms.

HECS can be paid in two ways: the up-front payment and the deferred payment. The scheme includes an incentive for paying up-front in that the fees are reduced by 25 per cent. To eliminate the possible barrier to access represented by up-front tuition fees, the deferred fee option was designed to provide students with access to higher education and the ability to pay the fee on an income-contingent basis after completing their studies and entering the labour market. Deferred fees have the distinct advantage (to the student) of being paid according to future income (Miller and Pincus, 1997).

Fee amounts depend on the year in which the student began her or his studies. According to Section 40 of the Higher Education Funding Act, the 2001 fee for students who began their studies before 1997 is $2,644. For those who began their studies after 1997 the fee level is related to the academic subject. The scheme categorizes each subject area into one of three bands:

1 Band One (Arts, Humanities, Social/Behavioural Sciences, Education, Visual/Performing Arts, Nursing, Justice and Legal Studies) contributes $3,521.
2 Band Two (Mathematics, Computing, other Health Sciences, Agriculture/ Renewable Resources, Built Environment/Architecture, Sciences, Engineering, Administration, Business and Economics) contributes $5,015.
3 Band Three (Law, Medicine, Dentistry, Dental Services, and Veterinary Science) contributes $5,870 annually.

Note that students who enrol in different subject areas can generate different HECS liabilities depending on the subject mix. For example, two students enrolled in a Bachelor of Arts course will pay different fees if one student takes all of her/his courses in HECS band one subject areas and the second takes a combination of band one and band two courses. Using

2001 figures, the first student would generate a HECS liability of $3,521 and the second, assuming that the student takes half band one subjects and half band two subjects, would generate a HECS liability of $4,268 (Ian Dobson, personal correspondence).

The Open Learning Deferred Payment Scheme

The Open Learning Deferred Payment Scheme (OLDPS) enables certain students undertaking undergraduate level units of study through Open Learning Australia to defer payment of part of the fee charged by Open Learning Australia by taking out a loan from the Commonwealth government. Students repay their loans through the taxation system once their income reaches a minimum level (Australian Higher Education, Contribution Scheme, 2003). Students who studied in or before 1996 or residents living in Australia for two or more years are eligible for the OLDPS. Students may defer payment of $352 per unit in 2001, but have to pay the balance of $73 per unit to Open Learning Australia.

The funds collected from the contribution scheme are reinvested in the education system in the form of scholarships, research funding and paying faculty members internationally competitive salaries (Miller and Pincus, 1997).

Repaying Debt

No interest is charged on the accumulated HECS debt; however, the debt is indexed annually through a cost of living adjustment. Payment begins when the student's income reaches the minimum threshold for compulsory repayment. In 2000–01 the income threshold was $22,346 (Table 4.8). Repayment income thresholds are recalculated each year to reflect any change in average weekly earnings. The HECS repayment is:

a) Taxable income for an income year; plus
b) Any amount the taxable income has been reduced by a net rental loss; plus
c) Total reportable fringe benefit amounts shown on the personal "Pay As You Go Payment Summary."

Students can make voluntary payments, in addition to compulsory payments, to the Australian Taxation Office at any time. The benefit of a voluntarily payment is that it immediately reduces the HECS debt, which may not be the case with a compulsory payment depending on the accumulated HECS debt, indexed increases to the debt, and the relationship between the participant's income and the minimum threshold. Bonuses of 15 per

Table 4.8
Income Thresholds and Repayment Rates
for Income Earned in 2000–01

Income Threshold	Repayment Rate (%)
Below $22,346	Nil
$22,346–23,565	3.0
$23,566–25,393	3.5
$25,394–29,456	4.0
$29,457–35,551	4.5
$35,552–37,420	5.0
$37,421–40,223	5.5
$40,224 and above	6.0

Source: Meek (2001)

cent are given if voluntary repayments are $500 or more. If an individual with a HECS debt dies, the debt prior to the date of death must be paid by the deceased's estate.

Financial Assistance

The Youth Allowance provides income support based on a student's personal and/or family circumstances. Austudy is an assistance program for eligible students over 25 years of age who are undertaking full-time studies. Abstudy provides support to Aboriginal and Torres Strait Island people who undertake full-time secondary or tertiary education courses, or correspondence or tertiary part-time studies. Some assistance is available for students over 14 who live at home. Assistance is available for post-graduate students through the Australia Post-Graduates Awards.

Impact of Australian Reforms on Higher Education Participation

Australian higher education policy reforms were broad-based and extended well beyond the discussion of public/private study costs, but a central objective was to increase enrolment in higher education while shifting the balance of public/private study costs so that the individual assumed a greater responsibility for the costs of his/her education. Enrolment in higher education has increased dramatically in the last two decades. The expansion of higher education has had a positive impact on the participation rates of some previously under-represented groups. Meek notes that "Indigenous Australians and persons from non-English speaking backgrounds with respect to overall participation have become over represented" (2001, 15). At the same time, however, "little or no progress has been made on the relative access by rural or isolated students, or by persons of low socio-economic status"; evidence indicates that the participation rates for persons of low socio-economic status have worsened (Meek, 2001, 15).

This concern about the participation of students from low socio-economic backgrounds has focused attention on the HECS, especially the recent increase in HECS charges and the lowering of the income threshold for repayment.[8] Enrolments of new domestic students in Australian universities declined for the first time in 2000, leading the Australian Vice-Chancellors' Committee to conclude that "Australia cannot afford to have rising fee income act as a disincentive to developing the knowledge and skills of its people ... and there is no justification for raising this burden still higher" (2001, 2).

Summary

Australian higher education policy reforms have sought to increase participation in higher education while shifting the cost of higher education from the state to the individual. The latter has been accomplished through the creation of HECS, an innovative scheme whereby students have the option of paying up-front fees or deferring payment until their studies have concluded and they have entered the labour market. If they choose to defer, the HECS liability is repaid through an income-contingent mechanism. While participation rates for some groups have increased, there are concerns about the participation of low socio-economic groups in higher education and the impact of recent fee increases.

DENMARK

Public financial support in Denmark is extremely high, with 0.63 per cent of GDP spent on higher education. In comparison with other European nations, this is second only to Norway, which spends 0.73 per cent of GDP, and far above the average European state contribution of 0.18 per cent of GDP (Eurydice, 1997, 22). This high level of support is reflected in the fact that students pay no tuition fees or any other kind of financial contribution to Danish educational institutions. In addition, parents are not legally required to financially maintain their children's cost of living or any other education costs. Student cost of living statistics are not compiled (Anthony, 1999; Mortensen, 1997) as students are seen as having the same living needs as other adults.

In Denmark students become legally independent at 18 years of age. The state provides student assistance through the State Educational Grants and Loan Scheme (*Staten Uddannelsessøte*), which is managed by the Danish Students' Grants and Loans Agency (*SUstyrelsen*) in collaboration with higher educational institutions, with oversight by the Ministry of Education (Anthony, 1999).

Student support consists of a combination of grants and loans. Loans are directly linked to eligibility for grants, i.e., if you are not eligible for grants you cannot get a loan. Grants and loans are only reduced when private earnings exceed the "free amount" (DKK 55,056). Student support is paid monthly and students must remain active in their course of study to receive the monthly grant. The grants and loans cover the student's cost of living and the purchase of books and other learning materials. In addition, students must complete their course of study in an "officially stipulated time." The study program and institution must be recognized by the state as full-time and non-paid, with a duration of at least three months. The system is based on a principle of "equal opportunity ... regardless of ... social background" (Mortensen, 1997, 98).

The Voucher System (klippekortsystemet)

The voucher system originated in the 1970s when Denmark instituted subsidized state loans and then in the late 1970s introduced market or bank loans for student assistance. The late 1970s were characterised by a sharp rise in loans while interest rates were rising as a result of the 1970s OPEC oil shock. In the 1980s the state realized that students and graduates found themselves with large debts that they could not pay. Radical reforms were introduced by the opposition in parliament and the "voucher system" was created. This flexible system is basically what is operational today, with some modifications, e.g., increased "free amounts" to allow for greater private earnings, support being independent of parental income, additional support for new parents, increased loan amounts, and transportation discounts (Anthony, 1999).

The voucher system provides the student with seventy monthly grants and loans (vouchers) for a five-year course. If necessary, a grace period of twelve months is provided to complete the five-year course. The vouchers have no time limit and students can change courses at the same or another institution (Anthony, 1999; Mortensen, 1997). New mothers are entitled to twelve additional vouchers and new fathers six vouchers. These vouchers are for DKK 3,551. Students with children under eighteen are entitled to increase their income (the free amount) by DKK 16,671 per child per year. In 1996, 11 per cent of grant recipients had children (Anthony, 1999).

The rationale behind the voucher system is that it enables students to organize their studies, and the division of monthly grants enables students to make personal decisions about when they want to use the support. For

Table 4.9
Grants and Loans for Students in Higher Education (DKK) 1998

Type of recipient	Grant[1]		Loan	
	Monthly amount	Annual amount	Monthly amount	Annual amount
Living with parents	1,852	22,224	1,907	22,884
Living independently	3,669	44,028	1,907	22,884
Finalisation loans			4,917	59,004

Source: SUstyrelsen, as shown in Anthony (1999)

example, if a student knows that she or he will earn more than the free amount, the vouchers can be saved for another period. Accumulated grants may be used in the last period of study as "double monthly grants" (Mortensen, 1997, 100). If students do not save up the support when they are earning income higher than the free amount they must repay the support at the end of the year in addition to 7 per cent of the amount (Mortensen, 1997, 100). The vouchers were introduced in 1988, but modified in 1993 to exclude those students enrolled in youth education programs (upper secondary school).

Grants and Loans

The Danish student support system provides one type of grant for students living at home and another for those living independently. Grants and loans are independent of parental income. As shown in Table 4.9, students living at home are eligible for a monthly grant of DKK 1,852 and a monthly loan of DKK 1,907. Students who have used up the ordinary support may use a finalisation loan (DKK 4,917) that is paid out for a maximum of twelve months.

Loan Repayment

During the period of study, interest of 4 per cent is charged on student loans from the moment they are paid out. After graduation, or if a student drops out, the interest rate is the minimum lending rate of the Danish Central Bank plus 1 per cent (Mortensen, 1997). Students must begin repayment of their loan one year after graduation. The loan must be paid within seven to fifteen years, unless the amount is less than DKK 10,000, when the loan must be repaid in seven years. Payments are made monthly in two equal installments on the basis of the amount of the debt, the repayment period, and the interest rate. According to Anthony (1999), in 1996, 92 per cent of student debtors paid less than DKK 12,000 per year.

Payments are not income dependent, but rather depend on the amount of the loan. If the student is unemployed or ill the payments can be eased or the payment period can be lengthened. Students who continue to have problems repaying loans can apply for cancellation, but it must be at least twelve years after graduation. New re-payment terms are usually agreed to at this point, but if the student debtor is unwilling the state can withhold tax refunds or ask the employer to deduct payment from employment income (Anthony, 1999). By the end of 1996, 241,000 people had student loans, at a total value of about DKK 9 billion. Loan repayments flow into the general national budget.

Additional Benefits for Students

In 1996 transportation discounts were introduced as a means of providing increased mobility to enable students to attend a greater number of institutions at greater distances (Eurydice, 1999). For a student to be eligible for the transportation discount, he or she must have applied for, and be entitled to, direct support (grant and loan) (Eurydice, 1999, 95). Meals are often subsidized, with the level of subsidy determined by the institution.

Summary

The Danish system of student assistance is very flexible and allows students to organize their program of study according to their preferences and earning possibilities. The use of loans in addition to grants introduces a measure of personal accountability into the system. Still, it is perplexing that a large number of students in Denmark work for pay while attending post-secondary education. According to Anthony and Elbrus (1997), in September 1996, 92 per cent of students at the University of Copenhagen were or had been employed during their studies.

SWEDEN

The higher education reforms of the 1970s created a centralized, planned university system in Sweden. The creation of a unified system was, at least in part, an attempt to deal with equity concerns based on the assumption that a higher education system with common standards could provide equal opportunities for students regardless of region. Reforms of the 1980s and 1990s have created a more decentralized system with greater levels of responsibility at the local and institutional level, but the Swedish system continues to assume that the state should pay for all direct educational costs and that student assistance is an entitlement for those who choose to pursue higher education (Lane, 1991; Svanfeldt, 1993).

Sweden's public higher education system has no tuition fees. The only fee that the student is required to pay is the compulsory student union membership fee of approximately 300 SEK per semester (Eurydice, 1999, 49). Currently, the general funding system is a state student finance system administered by the National Board of Student Aid (CSN) (Forss, 1997).

Sweden operates a grant and loan system of student financial aid. The Swedish approach is essentially to provide students with a guaranteed funding package that includes both a grant and an optional loan component. In 1996 the grant component represented approximately 27.5 per cent (1963 SEK) of the total amount of 7059 SEK per month available through the student-funding package. The student can decide not to access the loan component, or to access all or part of the loan component up to the maximum package value (Forss, 1997). The central assumption underlying the plan was that students should pay for the majority of their living costs while studying at tuition-free higher education institutions. The grant represents a mechanism for subsidizing these costs and the loan program provides a mechanism for financing all or a component of the remaining costs for students who require this assistance. The total funding package available to students is based on an assessment of the basic cost of living.

Reforms introduced in July 2001 shifted the balance between grants and loans, especially for students 25 years of age or older.[9] The funding package is now calculated in terms of an amount payable per week (1663 SEK for Spring term 2002) where the general grant (for students less than 25 years of age) would be 572 SEK (or 34 per cent of the weekly funding package) and the available loan would be 1091 SEK. Students 25 years of age or older are still eligible for a weekly funding package valued at 1663 SEK, but they receive a higher grant amount of 1364 (82 per cent of the weekly funding package) and the available loan amount is 299 SEK. These "higher grants" for students 25 and over "are awarded for as long as the government allocated funds last and in the order in which applications for student assistance reach the National Board of Student Aid (CSN)" (National Board of Student Aid, 2002, 1).

Students have been generally satisfied with the size of the funding packages, but concerned about the strong emphasis on loans. It was not uncommon for Swedish graduates to be paying back their student loans into their fifties (Klemperer, 1999). The 2001 reforms, designed to address issues related to student debt load and repayment associated with this system, assign the state a greater role in paying for student maintenance costs, especially for older students.

The Grant/Loan System

The basic grant/loan system is regarded as an entitlement, though the period of study time during which a student will receive support is limited.

Financial support for post-secondary education is payable for a maximum of 240 weeks of full-time study. Individuals over 50 years of age are generally ineligible for financial assistance, and entitlements to loans decrease after 40 years of age.[10]

The basic funding package of 1663 SEK per week assumes that the student is pursuing full-time studies. A point system is used to determine the rate of study (or "study tempo") and the funding package value will be prorated to 75 per cent or 50 per cent in parallel with the study load being undertaken by the student. Students who pursue less than half of a full-time load of studies are ineligible for support.

While the funding package is regarded as an entitlement, the level of support is reduced when the student's personal income exceeds a certain amount. Income is calculated for each calendar half-year during which a student is paid assistance, and the level of income that an individual can earn before student support is reduced depends on the number of weeks of paid assistance[11] and the study tempo (level of assistance as full, 75, or 50 per cent). For example, an individual who receives 20 weeks of full-time study support during a half-year period can earn up to 47,375 SEK during those six months. When income moves above this level, the value of the student assistance package is reduced by the excess amount. An individual who receives 20 weeks of student support at the 50 per cent level can earn up to 71,062 SEK during the six-month period without a reduction in the funding package (National Board of Student Aid, 2002).

Basic grant packages are not linked to academic achievement or economic need, though a supplementary loan (payable for a maximum of 120 study weeks) is available for students who had an income below a certain level during the year before they began their studies. This income level, like the income calculations described above, focuses clearly on individual personal income and there is no assumption that parents or a spouse have some responsibility to support the student's living costs.

Loans are interest bearing. The interest rate is determined by government; the 1996 rate was 6.1 per cent (Forss, 1997, 200) and the 2002 rate is 3 per cent.

Loan and Grant Statistics

Of all students studying at an institution of higher education in 1994–95, 77 per cent received financial aid. The state expenditure in the 1994–95 fiscal year for grants was 3,124,800,000 SEK, while loans were 6,105,000,000 SEK (Forss, 1997, 201). The amount of assistance is linked to the inflation rate and is adjusted annually.

In 1996, 1,200,000 people had outstanding student loans, with a value of 95,000,000,000 SEK (Forss, 1997, 200). The grant to loan ratio, according to Schäferbarthold, Held, and Schrameyer (1997, 45), was 70:30

(a function of the fact that the loan component is optional). This ratio will obviously change as a function of the student aid reforms introduced in July 2001, but data on the impact of these reforms are not yet available.

Repayment of the Loan

Repayment begins six months after the student receives assistance, but continuing students can apply to defer repayment and this request is usually granted. The original loan repayment approach was that 4 per cent of the individual's yearly income was paid until (a) the payments were complete, or (b) the individual reached 65 years of age. This simple structure became the subject of considerable debate, with loan repayment as the main concern. The approach was modified through a series of changes that were introduced between 1994 and 1998, including an increase in the percentage of the grant component of the student financial package and an increase in the age limit for support (Eurydice, 1999, 231).

The 2001 reforms further increased the grant component of the funding package, and the new loan arrangements involve annual repayments for a period of up to 25 years or until the student reaches the age of 60. The repayment period is shorter if the loan amount is small. Under the new regulations the repayment amount is normally 7 per cent of income (increased to create shorter repayment periods), though individuals under 50 years of age can apply to have the loan repayment amount reduced to 5 per cent of income.

Other Forms of Student Funding/Benefits

A number of other mechanisms are in place to subsidize or discount specific student living costs: students receive subsidized meals; and train, bus, and airline discounts are provided to those carrying valid student cards (Eurydice, 1999).

Summary

The Swedish approach to higher education policy is based on the assumption that the state is responsible for direct educational study costs. There are no tuition fees and university students are entitled to a funding package composed of a grant and a loan. Recent reforms to the student aid mechanism have increased the grant component of the funding package, and students 25 years of age and older can access a funding package where 82 per cent of the package's value comes in the form of a grant. The new regulations also consider personal income and include a mechanism whereby the level of entitlement is reduced when personal income is high. The new reforms are designed to address concerns related to student debt loads.

CONCLUSIONS

The six case studies presented above illustrate important differences in how public/private study costs of higher education are constructed in these jurisdictions. Each country, through public policies on fees and student financial assistance, has demarcated the responsibilities of the state for funding the costs of higher education and articulated the private responsibilities of the individual and/or family. The extreme differences in public policy in this area present a cogent reminder that there are no normative, universal assumptions of public/private study costs underlying this division, other than the presumption that the state has a substantive role in this policy area in all jurisdictions and that the state, rather than the individual student, has demarcated the boundaries between private and public costs. The case studies illustrate that these boundaries are arbitrary constructions.

The public policy assumptions underscoring public/private study costs can be discussed in terms of three major variables. The first is the way in which public policy deals with the direct costs of being a student, regardless of her or his living situation. The second is the way in which policy deals with maintenance or student living costs. The combination of these two variables provides the template for the division of private and public costs in each jurisdiction. The third variable is the state's approach to student financial support; that is, the assumptions underlying public mechanisms designed to subsidize or assist the student in the payment of costs that have been deemed as private.

Direct Educational Costs

The public policy assumptions underlying the boundaries between public and private direct educational costs differ substantially. In Sweden and Denmark all direct educational costs are regarded as the responsibility of the state. There are no tuition fees and grant entitlements are designed to cover the costs of educational supplies (books, etc.) as well as some component of maintenance costs. In Australia, Canada, the Netherlands, and the United Kingdom, public policy assumes a division of responsibility between public and private costs. It is assumed that the student should take responsibility for paying a component share of the direct costs of education.

While all four of these jurisdictions have established some form of tuition fee, these fees are understood in quite different ways by each country. The Netherlands has a standard fee regardless of academic program. There is no assumption that the fee bears any direct relationship to differential educational costs, personal rates of return on private educational investment, or other pricing strategies. In contrast, the fees charged in Australia, Canada, and the United Kingdom differ according to some assumption about private costs. In the United Kingdom, fees in England differ according to individual/family income. The government has set a maximum fee that is acknowledged as a modest share of the total cost of the educational program, but roughly half of all students do not pay any fee, and others pay less than the maximum fee.

Tuition fee levels in Australia appear to be based on two distinct types of strategies. The new, three-band approach used in this country relates private costs to program categories that seem to correspond to perceived differences in future employment income. The second strategy is to discount the fee for early payment. The fee schedule provides a pricing advantage to those who have the capacity to pay the fee up-front. Private costs vary both by program type and by when the fee is paid.

While the other five countries have established relatively clear national approaches to private/public dimensions of direct educational costs, the Canadian approach has been decentralized. Policies concerning private direct costs of education have been made by the provinces. While all provinces have established some form of tuition fee arrangement, the approach to establishing this fee has varied by jurisdiction. In terms of general themes, however, the fee level varies by academic program, based on some assumption related to either educational costs or future employment income. In some provinces, such as Quebec and British Columbia,[12] tuition levels have been tightly regulated and controlled by government. The Ontario government has restructured private educational costs by creating regulated and deregulated program categories: regulated programs have fee levels controlled by the provincial government; unregulated programs have fee levels set by the public university. In other words the private share of direct educational costs in Canada varies by province, academic program, and institution. In the case of the latter, the state is assuming that private costs should somehow relate to market forces through some combination of pressures associated with demand, costs, future employment income, and competition between public institutions.

Our final observation is that in four of the jurisdictions, Australia, Canada, Sweden, and the United Kingdom, the boundaries between public and private direct costs of education have shifted. In Australia, Canada, and the United Kingdom, recent policy changes have increased the private costs dimension of the equation. Recent changes in Sweden have shifted this balance in the opposite direction, especially for older students.

Maintenance/Living Costs

The case studies suggest three approaches to dealing with the private/public dimensions of student maintenance/living costs. Australia, Canada, and the United Kingdom have policies that assume that student living costs are clearly in the private domain. All three countries have developed mechanisms to assist certain students in paying these costs, as we will discuss below, but all three assume that these are private costs.

The second approach, associated with Denmark, the Netherlands, and Sweden, assumes that the majority of student living costs are a matter of private responsibility, but guaranteed grants involve the assumption that there is also some public responsibility. The non-targeted guaranteed grant mechanisms in Denmark and Sweden provide students with maintenance support in an environment where there are no tuition fees. The minimum grant in the Netherlands provides support in an environment where there are fees, but transportation costs (through the provision of transportation passes) are also taken into account.

The third approach, which has been documented in more detail (Eurydice, 1999), is that the state can play an active role in reducing private maintenance/living costs. In other words, while some costs may be assumed to be private, the state has determined that reducing the nature of these costs through subsidized meals, housing, transportation, and other areas of living costs is in the public interest. While there are examples of this approach in Denmark and Sweden, it is uncommon in Canada where most provincial governments require universities to operate ancillary services without public subsidy (or create a funding environment where institutions are encouraged to increase revenue generation).

Public Support for Private Costs

The two variables described above provide the broad template for the division of public/private study costs. However, having created a series of mechanisms that define the boundaries of private and public responsibility, each country has also developed mechanisms to assist the student, under certain circumstances, in paying what the state and the public higher education system has deemed to be private costs.

These mechanisms take a wide variety of forms and involve a number of assumptions about the role of the state in assisting students with private costs. A central variable is eligibility, that is, the assumptions that underlie the determination of whether a student should receive some form of assistance. Sweden, for example, has no eligibility requirements (other than student status) for the basic funding package. The assumption is that students will obtain the grant and access the loan component when needed to deal with private costs. Eligibility requirements are involved if the student wants to modify the standard package or access the "higher grant" package, which is primarily designed to encourage older students to pursue higher education in an economic environment where differences in average income by educational level are not as great as in some other jurisdictions.

In most jurisdictions, the central eligibility requirement involves some assessment of financial need. Need may be assessed in terms of personal and/or family income, but the assumption is that the state should provide some form of financial assistance to students who, because of their economic circumstances, cannot pay private study costs at the time that these costs are incurred.

In most cases the mechanisms to provide financial support include some combination of grants and loans. Grant mechanisms are based on the assumption that, under certain circumstances, the state should pay the student for a component of private study costs. Aside from financial need, other eligibility requirements for grants may include academic progress/standing, as in the Netherlands. Grants represent a mechanism for shifting the boundaries of private/public study costs for a subcomponent of the student population.

Loan programs, on the other hand, do not shift this boundary but represent a mechanism for deferring or bridging private costs, and they continue to be the major student financial assistance mechanism in Canada and the United Kingdom, and a major component of the Swedish system. Policies for loan repayment vary by jurisdiction, with several jurisdictions (for example, the United Kingdom, Sweden, Australia) assuming that the speed and magnitude of repayment should relate to the graduate's employment income. In other words, capacity to repay, as assessed through employment income or the taxation system, becomes an important factor in this type of loan mechanism. The Canadian loans mechanism, in contrast, assumes that loans for private study costs should be repaid regardless of the graduate's financial circumstances following graduation; even the nation's bankruptcy laws have been revised to strengthen the provisions for Canada Student Loan repayment.

CANADA IN COMPARATIVE PERSPECTIVE

The discussion above illustrates some of the major differences between how public/private study costs are defined in Canada compared with five other nations. Very different assumptions underlie the balance between private and public costs in different countries, and understanding these differences can provide policy-makers with a clearer sense of policy alternatives.

Underlying the discussion of public/private study costs, however, is the issue of the relationship between study costs and participation rates. It is important to recognize that Canada's rates of participation in higher education, at least as measured by major international indicators, are much higher than those in the other five jurisdictions included in this analysis. If aggregate participation rates are regarded as the core objective in terms of policy reforms related to study costs, then one might conclude that the other nations included in this study could learn more from the Canadian experience than vice versa. However, the policy challenge for Canadian higher education might be more accurately described as the search for mechanisms that will encourage the participation of all socio-economic classes, and some recent studies suggest that Canadian public policy is failing. This is not a uniquely Canadian problem, and recent studies in both the United Kingdom and Australia indicate problems in terms of the participation rates of lower socio-economic groups. However, the Canadian approach has at least two important differences from the approaches adopted by the other countries in this study, in addition to those discussed above.

The first is Canada's approach to providing public support for private costs, and in particular our strong reliance on student loans as a mechanism for supporting the private educational costs of economically disadvantaged groups. While other countries also use loans, several of the countries in this study have developed policies that modify repayment arrangements depending on future employment income or maximize the term of repayment. For potential students who are concerned about the risks associated with taking out substantive loans to finance their education, these policy approaches serve to redefine this risk in terms of either relating repayment to future success or establishing a maximum period of time during which the loan will be actively considered. These mechanisms, which vary substantively among the different jurisdictions included in the study, mean that loan default rates and the long-term effects of student loans are not major policy issues in some other jurisdictions.

The second is that the level of clarity and transparency associated with the approach to public/private study costs in the five other jurisdictions is greater than that in Canada. The Canadian situation involves significant differences in tuition and tuition policy by province (and in some provinces by institution) and academic program, and student financial assistance mechanisms that involve a range of actors, including the federal government, the provincial governments, and institutions. To some extent the lack of transparency may be a function of Canada's decentralized approach to higher education policy in the context of federalism, but even taking Canada's unique federal arrangements into account, Canadian methods for providing public support for private study costs involve a diversity of policy approaches and actors. For a student considering whether to invest in post-secondary education in Canada it is more difficult to obtain a clear sense of the total costs, the availability of student financial assistance in all forms, and the terms under which assistance in the form of loans must be repaid.

NOTES

1 Note that "study costs" may be defined differently in different jurisdictions. In Canada, for example, university operating expenditures support teaching,

research, and service activities; no national data separate the costs of teaching from the costs associated with research and/or service. This separation of expenditures by function is more established in some other jurisdictions, either because operating grants distinguish between functional areas or because of some agreement on reporting (such as the reporting protocols of the American Association of Universities). In our analyses we focus on study costs as understood by the student, namely direct educational costs such as tuition fees and maintenance (or living) costs.

2 While higher education in Canada and the public higher education sector in the United States have many similarities, including their shared Anglo-Saxon roots, common university degree structures, and, to some extent, institutional forms, they also have important structural differences that serve to minimize the degree to which discussions of the American experience can contribute to Canadian policy deliberations. The substantial private, non-profit university sector in the United States adds another layer of complexity to the discussion of public/private educational costs, and finding financial aid mechanisms that increase the level of access for students from low-income groups to the high status institutions in the private sector is a major policy concern (see Advisory Committee, 2001). The increasing importance of the proprietary, "third-sector" of American higher education adds yet another layer of complexity, as does the fact that the national student assistance programs are linked to a web of accreditation mechanisms that effectively differentiate between institutions where students can access public support for private study costs and those that operate completely in the private domain.

3 We would particularly like to acknowledge the assistance of Hans Vossensteyn and Ann Klemperer from the Centre for Higher Education Policy Studies at the University of Twente, the Netherlands, who shared data from their comparative analyses of student funding arrangements in Europe and facilitated our contact with other European scholars. Professor Vossensteyn also provided us with feedback on an initial draft of the Netherlands case. Professor Ian Dobson of Monash University provided important feedback on an early draft of the Australian case. We are also indebted to Bobby Deogan, Senior Consultant, Financial Aid for Studies Abroad, of the National Board of Student Aid in Sweden (CSN) who alerted us to the July 2001 changes to the Swedish student assistance program long before English-language documents summarizing these reforms became available in January 2002.

4 The Canada Student Loan Program (CSLP) remains the core component of Canada's student financial assistance policy. As its name suggests, this program provides loans to students who are assessed as having financial "need" given their expected expenditures for post-secondary education and their personal/family resources. At one point many provinces supplemented the core program by providing grants to students assessed as having high financial

needs, but these grant programs were gradually eliminated in most provinces. On a national level, an important exception to this trend has been the grant programs introduced by the Canada Millennium Scholarship Foundation. The Foundation programs are built on the assessment mechanisms associated with the CSLP and, in most provinces, though not all, provide direct grants to students.

5 Until 2000, students had to complete their program within six years, but because many students have part-time jobs and also want to be involved in student activities, the period was extended to ten years.

6 de Jong, U., D. Webbink, H. Meulenbeek, M. Voorthuis, F. Haanstra, and F. Verbeek (1996), *Uitstel of afstel? Een onderzoek naar de achtergronden en motieven om niet direct verder te studeren,* Stichting voor Economisch Onderzoek (SEO) / SCO-Kohnstamm Instituut, Universiteit van Amsterdam, Amsterdam) as cited in Vossensteyn 2002, 30.

7 Recent reforms in higher education policy have involved a decentralization of authority to Scotland, Northern Ireland, and, in some situations, Wales. Unless otherwise noted, the description that follows focuses on England. Note, for example, that Scotland, following a major political debate, did not introduce student tuition fees for Scottish students though tuition was charged to English students attending Scottish universities.

8 Meek notes that the new differential HECS "resulted in a 92 per cent fee increase for engineering and business students and a 125 per cent increase for law and medicine students. This has made tuition fees for Australian university students on the average amongst some of the highest in OECD countries" (2001, 17).

9 Note that admission requirements for Swedish higher education include either completion of upper secondary school (or equivalent) or for the student to be at least 25 years of age and have at least four years of work experience. Given that income differences between higher education graduates and non-graduates are not as great as in some other jurisdictions (see Klemperer, 1999), the new "Higher Grant" mechanism represents an incentive for students who did not complete upper secondary education (and completion rates differ by family economic status) to pursue further education.

10 For example, at age 41 an individual is only entitled to loans for 220 weeks of study. The number of weeks of student loan entitlements decrease each year by 20 (at age 42 the entitlement is 200 weeks, at age 43 it becomes 180, etc.) until age 50 when the entitlement becomes 40 weeks. Forty weeks corresponds to one academic year of university study.

11 Note that student assistance packages are available for programs of study as short as three weeks.

12 As we were revising this chapter for publication, the newly elected Government of British Columbia announced the deregulation of university tuition fees.

REFERENCES

Advisory Committee on Student Financial Assistance (2001). *Access denied: Restoring the nation's commitment to equal educational opportunity.* Washington, DC: Advisory Committee on Student Financial Assistance.

Anthony, S. (1999). "Student income and study behaviour in Denmark." *European Journal of Education, 34*(1), 87–94.

Anthony, S. and Elbrus, J. (1997). *Staten Uddannelsesstøtte-et effektivt uddannelsespolitisk styringsinstrument.* Copenhagen, Denmark: Institute for Statskundskab ved Københavns Universitet, Speciale.

Australian Higher Education (2003). *Contribution scheme.* Retrieved 3 August 2004, from www.hecs.gov.au

Australian Vice-Chancellors' Committee (2001). *Public under-investment in higher education.* Canberra, Australia: Australian Vice-Chancellors' Committee. Retrieved 4 August 2004, from www.avcc.edu.au

Bell, S., Plickert, G., and Anisef, P. (2000). *Accessibility to higher education in Canada: Are student loans and debts indenturing a new generation of Canadians?* Ottawa: Human Resources Development Canada.

Bowlby, J. and McMullen, K. (2002). *At a crossroads: First results for the 18 to 20-year-old cohort of the youth in transition survey.* Ottawa: Human Resources Development Canada.

Callendar, C. and Kemp, M. (December 2000). *Changing student finances: Income, expenditure and the take-up of student loans among full- and part-time higher education students in 1998–99.* Research Report No. 213. London: United Kingdom, Department of Education and Employment.

Canada Millennium Scholarship Foundation (2001). *Student financial survey: Baseline results.* Torornto: Canada Millennium Scholarship Foundation.

Canadian Education Statistics Council (2000). *Education indicators in Canada. Report of the Pan-Canadian Education Indicators Program 1999.* Catalogue No. 81-582-XPE. Toronto: Canadian Education Statistics Council.

Clark, W. (1998). "Paying off student loans." *Canadian Social Trends, 51,* 24–48.

Clift, R., Hawkey, C., and Vaughan, A.-M. (1998). *A background analysis of the relationships between tuition fees, financial aid, and student choice.* Paper presented at Canadian Society for the Study of Higher Education Conference, St John's, Nfld (June).

Conner, H. (2001). "Deciding for or against participation in higher education: The views of young people from lower economic backgrounds." *Higher Education Quarterly, 55*(2), 204–24.

Daniel, H.-D., Schwarz, S., and Teichler, U. (1999). "Study costs, student income and public policy in Europe." *European Journal of Education, 34*(1), 7–22.

de Broucker, P. and Underwood, K. (1998). "Intergenerational educational mobility: An international comparison with a focus on postsecondary education." *Education Quarterly Review, 5*(2), 30–51.

Department for Education and Skills (United Kingdom) (2001). *Financial support for higher education students in 2001–2002.* Retrieved 4 August 2004 from http://www.dfes.gov.uk/studentsupport/finance2001.cfn

Deutches Studentenwerk (1997). *Current developments in the educational assistance systems in Western Europe in connection with the family burden equalisation systems.* Bonn, Germany: Deutsches Studentenwerk.

European Commission: Education, Training, Youth (Eurydice) (1999). *Financial support for students in higher education in Europe, trends and debates. Key topics in education – volume 1.* Luxembourg: Office for the Official Publications of the European Communities.

Fischmann, G. and Stromquist, N.P. (2000). Globalization impacts on the third world university. In J. Smart, ed., *Higher education: Handbook of theory and research, vol. 15.* New York: Agathon. 501–21.

Forss, M. (1997). Educational assistance in Sweden. In Deutsches Studentenwerk (Eds.), *Current developments in the educational systems in Western Europe in connection with the family burden equalization systems.* Bonn, Germany: Deutsches Studentenwerk. 89–94.

Girdwood, A. (2000). *Tertiary education policy in Ghana, An assessment: 1988–1998.* Washington, DC: World Bank.

HRDC (1998). *Student loans: Insights into borrowing and repayment patterns.* Retrieved 3 August 2004, from http://www.hrdc-drhc.gc.ca/stratpol/arb/publications/bulletin/vol4n1/v4n1c05e.shtml

Huisman, J., Kaiser, F., and Vossensteyn, H. (2000). "Floating foundations of higher education policy." *Higher Education Quarterly,* 54(3), 217–38.

Jones, G.A. (1997). *Higher education in Canada: Different systems, different perspectives.* New York: Garland Publishing.

– (1998). "Diversity within a decentralized higher education system: The case of Canada." In V.L. Meek, L. Goedegebuure, O. Kivinen, and R. Rinne, eds. *The mockers and mocked: Comparative perspectives on differentiation, convergence and diversity in higher education.* Oxford, U.K.: Pergamon. 79–94.

Klemperer, A. (1999). *Higher education in Sweden. CHEPS – Higher education monitor country report.* Enschede, The Netherlands: Centre for Higher Education Policy Studies, University of Twente.

Lane, J.E. (1991). "Sweden in the aftermath of educational reform." In G. Neave and F.A. Van Vught, eds. *Prometheus bound: The changing relationship between government and higher education in Western Europe.* Oxford, U.K.: Pergamon. 145–64.

Magnusson, J.-L. (2000). "Canadian higher education and citizenship in the context of state restructuring and globalization." Special Issue: Building common spaces: Citizenship and education in Canada and Spain. *Encounters in Education,* volume 1, Fall. Faculty of Education, University of Manitoba. 107–23.

Meek, V.L. (2001). *On the road to mediocrity? Governance and management of Australian higher education in the market place.* Paper presented at the International Seminar on University Governance, Douro River, Portugal, October.

Miller, P. and Pincus, J. (1997). "Funding higher education: Performance and diversity." In *Evaluations and investigations program*. Australian Department of Employment, Education, Training and Youth Affairs. Retrieved 4 August 2004, from www.detya.gov.au/archive/highered/eippubs/eip97-19/exesum.htm

Mora, J.-G. (1998). "Financing higher education: Innovation and changes." *European Journal of Education*, 33, 113–29.

Mortensen, H. (1997). "Educational assistance in Denmark." In Deutsches Studentenwerk, eds. *Current developments in the educational systems in western Europe in connection with the family burden equalisation systems*. Bonn, Germany: Deutsches Studentenwerk. 95–102.

National Board of Student Aid (CSN) (2002). *Information on Swedish student assistance*. Stockholm, Sweden: CSN. Retrieved 4 August 2004 from www.csn.se

Rowley, R. (1997). "Educational assistance in the United Kingdom." In Deutsches Studentenwerk, eds. *Current developments in the educational systems in western Europe in connection with the family burden equalisation systems*. Bonn, Germany: Deutsches Studentenwerk. 227–35.

Ryan, C. (22 January 2002). "Reforming student finance." *The Guardian*. Retrieved 4 August 2004, from http://www.education.guardian.co.uk/students/comment/0,9976,637096,00.html

Schäferbarthold, D. Held, M., and Schrameyer, C. (1997). A European comparison of educational assistance systems. In Deutsches Studentenwerk, eds. *Current developments in the educational systems in western Europe in connection with the family burden equalisation systems*. Bonn, Germany: Deutsches Studentenwerk. 13–84.

Statistics Canada (1997). *National Graduate Survey*. Ottawa: Statistics Canada.

– (2003). "Education in Canada." (Catalogue No. 81-229-XPB). Ottawa: Statistics Canada.

Student Loan Company (United Kingdom). *Student Loan Company*. Retrieved 31 July 2004, from www.slc.co.uk

Svanfeldt, G. (1993). "Higher education policy in Sweden." In L. Goedegebuure, F. Kaiser, P. Maassen, L. Meek, F. van Vught, and E. de Weert, eds. *Higher education policy: An international comparative perspective*. Oxford, U.K.: Pergamon. 239–64.

Sweet, R., Anisef, P., and Lin, Z. (2000). *Exploring family antecedents of participation in post secondary education*. Ottawa: Learning and Literacy Directorate, Human Resources Development Canada.

Task Force on Higher Education and Society (2000). *Higher education in developing countries: Peril and promise*. Washington: World Bank.

Unesco (1997). Unesco Statistical Yearbook. Paris: Unesco.

Vergossen, F. (1997). "Educational assistance in the Netherlands." In Deutsches Studentenwerk, eds. *Current developments in the educational systems in western Europe in connection with the family burden equalisation systems*. Bonn, Germany: Deutsches Studentenwerk. 167–75.

Vossensteyn, H. (1998). *Student financial assistance in the Netherlands: A contextual report*. Centre for Higher Education Policy Studies Background Document for Eurydice Report. Enschede, The Netherlands: Centre for Higher Education Policy Studies, University of Twente.

– (1999). "The financial situation of students in the Netherlands." *European Journal of Education*, *34*(1), 59–68.

– (2002). "Shared interests, shared costs: Student contributions to Dutch higher education." *Journal of Higher Education Policy and Management*, *24*(2), 145–54.

Williams, G. and Light, G. (1999). "Student income and costs of study in the United Kingdom." *European Journal of Education*, *34*(1), 23–42.

5

Financing Lifelong Learning:
The Potential and Actual Role
of Individual Learning Accounts

HANS G. SCHUETZE

Lifelong learning has gained prominence on the policy agendas of many countries and academic literature has focused on many aspects of a system of lifelong learning. In spite of the abundance of articles, books, and policy reports on different aspects of lifelong learning, until recently few studies considered how such a system could be financed. After an initial discussion in the 1970s and early 1980s (Stoikov, 1975; Levin and Schuetze, 1983) the theme was not taken up again until recently, when a number of economists and one of the international organizations that had been an early promoter of lifelong learning (OECD, 1973) have started to plough the field seriously (Levin, 1998; Oosterbeek, 1998; Timmermann, 1996; McPherson and Shapiro, 2000; OECD 1997, 1999, 2000, 2001).

The renewed interest in lifelong learning is partly due to the concern shown by industry, which considers lifelong learning as the appropriate skill formation strategy for the "new economy" (Rubenson and Schuetze, 2000). This interest and the pressure from industry have caused policy makers to look for ways to implement and finance such a strategy. The difficulty of estimating the approximate cost of lifelong learning, the principles by which these costs are to be distributed among the various stakeholders, and, finally, the problem of translating these principles into viable financing schemes, pose considerable challenges. In this chapter, I concentrate on the financing issue, and also provide a brief discussion of what type and magnitude of cost need to be financed.

Lifelong learning had a number of precursors, in particular "lifelong education" (Faure, 1972) and "recurrent education" (OECD, 1973), two concepts that also postulated the distribution of organized learning over the entire life span rather than its concentration in a person's "formative" years. Let us briefly revisit the literature on financing for these earlier concepts. What were the principles discussed for designing financing systems to implement these earlier concepts, and to what extent are they still valid in a changed political and economic environment?

In the light of the earlier debate about various forms of financing and their suitability for lifelong learning, I discuss in some detail a particular financing model that focuses on lifelong learners rather than on system-wide financing models: specifically Individual Learning Accounts (ILAs), which have been discussed or implemented on a trial basis in several countries, for example, Sweden and the United Kingdom, and which recently were announced by the federal government as a system to bring about "Lifelong learning for all Canadians" (Speech from the Throne, Fall 2001). While different in both scope and design, these individual account models are of interest for a debate on lifelong learning financing as they reflect a shift from a focus on "education" and educational institutions to "learning" and individuals.

This chapter is structured as follows: first, I discuss the main characteristics and models of lifelong learning, a necessary if sometimes overlooked prerequisite for a discussion on financing lifelong learning; second, I briefly present and analyse the main financing systems that have been suggested for a lifelong learning system; third, I elaborate on the more recent model of ILAs and discuss their potential and actual role for financing lifelong learning.

MAIN FEATURES OF LIFELONG LEARNING

The concept of lifelong learning is based on three principles that break with the traditional notion of front-end formal education: lifelong learning is life-long, life-wide, and centred on learning rather than on education and educational institutions.

Life-long

That lifelong learning should be life-long is seemingly a tautology, but there is ample evidence that most of the expansion of learning opportunities in the last forty years has occurred in the formal sector of education and at the front end. (Schuller et al., 2002). Lifelong learning implies that people should continue learning throughout their lives, not just in informal ways as everybody does anyway (everyday learning), but also through organized learning in formal and non-formal settings.[1] Most writers and policy-makers take this to mean further or continuous learning after the phase of initial education (which is compulsory in all countries) and therefore concentrate on post-compulsory or post-secondary learning activities. However, there is general agreement that the extent and quality of education during the "formative" years are of crucial importance for the ability and motivation to engage in further learning later in life (Hargreaves, 2002). Therefore, a strategy for lifelong learning must also include these formative years.

The lifelong aspect of learning raises questions about the structure of the educational system and the interrelationships between different sectors. Since a crucial prerequisite for lifelong education is a system that allows and promotes smooth progression, has multiple access and exit points, pathways, and transitions, and has no programs leading to dead ends, this would require some fundamental reforms. Transitions entail not only pathways between different parts of the education system but also mechanisms for the passage from school to work, as well as, conversely, from work to education and training (Rubenson and Schuetze, 2000).

Life-wide

Organized learning occurs not just in schools, colleges, universities, and training institutions, but in a variety of forms and settings, many of them outside the formal educational system. In a system of "life-wide" learning the assessment and recognition of knowledge acquired outside the formal education system become a necessity. Simple as this may appear, it poses a major challenge to the established hierarchy and to traditional validation of different kinds of knowledge, that involves the places where, and the mode in which, knowledge and know-how (i.e., the applied form of knowledge) have been acquired. If all forms and types of know-how are treated the same way no matter where and how they have been acquired, mechanisms are needed for assessing and recognizing skills and competencies (OECD, 1996). These mechanisms must assess individual knowledge and abilities, instead of formal qualifications or the reputation and quality of accredited or otherwise recognized formal educational institutions and their programs.

That formal qualifications and actual abilities are not identical has been demonstrated impressively by the recent International Adult Literacy Survey (IALS), which was designed to assess literacy levels of the adult population in various countries (OECD, 1995 and 1997). The survey showed that discrepancies of certified and actual know-how exist at both ends of the spectrum: while a relatively sizable percentage of holders of high school or even advanced education qualifications have only minimal levels of literacy, others with few formal qualifications have demonstrated literacy competence at advanced levels. From a lifelong learning aspect, both groups are ill served by the present system of front-end education: the former group relying on qualifications acquired during their youth, which are no longer adequate; the latter with know-how learned in non-formal settings and modes without the formal certification required for both admission to continuous studies in the formal system and access to good jobs in the labour market. Therefore, assessing and recognizing knowledge which has not been learned in and certified by the formal education system is a major conceptual as well as a practical problem.

From a policy perspective, the coordination of various programs and institutions is a major challenge. If learning is to become life-wide, the organization, regulation, financing, and so on of learning activities do not fall exclusively into the domain of ministers of education. They are also the responsibility of other government departments, such as culture, economic and social affairs, health, and employment. Such a learning system requires a certain degree of consistency regarding policies, procedures, standards, and so on of the various agencies concerned, and also efficient mechanisms of coordination. Moreover, coordination is required not solely among different public agencies. With a great amount of non-formal adult education occurring at the workplace, public and private responsibilities need to be defined and coordinated to a greater extent than in the past. It follows that the issue of financing must also be addressed differently within a perspective of lifelong learning and a more diversified system of learning opportunities for adults.

Learning and Learner-centred

The third principle of lifelong learning, the change of perspective from "education" and "schooling" to "learning," entails an even more radical departure from the present system. Such a shift has a number of important consequences. The first of these is the recognition that a system of lifelong learning has little room for prescribed and rigidly structured and sequenced curricula or programs that apply to every individual belonging to the same age group. With the exception of the early years of formal learning, *what* is learned beyond initial education at home and in the early years of schooling and *when, where*, and *how* it is learned should be determined, in principle, by learners themselves – learning as a menu à la carte instead of a fixed meal. Second, in a learner-based system individuals have not only much more choice but also a greater responsibility for taking action and making meaningful – often difficult – choices among the various options open to them. The shift from a supply-led to a demand-based system also entails major changes in the way learning activities are financed (to be discussed further below).

Crucial for exercising such choice is the individual's ability to engage in learning beyond compulsory schooling. Lifelong and life-wide learning depend on the individual's possession of the personal characteristics necessary for the process. This principle is commonly discussed in terms of the learners' motivation and their capacity for learning, factors that depend on a number of others, especially socio-economic background, endowment with cultural and social capital, and quality of early childhood and primary education experience. From a lifelong angle, the capacity and motivation for further learning are also closely related to the structure and processes of day-to-day situations, especially the workplace (Rubenson and Schuetze, 2000).

PRINCIPAL MODELS

Because of its relative vagueness, the concept of lifelong learning has been compared to a chameleon whose colours change according to its environment. A closer look at the various policy reports reveals that different concepts or models use the same name but differ in essential features.

Real or potential demand for and support of lifelong learning comes from a variety of sources, but mainly from three: (1) an increasing number of better-educated adults who require continuous learning opportunities; (2) a still large population of people who lack the minimal qualifications needed for qualified work and for participation in civic and cultural life; and (3) the economy, i.e., the private sector which operates in environments where markets, technology, work organization, and hence skill requirements are frequently changing. These changes relate to the globalization of markets and major technological change. This economic imperative seems dominant in today's public discourse and is the reason why the call for lifelong learning is heard almost as often from employers and ministers of economic affairs as from educational leaders and ministers of education.

The dominance of an economic rationale is in stark contrast to the support for earlier reform concepts, such as the aforementioned strategies of "lifelong education" and "recurrent education," which had a strong egalitarian thrust and rationale for reforming the front-end, school-based education system. Whereas the proposed reform recognized the need for workers to adjust their skills to changing workplace requirements and the concomitant need for further training, its objective was primarily aimed at expanding access to general learning opportunities for people who had no or little previous education, because they came from less privileged socioeconomic backgrounds. Thus the model of lifelong learning that formed the base of the proposed reforms of the 1970s and early 1980s understood lifelong learning as having a strong emphasis on advancement of a free, equitable, democratic society, which would be accomplished through emancipation of the underprivileged by giving them equal opportunity with regard to education and hence life chances.

The present discourse about lifelong learning is marked by an erosion of this commitment to emancipation and democratization. In spite of some similarities between the earlier and present concepts, we can clearly see a shift from the emancipatory-utopian or social justice concept to a market-oriented model; from an understanding of opening up access to and participation in education as a means of achieving a more egalitarian society to a strategy of adjusting workers' skills to the requirements of changing production processes and global market conditions.

In summary, we can distinguish three different models, all sailing under the same banner of lifelong learning while charting different courses and advancing different models of education and learning, of work, and ultimately of society:

- A social justice model that advocates the notion of equality of opportunity and life chances through education in a democratic society (learning for all);
- A post-modern model that sees lifelong learning as the natural learning system for a post-industrialist, open, pluralistic, and multi-cultural society; and
- A human capital model where lifelong learning connotes continuous training and skill development to meet the need for a qualified, flexible, and adaptable workforce.

With this variety in concept and objectives, lifelong learning has been described as "both a cliché and an empty theoretical label: Motherhood and apple pie, all things to all people" (Frost and Taylor, 2001 51). However, behind these definitional differences stand concrete and diverging political agendas.

Of the three models, only the first is propagating lifelong learning for all, an idealistic, normative, and somewhat utopian concept. In contrast, the second and the third are more limited in scope, and the third model particularly is most specific about which types of learning activities, namely work and job specific, are included.

The second model is descriptive and typical of the situation in modern and open societies. It is normative in the sense that there should be no institutional barriers to learning opportunities for anyone who wants to learn. It embraces all developments that tend to eliminate such barriers, especially the modern information and communication technologies and education and learning at a distance, especially on-line learning. Unlike the first model – which would achieve its objectives by targeting specific populations that face specific barriers of a dispositional and situational nature (for the classification of barriers to adult learning, see Cross, 1981) and are therefore under-represented in formal education and training programs and non-formal learning activities – the second model holds individuals responsible for informing and availing themselves of learning opportunities.

The third model is the one most prominently advocated. It sees lifelong learning as a (continuing) training system appropriate for a knowledge-based economy in which a well-educated and adaptable (or "flexible") workforce is seen as a principal prerequisite for industrial innovativeness and international competitiveness. In contrast to the traditional view, which saw initial and continuing vocational or professional training as a responsibility of industry, the human capital notion of lifelong learning sees individual workers as primarily responsible for acquiring and updating their skills or for acquiring new qualifications to enhance their employability and career chances.

It follows from these differences in objective and scope that these models entail different financing mechanisms that reflect different principles and mechanisms for the distribution of costs among the various parties concerned, i.e., essentially private households, employers, and the state.

FINANCING LIFELONG LEARNING

In this section I deal with what types of learning activities these models cover and what financing models have been proposed for lifelong learning. In the two following sections, I discuss in more detail one recent financing model, Individual Learning Accounts (ILAs) and discuss how suitable these models are for a system of lifelong learning.

Financing What?

Lifelong learning is not just a special type of education, training, or other learning activity, such as adult education or web-based learning, but covers various forms of formal and non-formal learning that are now largely separate and operate in isolation from each other, including in the way they are financed. Table 5.1 shows which principal activities are constituents of a lifelong learning system and how they are funded at present.

In a system of lifelong learning, the various activities, programs, sectors, and providers would need to be more clearly articulated in relation to each other than they are at present. They would also need a certain degree of coordination to allow lifelong learners to navigate through the system without encountering unexpected road blocks, major detours, or dead ends that are the result of piecemeal sectoral or institutional policies and regulations. Besides some consistencies of such policies and regulations such a better articulated or better coordinated system would also require a transparent system of reliable information that would enable the lifelong learner

Table 5.1
Formal and Non-Formal Learning Activities and Their Financing

Types of non-formal education and training	Funders/financing instruments	Types of formal education and training	Funders/financing instruments
Voluntary sector-based	Member and user fees, state subsidies		State and/or private households
		Compulsory schooling	State
Community-based	Local taxes and user fees, state subsidies	• primary	
		• lower secondary	
Workplace-based	Employers and/or parafiscal funds	• upper secondary	
		Post-secondary education/training	State and/or private households
Organized individual	Individual households	• college	
		• university	
		• private training institutes	
		Continuing education/training	Private households, employers

articulation
coordination
integration

to find out about available options and make informed decisions. At the end of such a development of articulation and coordination of the existing elements stands the vision of an integrated system of lifelong learning. Whether this is seen as a necessary or desirable cornerstone of a future system is debatable and probably depends as much on feasibility and practicality as on the observer's trust in market mechanisms and voluntary arrangements as opposed to a coordinating role of the state or other public body.

Another question is whether the present variation of financing mechanisms should be further developed into a more comprehensive or unified system of finance for all lifelong learning activities. Financing systems for the different learning activities vary a great deal, depending not only on type of program or institution but also on factors such as personal background (especially age, socio-economic background, and national or ethnic origin), geographical location, and employment status. The question of whether a financing system for lifelong learning should be comprehensive, in the sense that it includes all learning activities and learners, or allow for a variety of financing schemes so long as they are consistent and equitable, is probably more a question of practicality than of necessity.

Financing Models

For the various concepts of lifelong learning proposed in the 1970s and 1980s, the suitability of a number of financing models was discussed and assessed. More recently, the idea of individual learning accounts emerged and was embraced by a number of countries that wanted to increase individual choice and hence motivation for work-related skill development training. Seven basic models (or eight, if financing by individuals of all their costs associated with learning is seen as a model), can be distinguished, ranging from single funder and single purpose to more comprehensive models (see Table 5.2). Most of these models do not cover the whole gamut of learning activities that fall under a comprehensive lifelong learning concept, nor do all cover the various costs involved in learning, both direct, such as tuition and other closely associated costs, and indirect, primarily the cost of living while learning (and therefore not being in full-time employment). In other words, the different models vary widely with respect to their comprehensiveness in terms of financing of the range of learning opportunities they cover. While some support only specific activities or target specific groups (for example, labour-market training for the unemployed or language education for immigrants), others provide a single financing system for all lifelong learning activities. Three basic types can be distinguished with respect to their scope: (1) single financing systems for all lifelong learning activities (integrated model); (2) multiple systems for different activities and/or populations, with a certain degree of consistency and a certain level of coordination (coordinated model); and (3) single purpose or program systems, unconnected to and complementing others (complementary model).

Of the seven financing models, only the drawing rights model would fall under the first, whereas voucher systems would probably fall under the second, depending on their design. Parafiscal funding for labour market training is an example of the third category. Single-employer funding normally covers strictly work-related activities, mostly during working time and on employers' premises, not activities that are pursued during non-work time and not directly work-related. However, employer-funded activities are commonly pursued during working time and workers' wages are maintained in full.[2] Conversely, state funding for education and training institutions would cover the whole or, in countries in which public institutions charge student fees, the bulk of the tuition cost but not, except in the case of needy students, indirect costs. This applies

Table 5.2
Financing Models for Lifelong Learning and Their Coverage

			Costs covered	
Financing Models	*Characteristics*	*Scope*	*Direct**	*Indirect***
Self-funding	Participants bear all costs (pay-as-you-use)	not applicable	all	all
(Single) employer funding	On-the-job-training, apprenticeship, and professional continuing ed.	complementary	all or some	all
State funding	Institutional funding from general tax revenues or through specific taxes	complementary	all or some	some
Parafiscal funding	Funding from employers' and workers' contributions and public subsidies administered through autonomous public bodies	complementary	all or some	some
Income-contingent student loans	Deferred financing by the individual; however, partly subsidized and risk of non-completion of studies or not finding a job with commensurate income alleviated	complementary	all or some	none
Individual learning accounts	Tax-friendly individual savings for the purpose of increasing vocational skills, augmented by contributions by the state	complementary	all or some	none
Individual entitlements	Public funding given to students/learners instead of to institutions, mostly covering fees	complementary	all or some	none
Individual "drawing rights"	Comprehensive transfer system of extending social security to cover all non-work activities	integrated	all	some

Notes: * Primarily the cost of tuition, but also books or tools and transportation
   ** Living costs during full-time education learning if learner is not receiving income from (full-time) work

also to public funding given to students in the form of individual entitlements or vouchers: these are in most cases meant to cover tuition costs
(fees) but not indirect costs (Levin, 1983 and 1998). In these cases, the
individual learner contributes to their learning by assuming a number of
cost items from their own sources.

Financing through collective funds that are financed by contributions
from employers and workers, in some systems topped up by public funding, is designed for workplace-related skill development but usually not
general education. Such collective funds exist in several countries and
are the result of either legislation or collective bargaining agreements
(Clement, 1983). Examples are the funds for continuing education and
training ("formation continue") in France (Caspar, 1983); the parafiscal
funds for labour market training in Germany, Austria, and the Scandi-
navian countries; and industry-specific levy-grant schemes such as the
former Industrial Training Boards in the u.k in the construction and
roofing trades.

By far the most extensive of the various financing systems proposed is
the "drawing rights" model (Rehn, 1983), an integrated financing system
that would cover the essential parts of the costs of post-compulsory learning activities over a person's lifetime. The drawing rights model is not limited to education or learning, however. It is a "single comprehensive system
for financing all periods of voluntary or age-determined non-work that
would (not only) replace the present systems of financing youth education,
(and) adult studies (but also) vacations, old age retirement, and other leisure periods that need income maintenance (such as) sabbaticals, long service leave and temporary retirement" (70). Because it is built on the idea
of an individual account, this model resembles the ilas (discussed below).
It is, however, quite different with regard to its objective and scope. Drawing rights are primarily an income maintenance financing system for all
types of non-work activities, funded by contributions from the individuals
themselves, but also their employers and the state. It could be used, however, for financing various learning activities after compulsory schooling,
and financial incentives could be provided within it for individuals to use
their assets for learning.

Other innovative systems were proposed and discussed, and in some instances implemented, in the late 1980s and 1990s. Prominent among
these are the income-contingent loans, an idea on which the Australian
Higher Education Contribution Scheme (hecs) system is based. The Australian model has been emulated, or is under discussion, in several other
countries that wish to shift public funding, or parts thereof, for post-
secondary education from funding for educational institutions to more
learner-centred forms of support.[3]

ILAS

More recent financing models for post-secondary education and training include ILAs (or alternatively training or development accounts). These have the objective of giving individuals more personal choice and ownership of their learning. Such individual accounts provide learners with money to pay for their learning activities, mainly tuition fees. In all cases where such accounts exist or are being discussed, eligible learning activities are confined to participation in programs related to skill or competency development.

ILAs are innovative financing mechanisms that are presently under discussion in some countries and have been introduced, in some cases on a trial basis, in a few others. While they differ in important details, they are discussed or implemented in these countries "as a means of putting flesh to the bones of the lifelong learning vision" (OECD 2001, 122). From a political economy perspective, they are an instrument for shifting from an institutional to a learner-centred approach, or, in economic terminology, from a supply to a demand approach. To the extent that it is primarily the savings of the learners and not government-provided funds that replenish these accounts, it is also a shift in the distribution of the financial burden and thus a shift from a welfare to a market approach to (post-compulsory) education and training.

If the eligibility for such learning accounts, or the size of government contributions to them, depends on the socio-economic background of the individuals, learning accounts "are part of a general class of policies aimed at individuals, especially from a population that traditionally has not participated in such activities, to increase their asset holdings and, with that, their 'stake-holding'" (OECD 2001, 122), in this case in their own learning after compulsory school or, more specifically, in their skill development.

ILA programs in the U.K., Sweden, and the U.S.

Three countries have introduced ILA programs or are in the process of doing so: the U.K., the U.S., and Sweden. These programs are briefly introduced here, as they provide important evidence and clues for a discussion of the Canadian project related to such accounts, even though the latter has been abandoned.

THE UNITED KINGDOM ILA PROGRAM

A system of ILAs was introduced in England in 2000, with similar programs being launched in Scotland, Northern Ireland, and Wales. ILAs made public money available for individuals to gain the skills they need for employment.

The overall aim was to widen participation in learning and to help overcome financial barriers to learning faced by individuals (Payne, 2000).

The program in England was funded by £150 million from Training and Enterprise Councils (TECs). This offered a contribution of up to £150, alongside small contributions from individuals (£25), which together funded certain training opportunities. Employers were encouraged to make voluntary contributions to these funds.

The ILA program was universal; everyone aged 19 or over (subject to some nationality and residency conditions) had a right to an ILA, except those in full-time education. ILAs were designed to develop in everyone a commitment to lifelong learning and to give individuals control and freedom of choice. ILAs were individual, universally available accounts, but provided *discounts* for learning. The level of discount had to be sufficient to act as an incentive to individuals to manage, plan, and invest in their own learning throughout their lives, whilst ensuring they retained a personal stake through individual contributions.

Stated program objectives were:

- to contribute to creating a better-equipped workforce
- to encourage people to have a personal stake in lifelong learning, with greater control over their personal development
- to increase levels of private (individual and employer) investment in learning
- to increase levels of participation and achievement in learning activities particularly amongst targeted groups where levels are traditionally low by providing discounts on the cost of learning as incentives to encourage individuals to register for ILAs, particularly from the target groups, e.g., ethnic minorities, women labour market returnees, younger workers aged 21–30 with low skills or few qualifications, and self-employed people
- to encourage the development of wider choice and innovation in the delivery of training and to attract new providers, particularly those operating in smaller niche markets with new, non-traditional learners (Department of Education and Skills, 2002).

The non-bureaucratic nature of the program, designed to reach non-traditional learners, was successful – 1.4 million learning episodes were booked, 16 per cent of ILA redeemers had no previous qualifications, and 22 per cent had not participated in any training/learning in the twelve months preceding ILA use – yet there was also some "deadweight," as it was estimated that over half (54 per cent) of redeemers would have been able to pay for their most recent ILA-supported course without their ILA.

By May 2001 the commitment to reach one million ILAs (964,000 in England) had been met, a year early, and an average of 3,000 accounts were

being opened each day. Expenditure on the program had reached some
£90 m and the majority of this was on payments to learning providers for
the introductory £150 ILA incentive using recycled TEC resources. By
September 2001 expenditure on the program had reached some £180 m,
reflecting the rapid program expansion over the period and exceeding all
expectations. This raised further concerns about the way the program had
been promoted and sold, particularly in the light of growing evidence that
some companies were abusing the system by offering low-value, poor-
quality learning (Thursfield et al., 2000).

In November 2001 the program, which had figured prominently as a
plank in the Labour Party's educational policy platform, was suddenly
suspended because of major irregularities and fraud. The ministry announced that it would introduce a successor program, but that the new
program would be part of a wider review of the funding of adult learning
and a skills strategy for the future. The program was also closed down in
Scotland, Wales, and Northern Ireland.

At the end of 2003 plans for a similar program were still on hold, although the responsible ministry has repeatedly insisted that it will be continued once the flaws in the implementation of the program have been
analysed and eliminated. The new Skills Strategy White Paper that the U.K.
government launched in Summer 2003 (Department for Education and
Skills, 2003) makes no mention of ILAs, although it incorporates several of
the successful elements of the ILA program. The White Paper stresses individual responsibility and choice, postulates an entitlement for all adults to
access training to increase their skills to the basic level of employability,
and affirms the principle that the costs of higher level skills development
must be shared with individuals and employers. Which form such an entitlement is going to take is still unclear.

In Wales, a follow-up program launched in 2003 targets people with low
or no qualifications (www.ilawales.com). The level of funding is determined by the learners' qualification levels and their employment status,
with a maximum of state funding of C$440. Because of the objective of
widening participation in learning by less qualified people, no financial
contribution is required from those unemployed, while those with higher
levels of qualifications who are employed are required to contribute 50 per
cent of the cost of the education or training chosen.

THE SWEDISH ILA PROGRAM
A financing system for "individual competence development" has been
discussed for several years in Sweden, especially between employers and
unions. In April 2002 the Swedish government presented to the Swedish
Parliament a so-called Guideline Bill on Individual Learning and Skills Development. The bill provides for saving accounts in which individuals can

set aside a certain amount of money and receive a tax reduction for the amount saved. Withdrawals from the account can be made for all purposes and are subject to the usual income tax. However, when money is withdrawn for learning purposes, a so-called competence premium will be granted. The ILA system is not designed to replace the existing public support for adult education and training, but to complement and add to the present support for "competence development."

The main purpose of the ILA scheme is to create a voluntary system that permits individuals to open a "learning account" on their own initiative and to determine how the money, basically their own savings – plus a tax premium when used for learning, and possibly contributions from their employers – is to be used.

Individuals who choose to set up a learning account can put deductible savings into their account. These are limited to 25 per cent of a base amount, i.e., SEK 9,500 (approx. C$1,620) per year. The account is liable to the usual capital tax (30 per cent) and funds withdrawn from the account are liable to income tax. However, if funds are being used for learning, a competence premium is granted. This premium may not exceed 50 per cent of the amount withdrawn. On top of that tax premium there is a fixed amount grant (SEK 1,000, or C$170) which applies for learning programs of more than five days' duration. Employers can contribute to an individuals' learning account up to half a base amount. These contributions are treated as salaries and are thus neutral in terms of costs (Ministry of Industry, Employment and Communications, 2002).

The government expects that 10 per cent of the labour force, or 650,000 individuals, will start a learning account during the first year and that, over the first ten years, some 30 per cent of the workforce (2 million individuals) will have active learning accounts. In Winter 2003 the plan to launch a national system was still on hold, although a clear political will to launch such a system is indicated.

THE U.S. INDIVIDUAL TRAINING ACCOUNTS (ITAS)

Different from the U.K. and Swedish ILA schemes, ITAs have been in operation for a number of years. ITAs are vouchers given to individuals ("customers") who need occupational skills training to become gainfully employed or re-employed. Individuals may use their ITAs for training in any program on the list of eligible programs and providers.

ITAs are part of the tool box of the Workforce Investment Act of 1998, which has the objectives of meeting the needs of businesses for skilled workers *and* the training, education, and employment needs of individuals, and enabling adults to obtain the training they find most appropriate through ITAs. The act is based on the following principles:

- Training and employment programs must be designed and managed at the local level – where the needs of businesses and individuals are best understood.
- Customers must be able to conveniently access the employment, education, training, and information services they need at a single location in their neighbourhoods.
- Customers should have choices in deciding the training program that best fits their needs and the organizations that will provide that service. They should have control over their own career development.

Under the new Workforce Investment System, state workforce investment boards were established and states developed five-year strategic plans. Individuals are referred to a "one-stop" delivery system, with career centres in their neighbourhoods where they can access core employment services and be referred directly to job training, education, or other services. ITAs are designed to promote individual responsibility and personal decision-making as they allow adult customers to "purchase" the training they determine best for them.

ILAS IN CANADA

In Canada ILAs appeared prominently on the public agenda for the first time when the Liberal Party, in its 2000 platform for the election in Spring 2001, promised to "create Registered Individual Learning Accounts to help Canadians finance their learning needs" (Liberal Party program, 2000). In the Speech from the Throne (September 2000) it was made part of the program of the newly (re)elected government: "The Government will also help adults who want to improve their skills, but who may face difficulty in finding the time or resources to do this while providing for themselves and their families. It will create Registered Individual Learning Accounts to make it easier for Canadians to finance their learning."

Although the ILA scheme was annnounced in the party's electoral platform and the Speech from the Throne, considerable opposition to the program arose within the newly elected government, especially the Ministry of Finance, the sectoral councils, the unions, and officials within Human Resources Development Canada (HRDC), the department that would have been responsible for the implementation of the program.

The Ministry of Finance was concerned that ILAs contained nothing novel and were similar to Registered Retirement Savings Plans (RRSPs) or Registered Education Savings Plans (RESPs). Moreover, such a program was seen as difficult to implement, while benefits were doubtful. Sectoral councils and the unions found this approach was too individualistic, arguing that it would be much more effective if the money was invested in sectoral activities in which unions could be involved, organizing the needed learning and training activities. The HRDC had two major concerns with regard to the objective of helping low-income Canadians to improve their skills or education. One was that this initiative would serve as a(nother) tax shelter program from which only people of middle- and upper-income levels would benefit. Poorer people, who were the original target group, would find it hard to accumulate disposable income to be put away in ILAs. Another major concern was that if the objective were to help adults learn, in most instances with ILAs it would take too long before people would be able to take up training. Thus, the project was never implemented; instead, it was quietly buried – without any explanation or public discussion.

However, a feasibility study and demonstration project related to the ILA concept was funded by HRDC and conducted by the Social Research and Demonstration Corporation (SRDC). This project (called learn$ave/$avoir en banque) will help, in conjunction with organizations in ten communities across Canada, more than 3,000 low-income Canadians to build savings to improve their training, return to school, or learn by starting a small business. Delivering Individual Development Accounts for learning, it matches the savings of low-income participants, dollar for dollar. The project, which started in Spring 2001, will be evaluated and its impact measured throughout and for up to two years after the project is delivered (Eckel et al., 2002). As this project was funded in 2000 for nine years, it can probably be safely assumed that it is attempting, albeit on a very small scale, to achieve what the ILAs were supposed to achieve on the national level.

As can be seen from the short description and review, ILAs in the four countries, albeit similar in name, have different features. Table 5.3 provides an overview.

SUMMARY

There is no "ideal" financing system that would benefit all potential lifelong learners in the same way. Rather, a number of different criteria have been identified that can be used to assess the various financing systems with respect to the multiple objectives a lifelong learning system is expected to realize (Timmermann, 1996). It is fairly obvious that providing incentives for further learning for high school drop-outs and illiterate adults will require different principles and mechanisms from those used to motivate highly educated professionals to engage in continuing professional education.

Learner-based financing systems emphasize the importance of individual responsibility for both investing in their further learning and choosing what, when, and how they learn. This emphasis on freedom of choice is closely linked to a more general move towards a privatization or marketization of education and training, and to consumer choice among different education service providers.

Table 5.3
ILAs in four countries

Country	Objectives/type of learning	Characteristics	Amount of contributions	Status
Canada	N/A	N/A	N/A	Abandoned before becoming operational; replaced by small pilot project
Sweden	Adult education and training for "competence development"	Individual savings accounts with contributions from the state and employers	Savings of up to C$1,600 p.a., tax deductible when used for education	Dormant
United Kingdom (England)	Skill training for employment	Individual savings accounts with sizeable contribution from state	Individual savings of C$55, state contribution of C$325	Abandoned after incidences of fraud; presently dormant
United States	Skill training for employment	ITAs are one of several instruments of the Workforce Investment Act of 1998	Variable	Fully operational

In the course of this shift, which reflects the progressive move from a welfare state model to a market model (Dale, 1997), governments that in the past have provided and financed a large array of formal education and training activities have more recently advocated and actively promoted private investments and individual choice in education by setting up a variety of "learner-centred" financing schemes.

Like some of the other financing models mentioned, ILAs are designed to stimulate investments by individuals in their own education and training. Financial incentives, particularly public grants or subsidies from the individual's employer, that can be put into these accounts, thereby increasing their cash balance, are thought to motivate individuals to undertake education and training activities in which they would otherwise not participate. This would be of particular importance for groups who are under-represented. Like vouchers, ILAs are instruments of demand-oriented financing, designed to empower the learner, who can make choices as to what to learn and with what provider. As such, ILAs could be an innovative response to some of the thorny problems concerning participation by under-educated adults in post-secondary education or training. To the extent that the scheme works as intended, such increased participation would raise the levels of overall participation in organized learning activities. Although the British experience with a full-scale program supports the view that ILAs are of 'honorable intentions, but ignoble utility' (Thursfield et al., 2002), the u.s. experience seems to justify a more positive judgment.

NOTES

1 "Formal" settings comprise the education system, i.e., schools, colleges, and universities whereas "non-formal" settings are places outside the formal sector where organized learning takes place (e.g. the workplace, museums, community centres, trade unions, sports clubs). By contrast, "informal" learning takes place anywhere, yet in an unplanned, unorganized, and mostly incidental manner. This informal everyday learning is not included in the discussion of the organization and financing of lifelong learning.

2 Exceptions are wages or allowances for apprentices, which are lower than those for a qualified worker.

3 However, in view of massive opposition from the tertiary sector, the Australian government has recently decided not to adopt a far more radical proposal for financing post-secondary education that would have combined a voucher system with an extended income-contingent loan scheme (Department of Employment, Education, Training and Youth Affairs, 1998; Harman, 1999).

REFERENCES

Caspar, P. (1983). "French law on continuing vocational training." In H.M. Levin and H.G. Schuetze, eds. *Financing recurrent education – Strategies for increasing employment, job opportunities, and productivity*. Beverly Hills: SAGE. 257–72.

Clement, W. (1983). "Intermediate ('parafiscal') financing schemes." In H.M. Levin and H.G. Schuetze, eds. *Financing recurrent education – Strategies for increasing employment, job opportunities, and productivity*. Beverly Hills: SAGE. 81–98

Cross, P. (1981). *Adults as learners: increasing participation and facilitating learning*. San Francisco: Jossey-Bass.

Dale, R. (1997). "The state and the governance of education: An analysis of the restructuring of the state-education relationship." In A.H. Halsey, H. Lauder, P. Brown, and A.S. Wells, eds. *Education – culture, economy, and society*. Oxford: Oxford University Press. 273–83.

Department of Education and Skills. (2002). *Individual Learning Accounts – A consultation exercise on a new ILA style scheme – Final Report*. Retrieved August, 2004 from http://www.dfes.gov.uk/research/data/uploadfiles/rr339.pdf)

– (2003). *21st century skills – realizing our potential: individuals, employer, nation*. Retrieved 26 November 2003, from http://www.dfes.gov.uk/skillsstrategy/docs/fulldoc.pdf

Department of Employment, Education, Training and Youth Affairs (1998). *Learning for life: Review of higher education financing and policy*. Final Report. Canberra: Commonwealth of Australia.

Eckel, C., Johnson, C., and Montmarquette, C. (2002). *Will the working poor invest in human capital? – A laboratory experiment*. Ottawa: Social Research and Demonstration Corporation.

Faure, E., et al (1972). *Learning to be*. Paris: UNESCO.

Frost, N., & Taylor, R. (2001). Pattern of change in the university: The impact of "Lifelong Learning" and the "World of Work". *Studies in the Education of Adults*, *33*(1), 49–59.

Hargreaves, D.H. (2002). Effective schooling for lifelong learning. In D. Istance, H.G. Schuetze, & T. Schuller, eds. *International perspectives of lifelong learning – From recurrent education to the knowledge society*. Buckingham: Open University Press. 49–62

Harman, G. (1999). "Vouchers or 'student centred funding': The 1996–1998 Australian review of higher education financing and policy." *Higher Education Policy*, *12*, 219–35.

Levin, H. and Schuetze, H.G., eds. (1983). *Financing recurrent education – Strategies for increasing employment, job opportunities, and productivity*. Beverly Hills: SAGE.

Levin, H.M. (1998). "Financing a system for lifelong learning." *Education Economics*, *6*(3), 201–18.

McPherson, M. and Shapiro, M.O. (2000). "Financing lifelong learning – Trends and patterns of participation and financing in US higher education." *Higher Education Management*, *12*(2), 131–56.

Ministry of Industry, Employment and Communication (SWE). (2002). *Individual learning and skills development (Press release of 15 April 2002)*. Retrieved 20 December 2002 from http://www.sweden.gov.se/sb/d/736/a/6034.

Oosterbeek, H. (1998). "Innovative ways to finance education and their relation to lifelong learning." *Education Economics*, *6*(3), 201–18.

Organization for Economic Cooperation and Development (1973). *Recurrent education: A strategy for lifelong learning*. Paris: OECD.

– (1995). *Literacy, economy and society*. Paris: OECD.

– (1996). *Lifelong learning for all*. Paris: OECD.

– (1997). "Lifelong investment in human capital." In Organization for Economic Cooperation and Development, eds. *Education policy analysis*. Paris: OECD. 29–43.

– (1999). "Resources for lifelong learning: What might be needed and how might it be funded?" In Organization for Economic Cooperation and Development, eds. *Education policy analysis*. Paris: OECD. 7–26.

– (2000). *Where are the resources for lifelong learning?* Paris: OECD.

– (2001). *Economics and finance of lifelong learning*. Paris: OECD.

Payne, J. (2000). "The contribution of individual learning accounts to the lifelong learning policies of the UK government: A case study." *Studies in the Education of Adults, 32*(2), 257–72.

Rehn, G. (1983). "Individual drawing rights." In H. Levin and H.G. Schuetze, eds. *Financing recurrent education – Strategies for increasing employment, job opportunities, and productivity.* Beverly Hills: SAGE.

Rubenson, K. and Schuetze, H.G. (2000). "Lifelong learning for the knowledge society: Demand, supply, and policy dilemmas." In K. Rubenson and H.G. Schuetze, eds. *Transition to the knowledge society: Policies and strategies for individual participation and learning.* Vancouver: UBC (Institute for European Studies). 355–76.

Schuller, T., Schuetze, H.G., and Istance, D. (2002). "Introduction." In D. Istance, H.G. Schuetze, and T. Schuller, eds. *International perspectives on lifelong learning: From recurrent education to the knowledge society.* Buckingham, UK: Open University Press.

Stoikov, V. (1975). *The economics of recurrent education and training.* Geneva: International Labour Office.

Thursfield, D., Smith, V., Holden, R., and Hamblett, J. (2002). "Individual learning accounts: Honourable intentions, ignoble utility?" *Research in Post-Compulsory Education, 7*(2), 133–46

Timmermann, D. (1996). "Lifelong education: Financing mechanisms." In A. Tuijnman, eds. *International encyclopedia of adult education and training.* Oxford: Pergamon. 300–03.

PART TWO

Families and PSE Planning

6

A Revolution of Expectations?
Three Key Trends in the SAEP Data

SCOTT DAVIES

The new economy is said to require historically high levels of skill which put a premium on higher education (Smith, 2001). This economy is likely to dramatically re-shape the labour market, rewarding workers with better skills, advantaging recent post-secondary graduates, and reducing the wages of those without advanced schooling.[1]

What will be the impact on Canadian universities and colleges? Expansion has already been pervasive over the past half century, as higher education evolved from an "elite" to a "mass" system, placing Canada among the world leaders in post-secondary enrolments (De Broucker and Underwood, 1998; Guppy and Davies, 1998). This expansion was accomplished by fostering relatively high educational aspirations among youth. In international comparison, Canada's high schools have relatively late and mild streaming, with the majority of students enrolling in non-vocational education. This has promoted an "opportunity consciousness" among youth, in which even mediocre secondary students feel encouraged to pursue further studies (Brint, 1998).

Yet the New Economy has been hailed as necessitating a further round of higher education expansion, one in which nearly all youth will eventually need to attend some type of post-secondary institution. Such growth will bring, some say, a new stage of higher education, an evolution from a "mass" to a "universal" system (Meek, 2000). Buoyed by ideologies of "life-long learning," post-secondary enrolments will be required to grow further, whether in the guise of corporate training, adult education, university, or college programs.

A question emerges: are Canadians ready to participate in this pro-claimed universal stage of post-secondary education? If so, what are its im-plications? Some policy-makers worry that many youth and parents have not reached this advanced mindset, so whether or not Canadians' educa-tional expectations have reached new levels is a key empirical question.

In this chapter I use the SAEP data to explore whether or not Canadians' educational expectations have reached these new heights. Using these data, I argue that three current trends are particularly noteworthy in light of decades of sociological research on this broad topic.[2] First, the sheer amount of educational ambition held by Canadian parents today does in-deed signal a revolution of expectations. Contemporary levels, when com-pared to those in the past half century, match the "k-16" or "universal" stage of post-secondary expansion that has been predicted by pundits. Sec-ond, despite these new levels of expectations, typical family traits predict their variation. The SAEP data largely reinforce generalizations that have been well established in sociological research over several decades. Third, the combination of higher expectations with old patterns of stratification has an important implication for community colleges: those colleges may face the spectre of becoming repositories for remedial students, that is, for students who in a past era would have certainly eschewed post-secondary education and may likely have dropped out of high school.

In the light of these trends I discuss three implications. First, universal expectations are likely to bring more inequality among higher education institutions. Second, the new era of post-secondary attendance is not likely to be any more equitable than in the past; that is, school expansion does not necessarily entail greater equity. Third, as more ill-prepared students enter higher education, particularly community colleges, a rise in student attrition and disappointment may follow if those institutions do not change their practices or standards.

FIRST TREND: RISING EXPECTATIONS
– TOWARDS A UNIVERSAL SYSTEM?

Are we witnessing a revolution of educational expectations? Historically, post-secondary schooling, particularly university, has been an elite enterprise. Even with the "massification" of colleges and universities over the past several decades, only a minority of Canadian adults currently possess a university degree. But do Canadian adults now have vastly higher expectations for their offspring? How many Canadian parents expect their children to study beyond high school?

While there is little past research on parent's expectations, several surveys have been done on previous teenage cohorts. For instance, Ontario data from the early 1970s showed that roughly one third of grade 12 students

Table 6.1
Expectations by Region and Rural-Urban Residence

	Parents' Educational Expectations for Their Children			
Antecedent Variables	None	College	University	Total
Region				
Atlantic	17%	25%	58%	184,739
Quebec	13%	36%	51%	516,537
Ontario	9%	31%	60%	873,025
West	14%	29%	58%	711,702
Rural-Urban				
Urban	11%	29%	60%	1,867,258
Rural/Remote	17%	40%	43%	418,744
Canadian Total	12%	31%	57%	2,286,002

Source: SAEP (1999)

expected to attend university, and about 55 per cent expected to attend either university or college (Anisef, 1974). Other data on high school students showed that between 38 per cent and 60 per cent expected to enter post-secondary education, depending on their gender and grade cohort (Porter et al., 1982).[3] Similar rates were found among Ontario high school students in the mid 1980s (Davies, 1992). Since then Canadian teens' education expectations have soared. The percentage of Canadians aged 15–19 who expected to graduate from university grew from 51 per cent in 1987, to 60 per cent in 1992, to 62 per cent in 2000. By 2000 fully 80 per cent of Canadian teenagers expected to graduate from some sort of post-secondary institution, and more believed they would at least attend such an institution. Only 8 per cent believed their formal education would end with high school (Bibby, 2001). In less than thirty years, therefore, the proportion of youth who expect to attend post-secondary education has risen from about 50 per cent to over 90 per cent. Youth expectations for post-secondary education, particularly university, continue to rise.

Do today's parents share these lofty hopes? Since the contemporary cohort of parents is the most educated in history, and since many are employed in service and knowledge sectors, we would expect high expectations, though it is sobering to recall that as late as 1991, only 11 per cent of Canadians possessed a university degree, while in the same year over half of Canadian teens expected to attain a degree (Guppy and Davies, 1998; Bibby and Posterski, 1992).

Are we witnessing a revolution of educational expectations? Table 6.1 shows that expectations are indeed very high.[4] Only 12 per cent of Canadian parents do *not* have post-secondary expectations (PSEs) for their children. University is expected by 57 per cent of parents, and fully 88 per cent have PSEs. In every region, a majority expect their children to opt for university. As one might anticipate (Butlin, 1999), Canadians living in rural and poorer regions have slightly lower educational expectations. With fewer available institutions, most have to leave their immediate locale, and so have greater financial and social burdens. Nevertheless, even with these disadvantages, the vast majority of rural parents expect their children to have a higher education. Nationally, roughly twice as many parents expect university rather than college. These levels are similar to those in a 2000 survey of Canadian teens (Bibby, 2001).

These data, in tandem with recent youth surveys, suggest that Canadian parents and their teenage offspring are revolutionizing their educational expectations. They are now "on board" when it comes to valuing post-secondary education in the new economy.

SECOND TREND: NEW LEVELS, SAME PREDICTORS

Though most Canadian parents have high expectations, not all do. What are the sources of variation? How do expectations vary by family characteristics? Decades of sociological research have shown that family characteristics greatly influence educational expectations, school performance, and youth's eventual status attainment (Buchmann and Dalton, 2002). Below I examine a series of bivariate relationships with two outcomes – whether or not parents expect their child to attend any post secondary institution, and whether they expect university or college – to examine three categories of independent variables.

Ascription: Gender, Race, Ethnicity, Language

What is the role of ascription in determining parental expectations? Do parents have higher expectations for their male or female offspring? What about linguistic and visible minority parents? Recent research on actual post attainment suggests a number of trends.

Through most of the twentieth century women were less likely than men to attend university, but since 1980 this pattern has been reversed, not only in Canada, but in many nations (Butlin, 1999; De Broucker and Underwood, 1998; Guppy and Davies, 1998; Bradley, 2000). Important gender differences persist in enrolments by fields of study, but these too are shrinking (Charles and Bradley, 2002). In terms of language and ethnicity, it is surprising to some that many non-Aboriginal ethnic, linguistic, and racial minorities actually attain greater levels of education in Canada than the national average (Davies and Guppy, 1998; Guppy and Davies, 1998;

Table 6.2
Expectations by Gender, Language, Ethnicity

| | *Parents' Educational Expectations for Their Children* | | | |
Antecedent Variables	None	College	University	Total
Child's Gender				
Male	15%	33%	52%	1,169,594
Female	9%	29%	62%	1,116,407
Language Spoken				
English	12%	31%	57%	1,536,318
French	14%	38%	48%	493,205
Other	6%	15%	79%	220,394
Mother's Ethnic Background				
Canadian	13%	37%	50%	676,020
English Canadian	11%	27%	62%	72,539
French Canadian	11%	37%	52%	191,808
Asian (Chinese, South Asian)	–*	–*	91%	87,380
English or Scottish	8%	26%	66%	225,346
Irish	–*	27%	56%	53,733
Western European (French, Italian, Dutch)	16%	33%	51%	127,859
Other European (Jewish, Polish, Ukrainian)	–*	–*	80%	70,530
Aboriginal	42%	–*	37%	39,645
Other Ethnic (Unidentified)	6%	26%	68%	273,741
Multiple	12%	32%	55%	453,341

Source: SAEP (1999)
Note: * Sample size less than 30 before weighting

Boyd, 2002). One reason for this is that Canada's immigration system is highly selective on education, and these immigrants pass on high expectations to their children. Another is that most non-Aboriginal minorities live in urban areas with close proximity to post-secondary institutions. Aboriginal Canadians, however, suffer by far the lowest attainments among all ethnic groups (Guppy and Davies, 1998; Davies and Guppy, 1998).

The SAEP data on expectations largely reinforce these patterns. Table 6.2 shows that Canadian parents have lower expectations for male than for female children, as 15 per cent do not expect their male offspring to attend a post-secondary institution, while 9 per cent do not expect their female offspring to do so. Parents are much more likely to expect their daughters to attend university. In terms of language, only 6 per cent of parents whose main language is neither English nor French do not expect their children to have a post-secondary education, and they are also far more likely to expect university than English and French speakers. The expectations of ethnic and cultural groups also differ distinctly. A significant number of Aboriginal parents (42 per cent) have no post-secondary expectations of their children. Some 37 per cent do, however, expect that their children will obtain a university education. Most other Canadians expect that their children will obtain a university education. University expectations do vary considerably among the different groups – ranging from 51 per cent to 91 per cent. Between one-quarter and one-third of parents of English-Scottish and Western European ancestry favour the more vocationally oriented college option. Asian parents have little or no interest in a college education for their children and overwhelmingly favour the university pathway (91 per cent).

Socioeconomics: Parental Income and Education

While gender and ethnic patterns of educational attainment have changed somewhat in recent decades, inequalities along socio-economic lines have remained far more persistent in Canada and many other Western nations (Shavit and Blossfeld, 1993; Davies, 1999; Gamoran, 2001; Wanner, 1999). Parental education remains a strong predictor of children's educational attainment in Canada, along with income and occupational prestige (De Broucker and Lavallee, 1998; Knighton and Mirza, 2002; Ryan and Adams, 1999; Quirke and Davies, 2002). Research shows that higher SES families have much more familiarity with educational prerequisites, demands, and rewards.

Table 6.3 confirms the expected effects of parental income and education. The lowest expectations are found in households with incomes below $40,000, where 20 per cent do not have post-secondary expectations, compared to 5 per cent of households earning $60,000 or more. Furthermore, wealthier parents are more likely to expect university over college. The effect of parental education is quite strong. When neither parent has attended university, 16 per cent have no post-secondary expectations, whereas, only 2 per cent lack these expectations when both attended university. Similarly, far more families expect university rather than college as parental education increases.

Social and Cultural Capital: Home Environment, Activities, Peers

Given these macro trends, what shapes parental expectations, irrespective of their social address? Beyond ascription and socio-economics, culture matters. Resources need to be activated via parental support, involvement, and establishment of an effective home-learning environment. Canadian

Table 6.3
Expectations by Parental Income and Education

	Parents' Educational Expectations for Their Children			
Antecedent Variables	None	College	University	Total
Household Income				
$0 – $39,999	20%	34%	47%	683,295
$40,000 – $59,999	11%	33%	56%	547,803
$60,000 and up	5%	26%	69%	824,751
Parents' Education				
No parent with U-level	16%	37%	48%	1,536,174
1 parent with U-level	4%	22%	74%	423,116
2 parents with U-level	2%	8%	90%	240,125
Others	9%	40%	51%	50,220

Source: SAEP (1999)

and international research on cultural capital generally supports these tenets (De Graaf et al., 2000; Kingston, 2001). Similarly, research on social
capital shows that parental support for school and extracurricular activities, along with positive peer cultures, enhances school attainment
(Connolly, Halchette, and McMaster, 1999; Ho and Willms, 1996; Norris,
1999; Portes, 1998; Schneider and Coleman, 1993).

The SAEP survey offers a number of indicators of child engagement that
can be used as proxies for cultural and social capital: organized activities,
such as sports and social clubs; cultural activities, such as music, art, dance,
or drama lessons; and a structured home-learning environment (having a
place to study or do homework, having a computer and reading materials
available). Similarly, parental support, in the form of spending leisure time
with children, and positive peer cultures represent forms of social capital.

These data show that these forms of capital are related to expectations.
For instance, Table 6.4 shows that parents who do not spend any leisure
time with their children are most likely (22 per cent) not to have PSE, compared to 10 per cent of parents who spend "lots of leisure time" with their
children. Also, expectations for university rather than college increase with
leisure time. Furthermore, children's greater involvement in a variety of
leisure activities is positively associated with parental expectations. The
greater frequency of a child's participation in organized activities (base-
ball, swim club, or hockey league), clubs (scouts, girl guides, etc.), church
groups, cultural activities (music, art, dance, or drama lessons), or social
clubs (music, band, or school plays) spawns expectations of university and
fewer non-expectations.

Table 6.4
Cultural and Social Capital: Child Engagement, Home Environment, Peers

Antecedent Variables	Educational Pathways			
	None	College	University	Total
Sports				
More than once	7%	25%	68%	621,588
About once	8%	34%	59%	397,086
Less than once	10%	28%	62%	202,168
Never	16%	34%	50%	948,088
Clubs				
More than once	10%	22%	68%	122,204
About once	9%	27%	65%	312,019
Less than once	8%	30%	62%	161,202
Never	12%	33%	55%	1,570,664
Cultural				
More than once	5%	16%	79%	162,039
About once	5%	25%	70%	333,127
Less than once	8%	30%	62%	107,868
Never	13%	34%	53%	1,570,040
School Extra Curriculum				
More than once	5%	25%	70%	474,526
About once	9%	27%	65%	421,235
Less than once	10%	31%	59%	435,715
Never	16%	37%	47%	828,308
Place to Work				
Yes	11%	31%	59%	1,973,820
No	16%	36%	48%	201,484
Computer				
Yes	8%	29%	63%	1,792,739
No	27%	39%	34%	425,546
Books				
Yes	11%	31%	59%	2,062,797
No	24%	36%	40%	157,026
Peers				
Do well	8%	29%	63%	1,596,875
Not do well	22%	38%	40%	251,562

Source: SAEP (1999)

Another source of cultural capital is the home-learning environment, indicated by items such as having a place to study or do homework, a computer available to do school work or assignments, and reading materials. While an overwhelming proportion of Canadian parents (90 per cent) provided a specific place for their children to study, a slightly higher proportion (89 per cent) whose children have a place expect some post-secondary education than do parents who do not establish a specific place (84 per cent), and the former parents are more likely to expect university. Having a computer has larger effects. While 27 per cent without a computer in the home do not anticipate further schooling, only 8 per cent of those who have computers do not have those expectations. In addition, figures are comparable for those without/with appropriate reading materials: 24 per cent and 11 per cent respectively. Computers and home reading materials foster university expectations.

Similarly, having positive peer cultures as a form of social capital tends to foster expectations. Table 6.4 shows a large difference between parents who report that their children's peers do well in schools and those who do not. Whereas only 8 per cent of parents whose children's peers do well do not have post-secondary expectations, fully 22 per cent of those whose children's peers do not do well lack such expectations – almost three times more. Only a minority of parents (40 per cent) whose children's peers do not do well expect university, while almost two-thirds of the other category have expectations for university.

In sum, the SAEP data tend to reinforce established findings in the sociology of education. Parental income and education have the anticipated impact on expectations. Parental expectations are greater for females and students from certain linguistic and ethnic minorities, while the activation of cultural and social capital spawns greater expectations. When these patterns of stratification are combined with the previous finding – that of near-universal expectations – what are the implications for colleges and universities?

UNIVERSITY FOR MOST, COLLEGE FOR ALL?

Tables 6.1 through 6.5 show that parents regard university as their "first" choice, with community colleges a distant second. University is favoured particularly by more advantaged parents, leaving expectations for college largely to those who are either less socially advantaged or have poor academic profiles. This preference stems in part from the greater income opportunities that university degrees offer. A long line of Canadian research has established that the average returns to university graduates generally exceed those of college graduates (Guppy and Davies, 1998; Finnie, 2000; Walters, 2002; Wanner, 2000).

College is clearly a lesser choice among Canadian parents. While this preference may not be new, what is new is that many students who a generation ago would have been considered ill-suited for further schooling now expect to go to college. As post-secondary expectations reach near-universal proportions, many young people who in previous eras might have even dropped out of high school are now contemplating college. Many of these students lack academic profiles that are attractive to these institutions.

Consider the following findings from Table 6.5, which presents three indicators of student quality: parental judgments of their child's attitudes to school; their perceptions of their child's school achievement; and their estimate of the amount of time their child spends on homework. All of these measures are consequential for school success (Butlin, 2000; Connolly et al., 1999). The historical image of the post-secondary student is one who achieves above average grades, enjoys school to a moderate extent, and puts forth some effort in the form of homework.

But this image may need revision. Certainly these indicators distinguish between different types of expectations. Those parents who report that their child "likes school very much," has "above average achievement," or does "a lot" of homework overwhelmingly have post-secondary expectations, ranging from 94 per cent to 97 per cent, with most expecting university. These figures are in stark contrast to parents who report that their child "dislikes school very much," has "below average achievement," and in terms of homework, does "none at all." Expectations among these parents range from 53 per cent to 78 per cent, a markedly lower level, with only small minorities expecting university.

What is striking about these data are the relatively high rates of these parents who have expectations for community college. Whereas in previous eras a student who disliked school, fared poorly, and did no homework would seldom be encouraged to pursue advanced studies, now many of their parents expect them to at least attend a community college. These parents are now more or less evenly split between those who have no post-secondary and those who have college expectations. For instance, 41 per cent vs 40 per cent of those who report their child as "disliking school very much" expect college over no post-secondary; the corresponding percentages for "below average achievement" are 43 per cent vs 37 per cent; and for doing "no homework at all," 42 per cent vs 47 per cent.

Thus, these measures sharply distinguish expectations among parents, but in an era of near-universal expectations, even those scoring at the bottom still expect community college in high numbers. This is a sign of the times. It illustrates how the rhetoric of universal higher education has pervaded the mindset of most Canadian parents. It signals a profound social change, an outgrowth of the new economy: that community colleges will be increasingly expected to be a repository for remedial students, to take on all comers.

Table 6.5
Student Quality

Antecedent Variable	Educational Pathways			
	None	*College*	*University*	*Total*
Attitude Toward School				
Liked very much	4%	15%	80%	509,389
Liked it	7%	31%	62%	954,338
Neither	15%	41%	44%	382,983
Disliked it	24%	45%	31%	253,432
Disliked very much	40%	41%	19%	70,861
Achievement				
Above average	3%	17%	80%	963,010
Average	14%	42%	45%	1,004,939
Below average	37%	43%	20%	208,611
Homework Time				
A lot	6%	22%	72%	515,976
A fair amount	9%	30%	61%	1,093,807
Very little	18%	40%	42%	511,898
None at all	47%	42%	11%	32,637

Source: SAEP (1999)

CONCLUSIONS:
THREE TRENDS, THREE IMPLICATIONS

Canadian parents now have very high educational expectations for their offspring, especially for university. The vast majority expect their children to attend a post-secondary institution. But as the new economy greatly alters the *level* of parental expectations, it is not changing established variations between different groups of parents. When contrasting this majority to those parents without post-secondary expectations for their children, the usual predictors of variation emerged and a similar pattern emerged when contrasting parents who expected university and those expecting community college. A key conclusion, therefore, is that the new economy is greatly altering the *level* of parental expectations, but not differences among parents. Canadian families will likely remain educationally stratified, albeit at higher levels, with some of the most disadvantaged and low-achieving students aspiring to enter community colleges. What are some of implications of these trends? The remainder of this chapter discusses likely consequences of these three findings.

Rising Expectations and Institutional Stratification

A likely result of a universal era of post-secondary expansion is that system growth will lead to greater institutional differentiation and stratification. As the market for credentials expands further, demand will become more segmented. With larger and larger flows of youth entering the system, institutions, particularly those that are currently advantaged, will try to distinguish themselves. The future of higher education appears to be one of many disparate, loosely related segments, each with its own trajectory, and of the emergence of new specialist institutions (Kerr, 2002).

In Canada, this may take the form of a more elaborate hierarchy of colleges and institutions. Currently, Canadian universities are not graded by a steep prestige hierarchy as in other nations, such as the United States, which has a vast continuum ranging from the elite Ivy League to lowly state community colleges. But some prevailing forces may change this. As Canadian universities and colleges are increasingly expected to generate more of their own revenues, whether via large external research grants, corporate funds, alumni donations, or steeper tuition, some will clearly be more successful than others. Older and larger research-intensive universities enjoy advantageous resources such as multiple professional schools, and large bodies of wealthy alumni and corporate contacts. These universities will be more able to attract top faculty and run generously endowed academic programs. Gaining prestige, they can raise their admission requirements and compete for the top students by guaranteeing residence for first-year students and building more on-campus residence spaces, consequently leaving smaller and less wealthy institutions behind. If wealthier institutions are perceived by students and employers to offer a superior education, it may bring an intensified pecking order within the Canadian higher education.

In this way, a universal post-secondary system will absorb much of the selection and streaming functions that have been historically performed by high schools (Davies and Guppy, 1997a). Colleges, it appears, will increasingly become like the lower streams of high school. Since these ideas are speculative, we need more research on distinctions and stratification in Canadian higher education.

Expansion Does Not Bring Equalization

International research shows that as higher education expanded over the twentieth century, it rarely brought greater equity. Amidst expansion, students from more affluent backgrounds largely retained their advantages, albeit with all populations attaining higher levels of education. This process has been dubbed "maximally maintained inequality" (Blossfeld and Shavit, 1993; Gamoran, 2001; Raftery and Hout, 1993; Walter, 2000). That is, as school systems expand to take in previously excluded groups, advantaged populations can retain their advantages by attaining further, advanced levels of education and by monopolizing elite sectors (the most prestigious institutions, and/or lucrative programs). As post-secondary expansion absorbs groups traditionally low on status hierarchies, the value of credentials accumulated earlier declines, as has happened with the high school diploma. This devaluation generates a demand for further schooling, leading to a spiral of educational expansion to maintain or better one's status. This process ensures that as more young people are included in the post-secondary system, the competition for desired spots *within* the system becomes more intense, with students from affluent backgrounds being best equipped for this competition.

Because there is a clear ranking of post-secondary credentials, educational competition hardly ends when a student enters higher education. Some credentials are valued more than others. While this line of research is well developed in the u.s. (Davies and Guppy, 1997b; Karen, 2002), similar work on Canada is only beginning (Walters, 2002), and more is needed.

"College for All" and Student Preparation

Will near-universal expectations be matched by new levels of student performance? Current research suggests that rising expectations and enrolments may bring rising levels of student attrition and parental frustration. Parents generally have loftier expectations for their children than do the latter's teachers (Norris, 1999). With less-prepared students entering colleges (and universities), we should expect to see rising attrition rates, at least among below-average high school graduates. Canadian research shows that post-secondary students who had low high school grades are more likely to drop out of colleges and universities (Butlin, 2000).

Some instructive lessons from the u.s. have appeared recently, as some now lament the implicit "college for all" norm that has pervaded American high schools (Rosenbaum, 2002). The American experience of the "college for all" mentality is that many enter post-secondary institutions ill-prepared, and do not complete their degrees and/or diplomas as a result. Rosenbaum reports that many low-achievers in high school believe that effort has little relevance for their future schooling or career, and show a remarkable complacency that is at odds with their chances of success in higher education. Rosenbaum argues that an implicit "college for all" policy gives students a mistaken impression that low high school achievement is not an obstacle to their academic future, and that this impression is much more pervasive than in previous eras.[5] Rosenbaum and his colleagues have further found that high school counsellors have recently changed their role. Whereas they have been historically portrayed as gate-keepers who cooled out students, they now find themselves criticized for promoting unrealistic expectations in ill-informed youth (counsellors respond that if they warn students about college difficulties, they will be criticized for having "low expectations," but face no complaints when they are encouraging).

In Canada we should therefore expect that if our post-secondary system continues to pursue its mission of admitting all qualified applicants without altering its current practices or standards, then near-universal expectations will engender significantly high attrition rates in post-secondary institutions. Many of these "college-bound" students will soon be "work-bound." Canadians can learn from the American case by monitoring emerging attrition rates in PSE, particularly for below-average high school graduates. Of course, a different possibility is that some institutions will relax their standards to retain students, as hinted in recent studies that show evidence of grade inflation in universities (Anglin and Meng, 2000).

In conclusion, high expectations for post-secondary studies may be needed in the emerging new economy. However, we should not expect that a more equitable system will emerge. Rather, it will be likely marked by greater institutional stratification, more competition among students to enter more valued niches, and disappointments and frustrations among those who are least prepared.

NOTES

1 I do not dismiss supply-side or credentialist arguments that regard the key motor of educational expansion to be labour-market competition, rather than expanded employers' demand for cognitive skills. Both arguments are compatible with notions of a New Economy, though they identify different causal forces.

2 In this chapter I assume that parental *expectations* are similar to their initial *aspirations*, but have been modified in the light of their child's school performance and experience.

3 In past decades, the expectations of grade 12 students did not accurately mirror those of the overall age cohort, because of relatively high dropout rates. The expectations of those still in school would be markedly higher than for the age cohort as a whole. In other words, those surveys likely overestimate the levels of expectations for the entire cohort.

4 All tables report weighted data. Cell totals that are based on fewer than 30 unweighted cases are marked with an asterisk.

5 As a result, Rosenbaum warns that it is far too early for high schools to be closing or reducing their opportunities for vocational education, as some are doing.

REFERENCES

Anglin, P. and Meng, R. (2000). "Evidence on grades and grade inflation at Ontario universities." *Canadian Public Policy*, 26, 361–8.

Anisef, P. (1974). *The critical juncture*. Toronto: Ministry of Colleges and Universities.

Beattie, I.R. (2002). "Are all 'Adolescent Econometricians' created equal? Racial, class, and gender differences in college enrollment." *Sociology of Education*, 75(1), 19–43.

Bibby, R.W. (2001). *Canada's teens*. Toronto: Stoddart.

Bibby, R.W. and Posterski, D. (1992). *Teen trends*. Toronto: Stoddart.

Boyd, M. (2002). "Educational attainments of immigrant offspring: Success or segmented assimilation?" *International Migration Review*, 36, 1037–60.

Bradley, K. (2000). "The incorporation of women into higher education: Paradoxical outcomes?" *Sociology of Education*, 73, 1–18.

Brint, S. (1998). *Schools and societies*. Thousand Oaks, CA: Pine Forge Press.

Buchmann, C. and Dalton, B. (2002). "Interpersonal influences and educational aspirations in 12 countries: The importance of institutional context." *Sociology of Education*, 75, 99–122.

Butlin, G. (1999). "Determinants of postsecondary participation." *Education Quarterly Review* 5(3), 9–35.

– (2000). "Determinants of university and community college leaving." *Education Quarterly Review* 6(4), 8–23.

Charles, M. and Bradley, (2002). "Equal but separate? A cross-national study of sex segregation in higher education." *American Sociological Review*, 67(4), 573–99.

Connolly, J., Halchette, V., and McMaster, L. (1999). "Academic achievement in early adolescence: Do school attitudes make a difference?" *Education Quarterly Review*, 6(1), 20–9.

Davies, S. (1992). *In search of the culture clash: Explaining class inequalities in education*. Doctoral Dissertation, Department of Sociology, University of Toronto.

– (1999). "Stubborn disparities: Explaining class inequalities in schooling." In J. Curtis, E. Grabb, and N. Guppy, eds. *Social inequality in Canada: Patterns, problems, and policies*. 3rd edition. Toronto: Prentice Hall. 138–50.

Davies, S. and Guppy, N. (1997a). "Globalization and educational reforms in Anglo-American democracies." *Comparative Education Review*, 41(4), 435–59.

– (1997b). "Fields of study, college selectivity, and student inequalities in higher education." *Social Forces*, 75, 1417–38.

– (1998). "Race and Canadian education." In V. Satzewich, ed. *Racism and social inequality in Canada: Concepts, controversies and strategies of resistance*. Toronto: Thompson Educational Publishing Inc. 131–55.

Davies, S., Mosher, C., and O'Grady, B. (1996). "Educating women: Gender inequalities among Canadian university graduates." *Canadian Review of Sociology and Anthropology*, 33(2), 125–42.

De Broucker, P. and Lavallee, L. (1998). "Getting ahead in life: does your parents' education count?" *Education Quarterly Review*, 5(1), 22–8.

De Broucker, P. and Underwood, K. (1998). "Intergenerational education mobility: An international comparison with a focus on postsecondary education." *Education Quarterly Review*, 5(2), 30–51.

De Graaf, N., De Graaf, P., and Kraaykamp, G. (2000). "Parental cultural capital and educational attainment in the Netherlands: A refinement of the cultural capital perspective." *Sociology of Education*, 73, 92–111.

Finnie, R. (2000). "Holding their own: Employment and earnings of post-secondary graduates." *Education Quarterly Review*, 7, 21–37.

Gamoran, A. (2001). "American schooling and educational inequality: A forecast for the 21st century." *Sociology of Education* (extra issue), 135–53.

Guppy, N. and Davies, S. (1998). *Education in Canada: Recent trends and future challenges*. Ottawa: Statistics Canada.

Ho, E. and Willms, D. (1996). "Effects of parental involvement on eighth-grade achievement." *Sociology of Education*, 69, 126–41.

Karen, D. 2002. "Changes in access to higher education in the United States: 1980–1992." *Sociology of Education*, 75, 191–210.

Kerr, C. (2002). "Shock wave II: An introduction to the twenty-first century." In S. Brint, ed. *The future of the city of intellect*. Stanford, CA: Stanford University Press. 1–22.

Kingston, P.W. (2001). The unfulfilled promise of cultural theory." *Sociology of Education*, 74, (special issue).

Knighton, T. and Mirza, S. (2002). "Post secondary participation: The effects of parents' education and household income." *Education Quarterly Review*, 8(3), 25–31.

Meek, V. (2000). "Diversity and marketisation of higher education: Incompatible concepts?" *Higher Education Policy*, 13(1), 23–39.

Norris, C. (1999). "Parents and schools: the involvement, participation, and expectations of parents in the education of their children." *Education Quarterly Review*, 5(4), 61–80.

Porter, J., Porter, M., and Blishen, B. (1982). *Stations and Callings*. Toronto: Methuen.

Portes, A. (1998). "Social capital: Its origins and applications in modern sociology." *Annual Review of Sociology*, 22, 1–24.

Quirke, L. and Davies, S. (2002). "The new entrepreneurship in higher education: The impact of tuition increases at an Ontario university." *Canadian Journal of Higher Education*, 32, 85–110.

Raftery, A.E. and Hout, M. (1993). "Maximally maintained inequality: Expansion, reform, and opportunity in Irish education, 1921–1975." *Sociology of Education*, 66, 22–39.

Rosenbaum, J. (2002). "Beyond empty promises: Policies to improve transitions into college and jobs." Paper Prepared for the Office of Vocational and Adult Education, U.S. Department of Education, Washington, DC.

Ryan, B. and Adams, G. (1999). "How do families affect children's success in school?" *Education Quarterly Review,* 6(1), 30–43.

Schneider, B. and Coleman, J. (1993). *Parents, their children, and schools.* Boulder: Westview Press.

Shavit, Y. and Blossfeld, H. (1993). *Persistent inequality.* Boulder, CO: Westview.

Smith, M. (2001). "Technological change, the demand for skills, and the adequacy of their supply." *Canadian Public Policy,* 27(1), 1–22.

Tanner, J., Davies, S., and O'Grady, B. (1999). "Whatever happened to yesterday's rebels? Longitudinal effects of teenage delinquency on education and occupational outcomes." *Social Problems,* 46(2), 250–74.

Tanner, J., Krahn, H., and Hartnagel, T.F. (1995). *Fractured transitions from school to work: Revisiting the dropout problem.* Don Mills: Oxford University Press.

Teachman, J. (1987). "Family background, educational resources and educational attainment." *American Sociological Review,* 52, 548–57.

Trow, M. (2001). "From mass higher education to universal access: The American advantage." In P. Altbach, P. Gumport, and D. Johnstone, eds. *The enduring legacies: In defense of the American university.* Baltimore, Maryland: The Johns Hopkins University Press. 110–43

Walter, P.B. (2000). "The limits of growth: School expansion and school reform in historical perspective." In M. Hallinan, ed. *Handbook of the sociology of education.* New York: Kluwer Academic/Plenum Publishers. 241–61.

Walters, D. (2002). *The relationship between post secondary education and labour market outcomes: Comparing graduates over a four-cohort period.* Doctoral dissertation, McMaster University.

Wanner, R.A. (1999). "Expansion and ascription: Trends in educational opportunity in Canada." *Canadian Review of Sociology and Anthropology,* 36(3), 409–42.

– (2000). "A matter of degree(s): Twentieth-century trends in occupational status returns to educational credentials in Canada." *Canadian Review of Sociology and Anthropology,* 37(3), 313–43.

7

Distributing Scarce Resources: Parental Investment in Their Children's Post-Secondary Education

VICTOR THIESSEN AND E. DIANNE LOOKER

Canadian parents hold high expectations for their children's ultimate educational attainment. Recent increases in the costs associated with post-secondary education and the shifting balance away from the state and towards individual and familial responsibility for these costs creates dilemmas for families whose resources are limited in attempting to implement their aspirations. It also makes it necessary for them to take early and concrete steps to maximize the chances that their aspirations for their children's education are fulfilled. These steps are not limited to savings, but can take the form of encouraging their children's academic performance through a variety of activities collectively referred to as activation of parental social and cultural capital. Arguably, parents consider access to quality post-secondary education to be the single most important aspect of their children's future. Two recent U.S. surveys, for example, show that Americans feel a greater obligation to help their adult children than to help their elderly parents (Coleman, Ganong, and Cable, 1997; Goldscheider and Lawton, 1998). One manifestation of this is that almost all parents make some resources available to their children to pursue further education. One U.S. study reports that 92 per cent of students enrolled in post-secondary programs received some form of tangible parental support (Choy and Henke, 1992, 3). In the Canadian context, Bowlby and McMullen (2002, 56–7) found that parental contributions (as loans or non-repayable gifts) were second only to employment earnings as a source of income for youth who undertake post-secondary education (see also Junor and Usher, 2002). A second manifestation is that many parents start educational savings when their children are quite young. One U.S. study found that among parents who made educational savings, almost half started these savings when the child was in elementary school or even earlier (Choy and Henke, 1992, v).

This chapter uses the Survey of Approaches to Educational Planning (SAEP) to explore the educational savings investment decisions Canadian parents make when they have two or more children. The difficulties facing families with two or more children are, of course, especially severe. Given the rising educational expectations and aspirations of both children and their parents, it may not be possible for parents of several children to provide all of them the resources necessary for achieving these aspirations. Not only are the required financial outlays multiplied but also parents must decide how, or on what basis, to distribute their limited resources among the children. This chapter attempts to document the decision-making dynamics parents exhibit when distributing scarce resources among their children. Eight possible decision-making principles that can be assessed with the SAEP data are:

1) Equality: Resources are distributed equally to all children
2) Gender: One gender is favoured over the other
3) Birth order: Resources are distributed unequally on the basis of whether the child is first-born, last-born, or a middle child
4) Affective closeness: Children are treated differentially on the basis of how close the parents feel to a particular child
5) Merit: More educational savings are directed to the child who performs better in school
6) Effort: The child who works harder on academic pursuits is given more resources
7) Need: Familial financial support is distributed on the basis of the expected amount each child will require. The child who is expected to attend longer, and/or on a full-time basis, as well as the one who is expected to have less chance of obtaining scholarships or bursaries, will need more resources. Likewise, those who are expected to enrol in a more expensive institution or whose incurred costs will be larger, because of having to leave the parental home to pursue post-secondary education, might be given a larger share of the parental aid.
8) Parental aspirations and expectations for their children's education: Specifically in the context of investments in their children's education, parents may have different aspirations and expectations for their offspring. One would ordinarily expect these varying aspirations to be grounded in parental assessments of their children's ability and efforts, and therefore differential parental aspirations would be captured by the decision-making principles listed above. However, parents may have other, unmeasured, grounds for expecting or desiring more education

for one child than for another. For this reason, we consider parental aspirations and expectations a separate dynamic.

A ninth decision-making principle is whether the parent-child relationship is biological: Research indicates that biological children are provided more familial resources than step- and/or adopted children, even after controlling for a number of important determinants of parental educational investments, such as parental socio-economic status and children's educational achievements (Zvoch, 1999). It is not possible to investigate this relationship here since the data we employ does not distinguish between biological and other children.

LITERATURE REVIEW

Most of the empirical literature on familial investment in their children is concerned with interfamilial differences. These address important questions concerning the patterns of economic transfers to children and their relationship to family characteristics, such as parental socio-economic situation and the structure or composition of the family. As important as these issues are, Arrondel and Masson (1999) argue that intergenerational transfers of resources cannot be adequately understood without taking into account intrafamilial relationships, dynamics, and structure. More specifically, as Steelman and Powell (1991) note, an evaluation of interpretations of intergenerational transfers requires us to have information on parental savings with respect to each of their children. We agree with these assessments and therefore take both the family and each of the children within the family as the units of analysis and examine how intrafamilial dynamics influence the educational savings intentions and behaviours of the parents with respect to each of their children.

Although some scholars recognize the importance of internal-to-the-family structure and dynamics on educational savings, the empirical literature examining these issues is rather sparse. Nevertheless, in this literature review we focus mainly on what is known, or can be inferred, about intrafamilial aspects of intergenerational transfer of resources, since the other chapters review the relevant interfamilial findings. The distinction between interfamilial and intrafamilial approaches, although conceptually clear, is nevertheless quite difficult to make in practice, since the same attribute can function at both levels. For example, the ages of children relative to their siblings is an intrafamilial attribute, but age of children is also likely to be positively correlated with the magnitude and stability of familial resources, thus confounding the decomposition of interfamilial and intrafamilial effects. Hence it is important to keep in mind those attributes of households that are known to affect the likelihood and the amount of parental educational savings.

Among the more important interfamilial factors are household economic resources and parental education. Another factor is family structure, which is related to household income (Magee, 1998). Lone-parent families generally have less disposable income and therefore are less likely to make educational savings for their children. Choy and Henke (1992, 12) found that 58 per cent of students of single parents received a gift or loan from their parents, (the mean amount of the gift or loan was $2,923) compared to 80 per cent of those coming from two-parent families (the mean amount of these gifts or loans being $4,452). In general, any internal familial attribute that is also associated with between-family attributes will complicate the interpretation of the findings. With this caution in mind, we turn to a review of the literature most relevant to intrafamilial impacts on parental investment in their (multiple) children's education.

Equality

A fundamental feature of our society is its commitment to the norm of equality of access to educational resources. We assume that parents also apply this norm to the treatment of their own children, so that siblings are afforded equal opportunity to attain post-secondary educational qualifications. Hertwig et al. (2002) in their review of the empirical literature find considerable support for parental desire to treat their children equally. We suspect that this norm of equality is pervasive, applying to most aspects of parental treatment of their children, but especially to the distribution of any familial resources. Yet such norms are neither absolute nor likely to be adhered to universally. Various reasons can be found for justifying unequal (but not necessarily inequitable) treatment of children. That is precisely our point: parents who treat their children equally are not required to provide a rationale for such equality of treatment, whereas parents who treat their children differentially must account for their diverse treatment, both to their children and to others. Hardly anyone observing parental equality of treatment of their children would be puzzled by such parental behaviour, whereas they quite likely would be puzzled if they observed differential treatment, unless the reason for such differential treatment was obvious. This necessity to account for differential treatment implies the existence of a norm of equality. The justification of differential treatment is necessary to show that one is not treating siblings inequitably.

We start with the assumption that equality is a powerful norm in Canadian society; it is generally taken for granted that favouritism should not be shown to any of the children. In other words, children are to be treated equally, all other things being equal. But that phrase is the rub: all other things being equal. Typically, children are not equal and such inequalities in children's needs, attributes, behaviours, and capabilities can form the basis of unequal treatments. What we are postulating is that inequality of treatment cannot be capricious; it must be anchored in other prior differences that drive or explain differential treatment. As Clignet (1992) points out, there is an imperative for legitimacy in all forms of differential intergenerational transfers.

The assessment of the extent to which parental educational investment adheres to the norm of equality is an analytic priority; if parental educational savings are distributed equally to all their children, the question of within-family attributes becomes a moot point. If parents save identical amounts for each of their children, internal-to-the-family variations in dynamics and structure become irrelevant to the issue of parental educational investments. Although a norm of equality of treatment exists, it is nevertheless likely that differential treatment of children will sometimes occur. We next discuss the main justifications for differential treatment of siblings, and review the relevant empirical literature pertaining to these justifications.

Gender

Historically males have enjoyed more privileges than females and, in some respects, continue to enjoy relative privilege. This is part of our patriarchal structure and heritage. Even as recently as a generation or two ago, parents may have been inclined to save less for a daughter's education than for a son's, since sons were more likely than daughters to pursue at least a bachelor's or even a master's or a doctorate degree. Young women today, however, are more likely than their male counterparts to be enrolled in undergraduate studies, although still less likely to participate in graduate studies (Statistics Canada and the Council of Ministers of Education Canada, 2000). Despite the increased level of educational attainment of young women, some scholars would expect parents, on rational grounds, to invest less in their daughters' than in their sons' education. In the context of familial decision-making regarding investments in children's education, human capitalists contend that parents would choose to invest more heavily in those children for whom the return on their education would be the highest (Becker and Tomes, 1976; Becker and Tomes, 1986). Stated differently, investment decisions would be made to maximize the utility for the family as a whole. It is well-known that women's earnings are roughly three-quarters of those of men at comparable levels of educational attainment, and that mothers are substantially more likely than fathers to withdraw from the labour market for various periods of time following the birth of children. Both these factors would dampen the return on parental educational investments in daughters compared to investments made in sons.

Some support for this argument is found in Third World countries (Brinton, 1988; Greenhalgh, 1985). Lee (1998) reports that the presence of brothers is the most detrimental factor in women's educational attainment. Lee argues that family resources are directly diverted from sisters to younger brothers and that the preferential treatment of sons over daughters can be understood as a survival strategy of families with economic hardships. In Japan, Brinton (1988) finds evidence that parents are more likely to subsidize their sons' education. She interprets this from a human capital perspective, drawing attention to the wide gender earnings gap. In these cross-cultural studies, the gender differences are unfortunately intertwined with gendered future filial responsibility, with sons being expected to financially support the aging parent.

If gender plays a significant role in parental investment decisions at the familial level, then we would expect to find some gender differences at the aggregate level. The literature generally indicates that gender does not play a large role in parental educational savings behaviours (Choy and Henke, 1992; Flint, 1997; Hossler and Vesper, 1993; Steelman and Powell, 1991). In a study of mother-child dyads, Coleman et al. (1997) found that the gender of the child was irrelevant to whether the mother expected to provide material support under a variety of different conditions, such as attendance at a post-secondary institution. In data from the u.s. 1986–87 National Postsecondary Student Aid Study, Choy and Henke (1992, 5) found essentially no gender differences: sons were only one percentage point more likely to receive financial support of all kinds than were daughters. Likewise very little gender difference in the amount they received emerged, with sons receiving somewhat less on average than daughters ($4,219 versus $4,257, respectively, for gifts or loans). Similar small differences were found in gifts, although daughters received somewhat larger loans ($2,905 versus $2,550 for daughters and sons, respectively). Flint (1997, 339) too finds no gender difference in parental savings behaviours in the more recent 1990 National Postsecondary Student Aid Study. A few studies report gender differences but the effects found are contradictory. Focusing on students enrolled in a post-secondary institution in 1983 in the 1984 follow-up of the High School and Beyond survey, Powell and Steelman (1995) document that parents paid $110 more on average for their daughters' education than for their sons', a difference that remained statistically significant after controlling for a variety of background factors.[1] Likewise Davis (1977, 33) found that, in a sample of six colleges, parents contribute more to their daughters' education than to their sons'. In contrast to these studies, Stage and Hossler (1989) report that parents were more likely to be saving for their sons' education than for their daughters'. Although Steelman and Powell (1991) did not find a significant gender effect on actual parental savings, they did find that among those parents whose child had enrolled in college (but not for the total sample) parents were more willing to assume debt if their child was male.

Taken together, the empirical literature fails to support the human capital arguments, suggesting instead that in most Western societies, the gender of the child is generally a negligible factor in parental educational savings behaviours. The question is whether the same holds for Canadian parents.

Birth Order

A large body of literature has explored birth order effects on children (for example, Modin, 2002; Paulhus, 1999; Rodgers, 2000; Rodgers, 2001). Historically, birth order has been a key factor in the intergenerational transfer of familial resources. In rural societies the eldest son would often inherit the family farm. In general, primogeniture is the principle that the first-born has special rights and privileges with respect to inheritance. Human capital scholars provide a rationale for expecting greater parental investment in the first-born. They contend that parents invest more in earlier-born than in later-born children because the expected dividends would normally materialize earlier. Although at first glance there appears to be some cross-cultural evidence for this (Greenhalgh, 1985), the greater parental financial outlays for the first-born are more likely due to the filial obligation of the first-born to provide future support to the parents. Whether and/or in what circumstances this principle extends to greater access to educational savings in societies without such filial obligations is unknown.

Variations in parental labour market outcomes confound the examination of birth-order effects. Parents are, of course, younger when they first become parents than when they have additional children. Consequently, because of more labour market experience, they are likely to be better off financially by the time the last-born is ready to attend a post-secondary institution than they were when the first-born was of that age. Since parental income is an important determinant of the amount of educational savings, it becomes difficult to separate birth order effects from familial resources effects.

Potentially counteracting the effect of familial resources, the oldest child is the one for whom post-secondary expenses arrive first. Therefore parents with limited resources may, at any given point, be more likely to save for the first child's education than for the younger children's; this does not imply that they expect to treat their children differentially. Especially if the time interval between the first and second child is large, parents might intend to save for the second child after the first child has started/completed their post-secondary education. Fortunately, in the data set at hand, parents were asked not only about the savings they had made to date but also about the savings they anticipated making for each child by the time that child attends a post-secondary institution.

The available evidence suggests that being the first-born is not an advantage with respect to access to parental educational savings. Rather, it is the later-born who have a distinct advantage (Powell and Steelman, 1995; Steelman and Powell, 1991). Powell and Steelman (1995, 1473) report that the proportion of older siblings had a positive slope of $170, indicating that the more older siblings one had (i.e., the closer one was to being the youngest) the more parents paid for one's education. This finding is not solely an artefact of parental income, since parental income and education were included as additional variables in the regression.

Affective Closeness

In the context of our research question, affective closeness refers to how close a parent feels to a particular son or daughter. Finch (1989, 160) concludes that "the quality of the relationship, especially between parents and children, plays a relatively small part in determining whether support actually is given." She goes on to suggest that on the whole the normative prescription to give assistance is so strong between parents and children that the quality of the relationship is not allowed to override it and that "a good relationship 'defines in' that person to a structure of obligations, but a poor relationship does not necessarily 'define out.' This latter point applies to parent-child relationships with particular force" (Finch, 1989, 160–1). A somewhat indirect measure of affective closeness is parental discussion with their children about their education. Limited as it is, it is the only indication of affective closeness available in the data set. Using this measure, Hossler and Vesper (1993, 151) found a significant relationship with parental propensity to make educational savings.

Merit

Merit constitutes another aspect of parental decision making for allocating familial resources. Assuming that parents desire to maximize the return on their educational investments, if not for themselves then at least for their offspring, it would make sense for them to concentrate their savings on those children who show the greatest academic ability. Those who do well in secondary school and who have strong motivation to learn are more likely to pursue and complete post-secondary education (Gladieux and Swail, 2000). They are also most likely to reap the greatest benefit from this advanced education.

Consistent with this expectation, Powell and Steelman (1995, 1473) find that both high school grades and test scores from a standardized exam developed by Educational Testing Services show significant positive relationships with student-reported amounts of parental educational support.

Similarly, Steelman and Powell (1991, 1519) find that academic track as well as test scores show the expected relationship with the amount of money parents had set aside for their child's education at the time the child was in the final year of high school.

Steelman and Powell (1991, 1520) also show that parents whose child has enrolled in college were more willing to go into debt if their child's academic test score was low. The authors suggest that "(t)his counter-intuitive pattern may reflect parental willingness to sacrifice for their children when children cannot, by virtue of low test scores or grades, garner scholarship support."

In contrast to these findings, Flint (1997, 339), using data from the U.S. 1990 National Postsecondary Student Aid Study of dependant students, reports that "academic ability has no apparent independent influence on the money that parents provide." Similarly Hossler and Vesper (1993, 150) found that the student's grade-point average was not a significant predictor of parental likelihood of making educational savings, net of other familial characteristics.

What must be kept in mind is that the sampling frame for the studies reviewed here limits the eligible population to those households where the child in question is enrolled, or about to enroll, in a post-secondary institution. In this population, the variation in academic performance is considerably reduced, since it excludes those children who did not complete high school, as well as those who are not pursuing a post-secondary education, at least not immediately after graduation from high school. Hence, although the evidence with respect to actual academic performance and ability is mixed, it may well be that academic merit is positively related to parental educational investments in the general population of parents with dependant children. The consistent finding that parental educational savings increase with the parents' educational expectations and aspirations reinforces the conclusion that academic merit probably plays a significant role in parental planning. The acid test is whether, within families, parents are more likely to save, and to save more, for those siblings they perceive as performing better academically.

Effort

No literature was found that directly assessed the relationship between effort and parental educational investment decisions. Nevertheless, one would expect both a direct and an indirect relationship between children's academic effort and parental investment in their post-secondary education. The direct relationship is premised on the general norm that effort should be rewarded, even if hampered by limited innate talent. Effort can be seen as individuals making the best out of whatever talents they have. An indirect effect is also to be expected, since children who strive to succeed academically are, all other things being equal, more likely to succeed. Parents who observe that their child is working hard at their homework, for example, are likely to be more confident that the child will enroll in a post-secondary institution in the future and are therefore more likely to begin making educational savings for that child. Some evidence indicates that an early and continuing commitment to post-secondary education on the part of the children is an important incentive for the parents to make educational savings (Hossler and Vesper, 1993, 155).

Student Need

Several aspects of student need are known to be related to the likelihood, as well as the amount, of educational savings by parents. One aspect of student need is related to whether they are attending on a full-year, full-time basis or not. Choy and Henke (1992, 7) report that 80 per cent of full-time, full-year students received a parental gift or loan, compared to 61 per cent of part-year and 62 per cent of part-time, full-year students. Likewise the amounts they receive reflect their attendance status, with full-time, full-year students receiving $4,710 compared to $2,797 and $2,522 for part-time, full-year and part-year respectively.

Variation in tuition costs has direct effects on student need. u.s. information on parents' savings behaviours shows that this is a major consideration, but it must be kept in mind that costs of programs vary much more widely there than in Canada. One study reports that only 63 per cent of students attending an American post-secondary institution whose costs are under $1,500 received financial support from their parents, compared to 90 per cent of those attending an expensive ($10,000 or more) institution. Perhaps even more telling is the amount of parental support, ranging from under $2,000 for the least expensive to more than $8,000 for the most expensive (Choy and Henke, 1992, 15). We can see how class differences are maintained through sending offspring to expensive institutions, which usually are the elite institutions.

Length of the educational program is intertwined to some extent with the type of institution attended and reflects the likely educational expectations. Institutions whose programs take under two years to complete are quite different from those at which one can obtain a bachelor's degree, for example. Hence one would expect some relationship between the length of the programs offered and parental aid. Consistent with this expectation, Choy and Henke (1992, 15) found that 60 per cent of students attending an institution whose programs are under two years long received parental support compared to 84 per cent of those attending an institution that offers PhD programs. They also found corresponding differences in the amounts of support given.

Parental Aspirations and Expectations

Choy and Henke (1992, 7) found that the higher the expected educational achievement, the greater the likelihood of receiving parental aid, and the greater the amounts received as gifts or loans. The one "reversal" is that those who are expected to attain "some college" are both less likely to get financial aid and more likely to get smaller amounts on average than are those who are expected to complete vocational studies. This could reflect the possibility that those students who are expected to attend college but not to complete it are perceived as either not as capable or not as serious about their post-secondary studies as are those who are expected to complete vocational school. The percentage obtaining some form of financial support ranges from a low of 60 per cent (some college) to a high of 80 per cent (PhD or advanced professional degree). The amounts saved for students expected to attain a PhD or advanced professional degree are on average more than double those saved for those who are expected to attain "some college."

It is well known that better-educated and financially better-off parents have higher educational expectations for their children. Hence the relationship between parental aspirations and savings may be spurious, reflecting nothing more than their better financial and educational status. This possibility can be partially assessed by studies that use multivariate procedures. Two studies document that net of these parental and household background factors, parents who have higher aspirations for their children make larger actual contributions to their children's post-secondary education (Flint, 1997, 334; Steelman and Powell, 1991, 1519). Of course, other unmeasured interfamilial factors may lie behind this relationship. A stricter test is one in which parental savings are compared between siblings, as will be done here.

Interaction Effects

Quite possibly the structural location of families, such as their ethnic background, interacts with parental investment behaviours. That is, certain decision-making principles might operate in families with a particular characteristic and different decision-making principles may operate in families with different characteristics. Prior research in this respect is quite limited, particularly statistical research. However, some intriguing evidence suggests that gender interacts with parental income in determining parental contributions. Choy and Henke (1992, 19) present information separately for low-income (<$24,000), middle-income ($24,000–$49,999), and high-income ($50,000+) households. They show that among the low-income students, 48 per cent of females but only 39 per cent of males receive less than 75 per cent of the expected contribution from their parents.[2] This gender difference flips around among middle-income students, with 45 per cent of males and 41 per cent of females obtaining less than 75 per cent of expected parental contribution. Among high-income students, there is virtually no difference (31 per cent versus 30 per cent of males and females receiving less than 75 per cent of expected contributions). These findings are consistent with expectations from evolutionary biology, which predict that "as resources become more plentiful, parents do best by becoming gradually more egalitarian" (Hertwig, Davis, and Sulloway, 2002, 730). Although exploration of such interaction effects is important, space limitations require us to simply note that such effects may be present and should be assessed in future research.

DATA AND MEASUREMENTS

Definition of Eligible Population

Statistics Canada conducted the SAEP for Human Resources Development Canada (HRDC). This survey, conducted in October 1999, was administered to a sub-sample of the dwellings in the Labour Force Survey (LFS).[3] After completing the LFS, the person most knowledgeable (PMK) about the children living in the household and about any plans for their post-secondary education was interviewed. The SAEP collected information for up to three children 18 years of age or younger. For households with more than three children, a randomization grid was used to select three children for whom educational and savings information was obtained. Educationally relevant information was obtained for a total of 18,805 children, who were members of 10,628 households. These households form the primary basis of the analyses in this paper. At least one child was present in 10,628 households.[4] To explore intrafamilial decision-making we selected the 6,260 households in which at least two children are present.

This data design captures two levels of information: the household level and, nested within the household, the child level. For each household, a household weight was supplied to make the information represent the number of Canadian families with these attributes. Except where otherwise noted, this household weight is used to weight all statistics reported in this paper. Where statistical tests of significance are reported, the household weight was divided by the mean household weight in the sample so that the weighted sample size equalled the actual sample size used. By restricting information to children aged 18 and younger, the implicit assumption is that the children are still largely dependent on their parents. This assumption is generally valid. However, a total of 25 children were, or had been, married at the time of the survey. Since savings for these children may have been started prior to their marriage, and in the interests of maintaining maximum sample sizes, these cases were retained in the analysis. Other research shows, significantly, that one of the consequences of a child getting married is a decreased likelihood of receiving parental financial support (60 per cent versus 75 per cent for married and single children, respectively, for receiving gifts or loans); in addition financial support is substantially less ($2,179 compared to $4,301 for married and single children, respectively, for gifts and loans combined) (Choy and Henke, 1992, 5).

Data Anomalies

Several anomalies emerged in the course of our analyses. First, parents of 82 children held only primary school aspirations for these children. Although it is possible that some parents have such low educational aspirations for their children, this is quite unusual. A second puzzle is that some parents whose educational aspirations for their children are primary school or secondary school or learning a trade nevertheless made post-secondary educational savings for them.

A third anomaly concerns the relationship between educational aspirations and expectations. In the Canadian culture, a university education is generally regarded as the pinnacle of educational accomplishments. Somewhat lower in the educational hierarchy are community colleges and still lower trade schools (Thiessen and Looker, 1999, 105, 108). Not completing public school would be at the bottom. That is, where a child has the ability and the familial resources are available, parents would generally desire that their child obtain a university education. This hierarchy of educational accomplishments is important for assessing the relationship between educational expectations and educational aspirations. We would expect aspirations to equal or exceed expectations. Stated differently, it is anomalous to have expectations exceed aspirations. Nevertheless, among those parents who expected a university education for their child, 82 stated that they desired a community college education for that child, 49 stated that their desire was for secondary school and 7 desired a primary school education. Likewise in 64 instances a community college was expected but only secondary (61 cases) or primary (3 cases) education was desired. All of these combinations violate the assumed hierarchical structure of our educational system and most likely represent measurement error.

As is to be expected, the distribution of educational savings is positively skewed. The pronounced skew violates the assumption of normality, which may adversely affect the estimates of effects. To minimize this problem, analyses of the amount of savings were replicated using the natural log of savings. In all analyses reported here, identical results were obtained with respect to whether a relationship was statistically significant, indicating that the results are relatively robust. Not only are educational savings skewed, but a few outliers with savings greater than $100,000 were also found. Since such outliers unduly influence parameter estimates, these cases were included but capped (i.e., recoded) at $100,000.

Measures of Parental Educational Savings

Four parental savings behaviours are examined for each of the potential decision-making factors:

- Percentage having begun saving:
  "Have you or anyone else living in your household ever saved money for (this child's) post-secondary education?"
- Percentage planning to save:
  "Are you or anyone else living in your household planning to save or pay for (this child's) post-secondary education?" This percentage includes those who have ever saved for the given child and is therefore always at least as high as the first measure.
- Mean amount (in dollars) saved:
  "Since starting to save for (this child), how much in total has been saved for his/her post-secondary education? Do not include any earnings or interest." This mean is calculated only for those who report having begun saving. Hence it represents the average amount saved among those who have started saving for their child's post-secondary education.
- Mean anticipated total savings:
  "How much do you expect to have saved for (this child's) education by the time he/she starts post-secondary studies? Include all earnings and interest." Again, this amount is calculated only for those who report having begun saving.

STATISTICAL PROCEDURES

Cross-sectional survey research designs are not well equipped to answer questions of causality. Longitudinal designs are substantially better and experimental designs are best for answering questions of why. In an experimental design, initial differences are minimized through random assignment into control and experimental groups. The data set available here is neither longitudinal nor experimental. However, it can be thought of as permitting each respondent to be their own control through the felicitous feature that identical questions were asked about each child within a family. Hence, although income differences between families, for example, may account for differences in savings activity, such income differences cannot account for any differential treatment of children within the same family. In this respect, then, all familial differences are "held constant" when the analysis focuses on differential treatment of siblings. The presence of siblings overcomes some of the severe methodological shortcomings of cross-sectional survey data (see Warren, Hauser, and Sheridan, 2002). Except for assessing the extent of equality of parental educational investments, that is the analytic strategy used in this paper.

Of necessity, when assessing the role of sibling differences on parental educational investments, the analyses are restricted to those families in which at least two children are present in the household *and* one of the children differs from the other(s) on the attribute in question. For each potential decision-making criterion, we first had to determine whether the second child differed from the first with respect to that criterion. If they differed, the parental savings behaviours for those two children were compared. If they did not differ, then the first child was compared with the third child, if such a child were present in the household. If they differed, then the parental savings behaviours for these two children were compared. If the first child did not differ from either the second or the third child, then that household was deleted from that specific analysis. In other words, with respect to each potential decision-making criterion, the analysis is restricted to those specific households in which at least two children were present and one of them differed from the other on the attribute in question. Hence the number of cases for each analysis represents the number of households in which two children differed on the independent variable in question. With respect to gender, if the first child was a son, for example, then we determined whether the second or third child was a daughter. If the second child was a daughter, then the parental savings behaviours for the first and second child were compared. If the second child was also a son, but the third child was a daughter, then the parental savings behaviours for the first and third child were compared. If neither the second nor the third child was a daughter, then that household was not kept for that analysis. The maximum sample size for these analyses is 6,260, since that is the number of households in the sample with two or more children. When comparing savings made for the oldest child with those for the second-oldest child, the actual number of cases is close to this maximum.[5] On most attributes, the actual number of cases is considerably less than this maximum, since on many attributes the majority of parents do not perceive their children as different.

For all non-dichotomous independent variables, the magnitude of the difference between the siblings was ignored, and only the direction of the difference was maintained. For example, with respect to a variable such as educational aspirations, we noted for which child the aspirations were higher and for which child they were lower (but not how much higher or lower).

But of course not every prior difference necessarily justifies subsequent differential treatment. Some differences may be considered irrelevant for any given topic or domain. We have then two tasks. The first is to ascertain the extent of sibling differences on a variety of attributes that might conceivably be the basis for differential treatment. On what attributes, behaviours, or capabilities do parents perceive their children to differ substantially and on which ones are only minimal differences noted? The reported Ns in the difference-of-means tables indicate in how many families the children differed on the attributes being assessed in that table.

The second task is to determine which of these differences are related to differential treatment. Some sibling differences may be seen as either requiring differential treatment or at least justifying such differential treatment. For example, do parents who have both a son and a daughter make different educational savings for them? The reported differences of proportions and means answer these questions.

FINDINGS

Before we look at the ways in which families divide their resources amongst their children, we should examine the basic premise of this paper, which is that the larger the family size, the more severe are the financial pressures. One manifestation of such pressure would be that educational savings for their children would become both less likely and smaller in amounts. The relevant information is shown in 7.1. Note that the mean amount of educational savings declines monotonically with number of children in the household. The relationship of family size with likelihood of making educational savings is not quite as straightforward: 42 per cent of parents with an only child have made educational savings, a figure that increases by two percentage points when there are two children and thereafter declines steadily.

Table 7.1
Educational Savings Behaviour by Number of Children
aged 18 or Under

Number of children 18 or under	Percentage making educational savings		Mean amount of educational savings	
	%	N	Mean	N
1	42.0	(4,235)	2169	(3,871)
2	44.2	(8,666)	2134	(7,854)
3	36.9	(4,496)	1656	(4,037)
4	32.4	(1,006)	1090	(915)
5+	28.7	(346)	1075	(321)
Total	40.8	(18,749)	1927	(16,998)

Source: SAEP (1999)

Equality

Our first task is to assess the extent to which parents treat their offspring equally with respect to making educational investments, or its obverse, the extent to which parental educational savings behaviour differentiates between their children. The equality principle can be assessed in several ways. The simplest is to note in what percentage of cases savings were made (or planned) for either none or all the children. For those who have made savings, we can also note the percentage in which the amounts saved for each child are identical. The drawback with this latter measure is that it treats parental investment as different, regardless of the dollar amount of the difference in savings; i.e., a $1 difference is treated the same as a $1,000 difference. This drawback is overcome by a third approach, which estimates the variation in amount saved between siblings within families as a proportion of the total variation in educational savings. This can be estimated using hierarchical linear modelling (HLM).

In households with two or more children aged 18 or under, 91 per cent have an identical savings status with respect to all children about whom there is savings information. Equality of treatment is even greater if we look at intended savings, with 94 per cent of parents having identical savings status expectations for their children. Despite these high percentages, there is substantially less similarity in the amounts saved, with only 35 per cent of parents having saved the identical amounts for all three children. Nevertheless, almost two-thirds of parents (65 per cent) expect to have saved identical amounts by the time their children can be expected to enrol in a post-secondary educational institution.

It is of some interest to break down the similarity of savings behaviours into their constituent parts. This is most easily done by restricting our attention to households with two children: 52 per cent have not saved for either child; 41 per cent have saved for both children; and the remainder have saved for one child but not the other. Approximately three-quarters (74 per cent) of these two-children families expect to have made educational savings for both their children by the time they enrol, about one-fifth (21 per cent) don't plan on making any educational savings for either of their children, and only one in twenty parents plan to save for one child but not the other.

Hierarchical linear modelling techniques permit one to partition the total variance in familial educational savings into within and between family components.[6] The intra-class correlation coefficient indicates that only 5.6 per cent of the total variance in educational savings is due to within-family variation; 94.4 per cent is due to differences between families in their savings behaviour. Clearly, equality of treatment of siblings is the overriding principle in Canadian families.[7]

Of course, the low estimate of the within-family variation in educational savings reflects to some extent that non-savers were included in the analysis. The non-savers, by definition, have no within-family variation in educational savings. For this reason we obtained a second estimate of the proportion of within-family variance in educational savings, limiting our cases to those families in which educational savings had been made (N = 6,057 children distributed across 3,777 families). Among these savers, the mean savings per child is $5,228. The percentage of variance in educational savings attributable to differentiation in savings between children within families is approximately double that reported above (11.5 per cent). A third estimate was obtained using the natural log of educational savings. The primary purpose of obtaining the log of savings was to reduce the extreme skew, which it did, since the standard deviation is much smaller than the mean 1.24 and 7.91, respectively. However, this transformation had the unanticipated effect of giving a substantially higher estimate of the proportion of within-family variance in educational savings, namely 18.9 per cent. The direct implication of these estimates is that the maximum possible variance that can be attributed to differential treatment of siblings is between 5.6 per cent and 18.9 per cent. The main conclusion is that, with respect to educational savings, equality of treatment is the fundamental decision-making principle. The task now is to determine whether the relatively small amount of within-family variation is systematically related to differences in sibling attributes. This is done in the following analyses. The remainder of this section focuses on parental savings behaviours for siblings who differ on those attributes that are potentially relevant grounds for differential treatment.

Gender

Despite modest improvements over time, it remains the case in Canada today that men can expect to earn more than women with comparable educational qualifications and labour force experience (Baker et al., 1995; Drolet, 2002; Kidd and Shannon, 1997). Furthermore, within families it is still more likely that mothers rather than fathers will interrupt their labour force participation. Both of these factors are used by scholars who, from a return on investment point of view, predict that sons will be favoured over daughters in parental deliberations concerning educational savings for their children. The SAEP survey results indicate absolutely no supporting evidence for this expectation. As Table 7.2 shows, in households with both sons and daughters, parents were just as likely to have made savings for daughters as for sons, and just as likely to plan to make savings for both of them (the gender difference is just 1 per cent for both behaviours, and it favours daughters rather than sons). Furthermore, the amounts saved and the amounts expected to be saved for daughters are approximately equal to the corresponding amounts for sons. We therefore conclude that gender equality characterises the educational investment behaviour of parents in Canada today. This gender equality may be the result of the increasing tendency of young women to enrol in post-secondary educational institutions.

Before concluding this section, we should place the discussion of gender in the context of the academic performance of boys and girls. There is consistent evidence that right from the beginning of primary school, girls adjust better to school and obtain better marks in school than do boys (Thiessen, 2001). Given this gender difference at the aggregate level, one could surmise that in the microcosm of the family, more daughters than sons would be seen as adjusting and performing better in school. And this is the case: parents are twice as likely to see sons as daughters as disliking school (11 per cent versus 5 per cent for sons and daughters, respectively). Likewise, parents see one-third of the daughters (compared to only one-quarter of the sons) to be above average academically. To the extent that parents take such indicators of academic merit into account, we would expect them to invest more heavily in their daughter's than in their son's education. That they don't indicates that either they ignore academic performance when making educational investment decisions or they use other criteria that negate the differential academic performance of sons and daughters.

Birth Order

To assess the effect of birth order, we compared the parental savings behaviour with respect to the oldest child for whom there was savings

Table 7.2
Parental Educational Investments by Gender, Birth Order, and Amount
of Leisure Time Spent with Child

	Saved	Planned	Amount	Amount expected
	(%)	(%)	$	$
Gender				
Daughters	42**	74**	5,655	21,714
Sons	41**	73**	5,657	22,161
(N)	(3,591)	(3,591)	(1,038)	(808)
Birth order				
Younger	40***	73***	5,091***	23,591***
Older	45***	75***	6,230***	22,805***
(N)	(6,236)	(6,236)	(1,842)	(1,475)
Amount of leisure time				
Less	43**	72**	7,836**	15,785***
More	40**	69**	7,081**	18,588***
(N)	(878)	(878)	(259)	(199)

Source: SAEP (1999)

Note: Percentages and means are weighted at the household level but the number of cases are unweighted.

* p < .05

** p < .01

*** p < .001

information with that for a younger child. In most instances, this means that we are comparing savings for the first-born with savings for a younger sibling. In families with more than three children, the older child is not necessarily the first-born child, since random selection of children was used in such households and the first-born may not have been selected. With this methodological caveat in mind, there is clear evidence that, cross-sectionally, parents are more likely to have made savings, and to have saved more, for the first-born than for the younger child. Savings were made for 45 per cent of the first-born, with mean savings of $6,230; the comparable figures for the younger sibling are 40 per cent and $5,091 (see Table 7.2). Can we conclude from this that parents favour first-born children? Probably not, since parents actually expect to have saved more for their younger child than for their older child by the time they expect their children to start their post-secondary studies ($23,591 versus $22,805 for the younger and older child, respectively). From this we infer that parents, under conditions of limited familial resources, direct educational savings to their first-born initially, expecting to make savings for their younger child a priority at a later time when the family is in a more solid economic situation. This interpretation is reinforced by additional HLM results in which the confounding effects of father's age and children's ages can be separated (the confounding effect is the result of the fact that the children of older fathers are themselves on average older). In this application of HLM, we use one household-level (or level-2) variable (father's age, centred on the mean age of fathers) and one child-level (or level-1) variable (child's age, not centred). Among savers, the parameter estimates are $99 for age of father and $382 for age of child, with a Y-intercept of $1,823. That is:

$$\text{Estimated savings (\$)} = \$99 \text{ (Father's age} - \text{Mean age)} \\ + \$382 \text{ (Child's age)} + \$1,823.$$

The Y-intercept of $1,823 is the estimated amount saved during the child's first year after birth (i.e., when the child's age is 0) in families where the father is of average age. In families with two (or more) children, the parameter associated with age of child ($382) can be interpreted as the estimated difference in savings between children within the same family who were born one year apart. If they were born two years apart, this equation estimates that the savings made for the older child would be $764 (2×382) more than that made for the younger child. Note that since age of father is also in the equation, his age is "held constant," as it must be in families with multiple children (i.e., the father is the "same" age with respect to each of his children). The parameter estimate associated with father's age indicates that for each additional year, $99 more educational savings are made. This effect in all likelihood can be attributed to the improved financial security of the family due to the greater labour market experience of the father.[8] To summarize, these findings suggest two inter-related savings dynamics. First, families save more for their children's education as the financial security that comes with increasing age/labour market experience increases. Second, families save more for their children's education as their entrance to post-secondary institutions comes closer. Since the effect of children's age is almost four times as large as the effect of father's age, we conclude that imminence of attending a post-secondary institution is a substantially greater impetus for making educational savings than is father's age and all that it represents.

Affective Closeness

The only measure of how close parents feel to each of their children concerns the amount of leisure time they spend with each of their children. For each child, respondents were asked "How much leisure time did (child's) parents usually spend with him/her in a week? Leisure time means doing things together like playing a game, going shopping together, or other activities." Four response categories were provided, ranging from "a lot" to "none at all." In only 878 households was it reported that parents spent more leisure time with one child than with another, and it is only for these households that we can assess whether affective closeness is a basis for differential parental educational investments.

Although Table 7.2 reveals that all parental educational savings behaviours are significantly related to the amount of leisure time spent with their children, the relationships are not all in the same direction. Contrary to what one might expect, parents are more likely to have saved, to have already saved more, and to plan to save for the child with whom they spend less leisure time. In contrast, they plan to have saved more for the child with whom they spend more leisure time. On the face of it, these are contradictory results. However, the contradiction is to a large extent probably an artefact of age of child. Additional analyses revealed that the older the child, the less leisure time is spent with that child – the Pearson correlation coefficient between age of child and amount of leisure time spent with the child is -.30. But the older a child is, the more imminent is their enrolment in a post-secondary institution, and therefore this child is the one for whom educational savings are currently a priority. For the younger child (with whom they currently spend more leisure time), they expect to have saved more by the time this child enrols. Stated differently, since age of child is negatively related to amount of leisure time spent with that child, but positively related to amount of current savings, it produces a spurious negative relationship between amount of leisure time spent with a child and current savings. That parents expect to have saved more for the younger child by the time that child will enroll in a post-secondary educational institution also reflects the more stable financial situation the parents expect to enjoy by that time in their life stage.

We conclude that affective closeness, as measured here, has no direct effect on parental educational savings behaviour. The measure of affective closeness is too much affected by age of the child. As a consequence, the amount of time spent with a child is perhaps not a measure of emotional closeness but rather of how much time the child makes available to the parent. Hence the patterns of parental educational investments we observe here are precisely the same as those we documented for birth order.

Merit

Generally, academic merit refers specifically to the marks that students obtain in their schoolwork and to their academically relevant skills (often measured through tests of intelligence, literacy, and numeracy). We employ a broader definition that also includes a child's academic orientation, as indicated by liking schoolwork and surrounding themselves with friends who do well academically. Finally, because all of these factors likely contribute to the educational aspirations and expectations parents have for their children, we include these indirect components as well. These different aspects of merit are captured through the following questions:

- Academic performance: "Based on your knowledge of (child's) schoolwork, including report cards, how did he/she do *overall* in school?" The response options were "above average," "average," and "below average." Respondents were directed to focus on the child's performance in the last school year.
- Likes schoolwork: "How did (child) feel about his/her schoolwork?" Five response categories were provided ranging from "liked it very much" to "disliked it very much."
- Friends' academic performance: "Overall, did (child's) close friends do well in their schoolwork? (Yes/No)."
- Academic aspiration: "How far do (child's) parents/guardians *hope* that he/she will go in school?"
- Academic expectation: "How far do (child's) parents/guardians *expect* that he/she will go in school?" So that a reasonable basis for expectations existed, this question was asked only if the child in question was at least nine years old.
  For both of these questions, we ordered the available response categories from what we consider the lowest to the highest educational attainments as follows: "primary school," "secondary or high school," "learn a trade," "community college, technical college, or CEGEP," and "university."

The relationship of sibling differences on each of these indicators to parental educational investments is given in Table 7.3.

All five indicators of merit are related to parental educational investments in the expected direction, although not all the relationships are statistically significant. Of special note is that the most direct measure of academic merit shows among the weakest connections with parental savings. For example, parents are only one percentage point more likely to have begun savings for the child they see as doing better in school. Such a small difference might occur because many parents start their educational savings earlier, prior to knowing how well the child will do in school. Consistent with this possibility, we find a somewhat larger difference (3 per cent) with respect to whether they plan to make savings. Likewise, the difference in the amount they plan to save for the academically better-performing child is larger than for the amounts currently saved. Yet these differences remain relatively small. The

Table 7.3
Parental Educational Investments by Indicators of Differential Sibling Merit

	Saved	Planned	Amount	Amount expected
	(%)	(%)	$	$
Academic performance				
Lower	43**	70***	6,921	17,766
Higher	44**	73***	7,189	18,597
(N)	(1,805)	(1,805)	(535)	(437)
Likes school work				
Less	42	71**	6,397*	17,329*
More	43	72**	6,696*	18,171*
(N)	(2,195)	(2,195)	(637)	(523)
Friends' academic performance				
Less well	39	72**	6,709	16,741
Better	40	76**	7,057	17,465
(N)	(398)	(398)	(118)	(107)
Educational aspirations				
Lower	35***	63***	5,577**	15,429***
Higher	39***	70***	6,252**	17,683***
(N)	(1,042)	(1,042)	(253)	(196)
Educational expectations				
Lower	38**	66***	7,320	14,496***
Higher	41**	71***	7,859	16,774***
(N)	(848)	(848)	(214)	(187)

Source: SAEP (1999)

Note: Percentages and means are weighted at the household level but the number of cases are unweighted.

  * p < .05
 ** p < .01
*** p < .001

patterns are much the same for savings made for the children who differ in how much they like school as well as for those who differ in whether they surround themselves with academic peers.

On the other hand, sibling differences on the aspirations and expectations their parents have for them generally have sizable effects, especially on intended savings behaviours. For example, parents are seven percentage points more likely to expect to make savings, and expect to save $2,254 more on average (17,683–15,479 = 2,254), for the child for whom they have higher educational aspirations. Given that differential parental aspirations and expectations for their children play a substantial role in their educational investment behaviour, it is important to determine whether any gender difference occurs in this regard. We reported earlier that parents recognize that sons are less likely than daughters to perform above average academically. Hence it is not surprising that parents are more likely to expect their daughters rather than their sons to enrol in universities (68 per cent versus 60 per cent). Nevertheless, additional analysis provides no evidence that, at any given level of aspirations or expectations, one gender is advantaged over another. That is, where parental aspirations and expectations are comparable for sons and daughters, parental savings are also comparable (data not shown).[9]

That the most indirect measures of academic merit are the ones most strongly related to parental savings behaviours suggests that dynamics in addition to academic merit are at play here. The patterns documented above indicate that once parents have differentiated educational expectations and aspirations for their children, these differences have considerable effect on their intended savings behaviours. However, these differential aspirations and expectations seem not to be driven to any appreciable extent by their children's relative academic performance, since differences in this respect are only modestly related to parental savings behaviours. The puzzle that remains is on what other grounds do parents base their expectations and aspirations for their children.

Effort

Solid academic performance is easier for some children than for others, because of such factors as intrinsic ability. At the same time, some children, despite their ability, fail to realize their potential because of lack of effort. In this section we look specifically at whether parents are more apt to make educational savings for the child who is perceived to work harder. Four questions were asked to tap the extent of a child's academic effort:

- Working to potential: "How often did (child's) parents tell or remind (child) that he/she was not working to his/her potential?"
- Remind about homework: "How often did (child's) parents remind (child) to begin or complete homework?"
- Set limits on watching TV: "How often did (child's) parents decide how much television (child) could watch on school days?"
  For the above three items, four response categories, ranging from "very often" to "never" were provided.
- Amount of homework done: "In general, how much time did (child) spend doing homework?" Responses were recorded on a four-point continuum ranging from "a lot" to "none at all."

Table 7.4
Parental Educational Investments by Indicators of Differential Sibling Academic Effort

	Saved	Planned	Amount	Amount expected
	(%)	(%)	$	$
Working to potential				
Less	44	73*	6,448**	17,928**
More	44	74*	6,965**	19,033**
(N)	(1,772)	(1,772)	(525)	(433)
Remind about homework				
More often	43*	73**	6,529***	18,256
Less often	44*	75**	7,155***	18,615
(N)	(2,074)	(2,074)	(628)	(526)
Amount of homework done				
Less	42***	71***	6,423***	18,614
More	45***	73***	7,291***	18,699
(N)	(1,959)	(1,959)	(577)	(477)
Set limits on watching TV				
More often	43***	71***	6,420***	17,943
Less often	47***	74***	7,446***	18,165
(N)	(1,470)	(1,470)	(444)	(379)

Source: SAEP (1999)

Note: Percentages and means are weighted at the household level but the number of cases are unweighted.

 * $p < .05$
 ** $p < .01$
 *** $p < .001$

Table 7.4 shows the relationship of these measures of academic effort to parental educational investments. As can be seen, these measures are weakly but consistently related in the expected direction. Parents are more likely to make educational savings, plan to make educational savings, save more, and expect to save more for the child who is working closer to potential, needs fewer reminders about doing their homework, spends more time on homework, and requires fewer limits on watching TV. Although the patterns are consistent, the differences in parental savings behaviours are modest. At most there was a 4 per cent difference in having made educational savings (in favour of the child for whom limits on watching TV were less often necessary) and $1,105 in expected savings (for the child who was working closer to potential). Are these differences due to rewarding effort, or are they an indirect manifestation of the role of academic merit? There is some ground for concluding that merit accounts for some of these differences, since in general weak positive correlations were found between the measures of effort and the measures of academic merit. For example, the Pearson correlation coefficient of academic performance with working to potential is .31, and .24 with reminders about homework. The fact that parental savings are somewhat more strongly associated with differences in effort than with the direct measures of academic performance leads us to conclude that parents reward effort in addition to merit.

Need

Some children will likely be in greater need of parental financial contributions to their post-secondary education than others. Two factors determine their need: a) the costs associated with post-secondary education; and b) the resources that a child is expected to obtain from other sources, such as scholarships. Two indicators are available for assessing cost. First, respondents were asked "If (child) were to go on to post-secondary education, do his/her parents/guardians expect that he/she will live away from home?" We assume that a child living away from home will incur greater costs. Second, respondents were asked to estimate "the total cost of his/her education and living expenses." Respondents were asked to make these estimates in the light of whether the child was expected to live away from home or not. For other resources available to the child, respondents indicated whether or not they expected that the child would obtain "scholarships or awards based on academic merit," "grants or bursaries based on financial need," and "gifts or inheritances." All of these questions on need were asked only in those households where parents had already made educational savings or reported that they intended to make such savings, reducing still further the sample sizes. Hence the findings in this section are likely to be particularly unstable and the reported differences should be treated with caution.[10]

Both the anticipated cost of post-secondary education and whether the child is expected to live away from home show the expected results with the amount of money parents estimate they will have saved for their children's education (Table 7.5). That is, parents estimate they will have saved $2,468 more for the child whose educational costs will be higher, and $3,720 more for the child who will not live at home while pursuing post-secondary education. Yet these differences are not reflected in their current savings, since parents actually saved significantly less ($1,035) for the child whose post-secondary educational costs are anticipated to be higher, and there is no significant difference in the amounts saved if the child will live at home. From these patterns we conclude that parents intend to make their savings reflect the differential educational costs of their offspring but have as yet been unable to put these intentions into practice.

Table 7.5
Parental Educational Investments by Indicators of Differential Sibling Need

	Amount	Amount expected
	$	$
Anticipated cost of education		
Higher	7,413**	24,277***
Lower	8,448**	21,709***
(N)	(302)	(277)
Expect child will		
Live away from home		
No	9,294	18,472***
Yes	9,873	22,192***
(N)	(94)	(84)
Obtain a scholarship		
No	7,344	17,572
Yes	7,208	18,446
(N)	(226)	(194)
Obtain a bursary		
No	6,329	19,700
Yes	7,188	20,182
(N)	(93)	(73)
Obtain a gift or inheritance		
No	5,848**	23,573
Yes	8,693**	24,125
(N)	(55)	(50)

Source: SAEP (1999)

Note: Neither the percentages who made savings nor those who planned to make savings are reported in this table, since the various indicators of need were asked only of the sub-sample who had already made savings or who reported that they planned to make savings. Hence these percentages would be either misleading or meaningless. Means are weighted at the household level but the number of cases are unweighted.

  * p < .05
 ** p < .01
*** p < .001

The expectation of obtaining a scholarship or a bursary is not significantly related to parental educational investment behaviours. There is a large difference in current savings if a gift or inheritance is expected for one child but not for the other: savings are higher for the child for whom it was reported that they expect a gift or inheritance. Perhaps the gift or inheritance has already been given and is therefore included in the amount currently saved. In any event, in only 55 households is one child expected to obtain funds from such a source while the other is not, making generalizations in this respect hazardous.

DISCUSSION AND CONCLUSION

The design of the SAEP data obtained separate information about each of up to three children living in a household, which provided a rare opportunity to assess on what bases parents decide to distribute educational savings among their children. The difficult issue of families having to divide scarce resources is compounded by the fact that large nuclear families are faced with the challenge of providing for the educational costs of a greater number of children. Are educational savings divided equally between siblings or are savings more likely for children with certain characteristics, thereby disadvantaging post-secondary educational opportunities for those who do not possess these characteristics? If certain siblings are systematically disadvantaged, this jeopardizes the Canadian principle of equality of access to educational opportunities. The answer to this question has important policy implications, given that an ever-increasing share of educational expenses is being carried by parents. Our findings indicate that equality is by far the overriding feature of parental educational investments. Between 80 per cent and 90 per cent of the total variation in Canadian parents' educational savings are due to differences between families in their educational savings behaviour, rather than to differential treatment of siblings within the family. This implies that, at least with respect to educational policy issues, it is not unreasonable to treat the family as a single entity. That is, if a given family makes savings for one of their children, it is probable that they will make similar savings for the other children; vice versa, if parents fail to make savings for a given child, it is highly likely that they will also not make savings for the other children.

The amount of within-family variation in parental educational savings is nevertheless sufficiently large to empirically address the question of whether certain attributes of the children result in greater savings being made for them. Six types of sibling characteristics that we felt might form the bases for differential parental investments (gender, birth order, affective closeness, academic merit, academic effort, and need) were assessed. Although all of them were statistically related to parental educational savings behaviours, the patterns of the relationships suggest a rather different set of family dynamics. At the risk of being speculative, in this conclusion we will present what we consider the important underlying savings dynamics. First, and most important, is that unequal savings for children are primarily a function of two intertwined family life-course factors: the age of the parent and the age of a given child. These life-course factors affect parental savings in the following way: as attendance at a post-secondary institution becomes imminent for the first-born child, parents make savings for this child their priority. Hence, at a given point, they are more likely to have made savings, and to have saved more, for the first-born than for the younger children. However, this does not mean that the younger children will be disadvantaged. Indeed, just the opposite seems to be the case, since parents expect to have saved more for the education of their younger children. We suggest that this is because parents expect to be in a better financial situation by the time the younger children will attend a post-secondary institution. This implies that parents do not "choose" to invest more in the older or the younger children, but rather that they struggle to provide however much they can by using a longer time frame when making their investment plans. Educational savings are prioritized in terms of imminence of need and likely opportunities to make savings when their financial situation is more secure. Although their behaviour may ultimately result in larger savings being made for the younger children, this is not because the younger children are favoured, but simply because the familial financial resources will likely permit them to make greater savings later on in their life course. In short, the patterns suggest that, in the face of inadequate resources to meet all educational needs, parents dynamically balance current needs with anticipated future resources, rather than deciding to invest more in one child than in another. As a result, the patterns for current savings are often at odds with the anticipated savings. These inconsistencies are therefore more apparent than real. So, for example, younger siblings are at a disadvantage with respect to current savings but have an advantage with respect to anticipated savings. The same holds true for affective closeness; children whose parents spend more leisure time with them are at a disadvantage with respect to current savings, but not with respect to expected savings. These inconsistencies are resolved under the dynamic that we suggest underlies parental investment behaviours.

The second dynamic concerns the aspirations and expectations parents have for each of their children. Canadian parents in general hold extremely high aspirations and expectations for the education of their children. This commitment to the value of post-secondary education is as high as – if not higher than – those of the young people themselves (Thiessen, 1993). But when, for whatever reason, parents' expectations and/or aspirations are for one child to get a higher level of education than another, this is reflected in their savings patterns. What remains unclear is on what basis they come to have these differential desires and expectations. Whether one child does better in school or seems to like school more is certainly one factor, but it is a surprisingly small factor. Perhaps parents have distinct possible careers in mind for their children, and base their savings decisions primarily on the educational requirements of these careers, discounting to some extent the child's current academic performance.

The third dynamic is the parents' appraisal of the likely costs of the children's education and the likely resources that will be available to each of them. A minority of parents differentiates between the likely educational costs for their children. Those who judge that the costs will be greater for one child than for another also intend to save more for the child whose post-secondary education will cost more. Yet on average their intention has not been put into practice, since current incidence and level of savings are about equal for these siblings. This again suggests that parents of multiple children recognize the importance of making educational savings that are commensurate with the cost of post-secondary education but cannot, in the face of their day-to-day needs, implement their desired action.

A final dynamic concerns the parents' appraisal of the amount of effort their children put into their schoolwork. There is compelling evidence that parents invest more heavily in the sibling who is working closer to their potential, does more homework, does not have to be reminded about their homework as often, and does not need limits on watching TV as often. It is as though the norm of reciprocity is operating here, with parents in effect saying, if you work hard, we'll reciprocate by investing more in your education. This is the only basis on which it appears that parents actually "choose" to invest more in one child than another.

Note that parents invest equally in the education of their sons and daughters, while at the same time recognizing that daughters like school more, do better academically, and are more likely to attend a university than are their sons. At all levels of parental aspirations and expectations for their children's post-secondary education, investment in the education of their daughters is approximately equal to that for their sons. In the light of the continued lower earnings of women compared to men, and their greater likelihood of withdrawing at least temporarily from the labour market upon the arrival of children, this is just one of several findings that weaken the economists' argument that parents make their educational investments on the basis of the expected returns. Our findings, based on analyses of families with more than one child, suggest instead that parental educational investments are dynamically linked to a clear recognition and affirmation of the importance of post-secondary education for all of their children. This means that they plan their savings in a manner that they believe maximizes the possibility of all of their children participating in post-secondary education. In the face of limited resources, parents allocate their savings between their children primarily on temporal grounds, rather than on the basis of maximizing the return on their investment or on the basis of attributes that differentiate their children.

NOTES

1 This is based on the student's response to the question "How much financial assistance (in cash or gifts and support) did you receive from your parents or guardians in 1983?" (Students were asked to estimate the approximate dollar value of a variety of supports and gifts).

2 For policy purposes in the United States, "expected" parental contributions are determined on the basis of parental income and educational costs. The procedures used are referred to as "Congressional Methodology."

3 Further details on the sampling design and other technical aspects of the LFS are provided in Statistics Canada (2000).

4 The sample sizes reported here are for what is known as the shared file. The interviewers for Statistics Canada asked the respondents' permission to share the information with HRDC, and this permission was withheld for 1,548 children, representing a loss of 5.8 per cent of cases.

5 Savings information is not ascertained for a few families, and additionally there may occasionally be twins.

6 For the level 1 file on amount saved, all children for whom information on the amount saved was not reported were deleted (N = 1,907). This resulted in a drop from 18,805 to 16,998 children. Then all those who reported not making any savings (N = 10,941) were recoded as 0 for the amount saved. For the level 2 file, since some families failed to indicate the amount saved for a particular child, it was likely that some of these would have no children for whom there was information on the amount saved. Therefore such families were deleted. This reduced the number of households from 10,628 to 9,768. HLM on the amount saved was conducted with these 16,998 children distributed across the 9,768 families.

7 The figures reported here and in the remainder of this paper are based on household-weighted data.

8 Given the eligibility criteria for inclusion in the SAEP sample (e.g., the presence of children in the household who are 18 years of age or younger), it is not important to include a quadratic term for father's age to capture the diminishing returns generally found associated with earnings functions.

9 The one exception is for the small number of instances where parents have either aspirations or expectations for a child to enrol in trade school. In these cases, parents are less likely to save, and save smaller amounts, for daughters than for sons.

10 Some additional questions on other sources of financing for post-secondary education (such as the child working prior to and/or during their post-secondary studies, taking out loans, or interrupting their studies to work) were also asked of this sub-sample. However, the number of cases in which siblings were differentiated in these respects is too small to analyse. In addition, it is not clear whether children that are expected to work during their studies, for example, have greater or lesser need for parental support.

REFERENCES

Arrondel, L. and Masson, A. (1999). "Intergenerational transfers: The state, the market and the family." *Futuribles, 247*, 5–40.

Baker, M., Benjamin, D., Desaulniers, A., and Grant, M. (1995). "The distribution of the male/female earnings differential, 1970–1990." *Canadian Journal of Economics, 28*, 479–500.

Becker, G. and Tomes, N. (1976). "Child endowments and the quantity and quality of children." *Journal of Political Economy, 84*, 143–62.

– (1986). "Human capital and the rise and fall of families." *Journal of Labor Economics, 4*, 1–39.

Bowlby, J. and McMullen, K. (2002). *At a crossroads: First results for the 18 to 20-year-old cohort of the Youth in Transition survey.* Ottawa: Human Resources Development Canada, Statistics Canada.

Brinton, M. (1988). "The social-institutional bases of gender stratification: Japan as an illustrative case." *American Journal of Sociology, 94*, 300–34.

Choy, S. and Henke, R. (1992). *Parental financial support for undergraduate education.* National Postsecondary Student Aid Study, Research and Development Report. MPR Associates, Berkeley, CA. National Center for Education Statistics, ed. Washington, DC. Minnesota Private Coll. Research Foundation, St Paul. Lilly Endowment, Inc., Indianapolis, IN, District of Columbia, Minnesota.

Clignet, R. (1992). "Tuition and birth order: Higher education, heirship, and social change in America." *Wisconsin Sociologist, 29*, 107–24.

Coleman, M., Ganong, L., and Cable, S. (1997). "Beliefs about women's intergenerational family obligations to provide support before and after divorce and remarriage." *Journal of Marriage and the Family, 59*, 165–76.

Davis, Jerry S. (1977). "Paying for college costs: Does the student's sex make a difference?" *Journal of Student Financial Aid, 7*(3), 21–34.

Drolet, M. (2002). "Can the workplace explain Canadian gender pay differentials?" *Canadian Public Policy, 28*, S41–S63.

Finch, J. (1989). *Family obligations and social change.* Cambridge, U.K.: Polity.

Flint, T. (1997). "Intergenerational effects of paying for college." *Research in Higher Education, 38*, 313–44.

Gladieux, L. and Swail, S. (2000). "Beyond access: improving the odds of college success." *Phi Delta Kappan, 81*, 692–9.

Goldscheider, F. and Lawton, L. (1998). "Family experiences and the erosion of support for intergenerational coresidence." *Journal of Marriage and the Family, 60*, 623–32.

Greenhalgh, S. (1985). "Sexual stratification: The other side of 'growth versus equity' in East Asia." *Population and Human Development Review, 11*, 265–314.

Hertwig, R., Davis, J., and Sulloway, F. (2002). "Parental investment: How an equity motive can produce inequality." *Psychological Bulletin, 128*, 728–45.

Hossler, D. and Vesper, N. (1993). "An exploratory study of the factors associated with parental savings for postsecondary education." *Journal of Higher Education, 64*, 140–65.

Junor, S. and Usher, A. (2002). *The price of knowledge:Access to student financing in Canada.* Ottawa: Renouf.

Kidd, M. and Shannon, M. (1997). "The gender wage gap in Canada over the 1980s." In M. Abott, C. Beach, and R. Chaykowski, eds. *Transition and structural change in the North American labour market.* Kingston: Industrial Relations Press, Queen's University.

Lee, M.-J. (1998). "Gender and differential educational investment within the family." *Han'guk Sahoehak/Korean Journal of Sociology, 32*, 63–97.

Magee, P. (1998). *Symbol or structure: The effects of family structure on youth's education.* MA thesis, sociology. Acadia, Wolfville, Nova Scotia.

Modin, B. (2002). "Birth order and educational career: A study of school performance and achieved education of children born in early-twentieth-century Sweden." *Journal of Family History, 27*, 25.

Paulhus, Delroy L. (1999). "Birth order effects on personality and achievement within families." *Psychological Science*, November, 482.

Powell, B. and Steelman, L. (1995). "Feeling the pinch: Child spacing and constraints on parental economic investments in children." *Social Forces, 73*, 1465–86.

Rodgers, J. (2000). "Resolving the debate over birth order, family size, and intelligence." *The American Psychologist*, June, 599.

– (2001). "What causes birth order-intelligence patterns? The admixture hypothesis, revived." *The American Psychologist*, June/July, 505.

Stage, F. and Hossler, D. (1989). "Differences in family influence on the college plans of high-school males and females." *Research in Higher Education, 30*, 301–15.

Statistics Canada. (2000). *1999 Survey of Approaches to Educational Planning: Microdata users' guide for the shared data files.* Ottawa: Special Surveys Division, Statistics Canada.

Statistics Canada and the Council of Ministers of Education Canada. (2000). *Education indicators in Canada: Report of the pan-Canadian education indicators program, 1999.* Ottawa: Statistics Canada.

Steelman, L. and Powell, B. (1991). "Sponsoring the next generation: Parental willingness to pay for higher education." *American Journal of Sociology*, 96, 1505–29.

Thiessen, V. (1993). *Arguing with numbers: Statistics for the social sciences*. Halifax: Fernwood.

– (2001). *Policy research issues for Canadian youth: School-work transitions*. Ottawa: Human Resources Development Canada.

Thiessen, V. and Looker, D. (1999). *Investing in Youth: The Nova Scotia School-to-Work Transition Project*. Ottawa: Human Resources Development Canada.

Warren, J., Hauser, R., and Sheridan, J. (2002). "Occupational stratification across the life course: Evidence from the Wisconsin longitudinal study." *Amercian Sociological Review*, 67, 432–55.

Zvoch, K. (1999). "Family type and investment in education: A comparison of genetic and step-parent families." *Evolution and Human Behavior*, 20, 453–64.

8

The Effects of Region and Gender on Educational Planning in Canadian Families

PAUL ANISEF, GEORGE FREMPONG, AND ROBERT SWEET

While the government of Canada attempts to engage and prepare all Canadians for the emerging knowledge-based economy, concerns are raised over the differences between rural and urban communities, such as the absence of university education services in rural areas, which discourages parents from rural communities from preparing their children for a university education. Furthermore, the rising cost of post-secondary education and the increasing burden on parents to plan ahead for their child's post-secondary education decreases the chances of children from disadvantaged socio-economic backgrounds acquiring a post-secondary education. Recognizing the influence of a child's school outcome on parents' educational decisions, in this chapter we examine: differences between rural and urban families in educational planning for their male and female children; the effect of region (rural or urban), gender, and socio-economic status on university expectation; and how the university expectation of parents of a particular socio-economic background is informed by financial planning decisions, the availability of a post-secondary institution in close proximity, and the child's school performance and attitude.

Human Resources and Development Canada recently (2002) released a discussion paper, entitled *Knowledge Matters: Skills and Learning for Canadians*, that is intended to act as a catalyst for discussion on skills and learning in the twenty-first century. In this document, the government points to the knowledge-based economy as the source of an ever-increasing demand for a well-educated and skilled workforce in parts of the economy and in all parts of Canada. Among the factors identified are: a profound transformation in the ways we live and work as a result of the revolution in information and communications technologies and the rise of the global knowledge-based economy; skill change requirements among many conventional occupations; and the projection that, by 2004, more than 70 per cent of all new jobs created will require some form of post-secondary education and only 6 per cent of new jobs will be held by those who have not finished high school. The government declares that "By providing opportunities for all Canadians to learn and to develop their skills and abilities, we can achieve our commitment to economic growth and prosperity and demonstrate our social values of inclusion and equality" (1).

While Canada is described as a knowledge-based economy (KBE), some have argued that a KBE can be realized and sustained only within large urban metropolises. Other pundits disagree, arguing that contemporary rural Canada has become increasingly involved in the KBE, experiencing quick growth in high-knowledge occupations, an increasingly educated workforce, and a rise in computer and internet use (Industry Canada, 2000). Given the role played by post-secondary education (particularly university) in a KBE, it is important that we investigate whether parents in rural areas predispose their children to university education. Even more specifically, we need to distinguish the educational expectation levels of parents living in rural and urban areas of Canada. As Scott Davies documents in chapter 6, the sheer level of educational expectations held by Canadian parents signals a revolution of expectations. Contemporary levels, when compared to those in the past half century, match the "k-16" or "universal" stage of post-secondary expansion.

Any examination of the role played by parents in preparing children to enter a KBE must also account for major changes in student support policies. In the last decade Canadians have witnessed both an erosion of government funding to universities and colleges and a marked shift in student-support policies. Private costs for post-secondary education have consequently increased in relation to public costs. Private costs include not only monies earned by individual students and their families but also financial obligations in the form of direct loans and prepayment schemes in the form of Registered Educational Savings Plans. It is clear that as a consequence of government policies, parents now must assume greater responsibility for financing their children's post-secondary education. With this in mind, it is important that we determine whether there are rural-urban differences in the activation of financial capital by parents. Are parents in rural areas of Canada equally likely to invest in their children's post-secondary education in the form of total savings and RESPs?

The importance of a university education in a KBE coupled with substantial increases in the cost of a post-secondary education have prompted researchers in recent years to investigate issues surrounding university access. One factor of interest is the distance students must travel to gain physical access to a university. By way of illustration, Andres and Looker (2001) find that high school students from the late 1980s in Nova Scotia and British Columbia were less likely to attend university if they lived outside reasonable commuting distance (i.e., more than 80 km driving distance). A recent study by Frenette (2002) employs data from the Survey of Labour and Income Dynamics (SLID) to map the straight line distance between the homes of high school students prior to graduating and the nearest university (using postal codes). After controlling for family income, parental education, and other factors associated with university participation, students living outside commuting distance were less likely to attend than students living within commuting distance.

If students in lower-income families are unwilling to assume the heavier debt load, then the access gap across the income distribution may be larger among students living further away from university (Frenette, 2002, 1). In lieu of a distance variable, many researchers have employed a rural/urban dummy variable as a proxy in analysing university participation. However tempting, this variable remains imperfect in that some smaller urban areas may be outside commuting distance while some universities may be accessible to nearby rural residents. While the SAEP does not contain a specific measure of commuting distance to university, PMKs were asked whether they expected their children to live away from home while attending a post-secondary institution. We assume in this analysis that parents who plan for their children to attend university (and who indicate that their children will live away from home) understand that a university is beyond commuting distance.

Our intent in this chapter is to examine the selection of academic vs vocational pathways by a majority of students aged 9–18, none of whom were attending a post-secondary institution when the SAEP data were collected in 1999. More specifically, we seek to answer the following question: Why do a significantly lower proportion of rural than of urban children plan on attending a university? We first profile our working sample of children aged 9–18 by region and gender, in terms of educational planning by parents, socio-economic status, and children's attitude to school and school performance. The profile reveals that approximately 40 per cent of parents in rural and urban areas save for their children's post-secondary education and, in terms of total savings, there is little to distinguish rural and urban parents. When RESPs are examined, we find that rural parents are more likely to employ such savings for their female than for their male children, a finding that is reversed in urban settings. When we inspect school performance and school attitudes, rural females are found to achieve better results in school and possess more positive attitudes regarding schoolwork.

In the next stage, we acknowledge and investigate the influence of socio-economic status (SES) on post-secondary expectations, employing an index of SES composed of parental levels of formal education and income. An SES gradient analysis of university expectations that employs both region and gender shows few variations in university expectations at the high SES end. However, at low and middle ranges of SES we find significant variations in university expectations and these are strongly related to region and gender.

Given the results of this gradient analysis, we then employed a series of three logistic regression models, applied to the entire working sample and to the low and middle SES categories. In each instance, two main models were employed, with the first model including dummies representing rural males and females, and urban males and females, with rural males and the reference group. In the second model, we added variables that describe the ages of children, their school performance and attitude towards school, parents' financial planning (e.g., total savings, RESP savings), and whether parents anticipate that children will leave home to attend a post-secondary institution. The use of such models points to the efficacy of working with children of low and middle SES families to improve their school performance and attitude towards school. The regression analysis also documents the potential impact that an investment in RESPs by parents of comparable SES backgrounds and school outcomes could have on enhancing university expectations.

BACKGROUND

In this section we provide a context for understanding educational planning within families, some elaboration of how rurality has been conceptualized and operationalized in the research literature, and background information on the interconnections between gender and rurality.

Educational Planning

Educational and career planning is an important part of the high-school experience for virtually all adolescents, even those who leave or "drop out" before graduation (Jeffrey, 1996; Krahn, 1996). While the research on planning in schools is well documented in the career counselling literature, research on the educational planning processes that occur within families is limited and tends to focus on two aspects: the formation of post-secondary aspirations and the selection or choice of a college. Hossler et al. (1999) describe several models of college selection that incorporate the development of aspiration and the determination of a suitable post-secondary institution. Some of these are traditional rational-choice (economic) or status-attainment models, while the more recent formulations include cultural, social, and financial capital concepts.

The role of social, cultural, and financial capital is fundamental to educational progress. It is therefore essential to understand the role of capital as an important resource for children, as well as the structural factors that impede or facilitate a parent's ability to activate or construct capital. The socio-economic position of parents confers a distinct educational advantage on their children. To the extent that responsibility for their children's educational futures must be assumed by parents, it is important to better understand the effects of conditions such as region, gender, and socio-economic status on their ability to activate the various forms of capital required to ensure that their children are not excluded from the opportunities afforded by Canadian society.

Hossler et al. (1999) identified a number of issues related to the college choice process. Prominent in this list are questions about the family's capacity to finance their children's post-secondary education. In the Canadian context, it has been customary for students to take part-time or summer employment to relieve the family of the sole financial burden for their education. With widespread youth unemployment and rising tuition fees, increasing numbers of students and their families are unable to meet the financial requirements of full-time and continuous attendance. Among the many "side effects" of financial pressure on students is an increasing dependency on their parents as their attempts to make the transition from high school to some form of post-secondary education or training are delayed. While this has been recognized in the literature, little research has focused on the implications of prolonged dependency for adolescents and young adults (Schneider, 2000; Furlong and Cartmel, 1997).

In our analysis we consider parents' educational expectation levels. These are assumed to be similar to the aspirations parents initially formed for their children's educational future but have been modified in the light of the child's school performance. That is, expectations reflect a reasonably accurate assessment of children's academic potential and interest – based on information parents obtain from report cards and children's personal comments about their school experience. Parents' ability to gauge the most appropriate transition pathway for their children derives also from observations of activities such as homework and involvement in social, cultural, and sports activities in the community. Parents are seen to play an important role in encouraging their children's intellectual development as well as in fostering positive attitudes toward schoolwork.

The intentions and behaviours of parents and children must to some degree counter the influence of social context and structural features of the family on the formation of parents' expectations. Both structure and agency play important roles in shaping parents' expectations; they also have an indirect effect on other important facets of post-secondary planning, principally the commitment of parents to financially support their children's further education.

Region

It is important to bear in mind the significant differences in how "rural" is defined, both in conceptual terms and operationally, in official statistics provided by Statistics Canada. Different definitions lead to quite different classifications of people as either rural or non-rural, so that correlates of rurality will shift with different definitions (Looker, 2001, 1). The definition employed in this chapter is based on Statistics Canada's census, in which areas with a population of under 10,000, which are outside commuting zones for small cities or CMAs are seen as "rural."

The differences between urban and rural areas are more pronounced than simple variances in demography. The economic and social structures of communities vary significantly depending on numerous factors, such as the industrial, social, and cultural development of the region. The life course of rural residents is especially driven by their experiences within the social, economic, and cultural environment of the region.

In its *Annual Report to Parliament* (2000), the Ministry of Public Works and Government Services measures the quality of life in rural and remote Canada by examining such indices as geography, population, and employment, as well as economic and social well-being. While Canada's rural regions contain 31.4 per cent of the country's population, they employ only 29 per cent of the nation's workforce. The unemployment rate is generally higher in rural and small-town Canada, although the rate varies widely from province to province. However, the economy in rural Canada has recently become more diversified to match urban centres. The growth of manufacturing, trade, finance, communication, business and personal services, tourism, and transportation now accounts for a greater variety of employment opportunities in rural regions (Minister of Public Works and Government Services Canada, 2000, 2).

This past decade has also seen a dramatic change in rural economies and corresponding labour markets. The advent of the high-technology industry and the adoption of high-technology production and management methods are changing the education requirements for local jobs. The rural education system must remain competitive and meet the challenges of the new economy by better preparing its students for the higher-skill jobs coming to rural regions (Gibbs, 2000).

The average income of rural families tends to be lower than that of urban families. While rural households may pay relatively less tax, they pay more per household for transportation, food, and household operations. The average rural Canadian has less formal education than does an urban

Canadian, and rural Canadians are more likely to drop out of high school (Minister of Public Works and Government Services Canada, 2000, 3–4). Despite this, if we take into account family size and cost of living, fewer rural than urban families fall below Statistics Canada's low-income cut-off. Also, the proportion of low-income families living in rural areas is on a decreasing trend, while their incidence in urban areas has been increasing since the early 1990s (Looker, 2001, 3).

The rural education system is quite different from that of urban centres. The geographic location, small enrolment, and lack of specialized courses have had a significant impact on the decision to pursue higher education for some youth. It is evident from research on the subject that social, economic, and cultural differences between urban and rural society have helped to define parents' expectations and aspirations for their children regarding education and employment. The persistent gap in college attendance between urban and rural students in Canada can be attributed to a number of different economic, social, and cultural factors. The role of parents must also be considered in discussing the rural-urban gap in post-secondary attendance in Canada. Thus, Mackinnon and Looker (1999) find that parents of rural youth have lower educational aspirations for their children than do parents residing in urban areas.

Andres and Looker (2001) compare educational expectations and attainments of youth from metropolitan, urban/rural, and rural communities in British Columbia and Nova Scotia. Their findings suggest that students in rural areas have lower expectations and attainments compared to other students. Many other researchers have cited the reasons for this outcome. It is believed that students from rural communities have limited exposure to a wide range of educational and career opportunities because of differences in rural and non-rural labour markets (Dupuy et al., 2000; Haller and Virkler, 1993; Hektner, 1995; Sarigiani et al., 1990). "The aspirations and expectations of these individuals, particularly young people who are anticipating their adult roles, are constrained by what they define as available and possible" (Andres and Looker, 2001, 2). The decision to pursue an education or economic mobility is further complicated by what is perceived as the inevitable decision to leave family, friends, and community (Looker, 1993; Andres and Looker, 2001).

The federal government conducted a National Rural Workshop in 1998 to learn more about some of the key issues facing rural Canadians. Workshop participants stressed the limited opportunities available to rural youth in the areas of education and employment. It was suggested that youth do not feel confident about the future in their rural communities and that this was reinforced by the lack of optimism often expressed by parents. The workshop revealed a general lack of awareness among rural youth regarding the types of opportunities available to them. This was attributed to the absence of role models within the community and the lack of direction exhibited by parents and educators. The motivation to pursue a post-secondary education and favourable employment opportunities often depends on the encouragement of parents and their ability to manage family and work effectively (Government of Canada, 1999).

Gender and Region

Looker (1993) considers how both gender and geographic locale influence the transition from school to work. Her survey of youth in Hamilton, Halifax, and rural Nova Scotia provides insight into some of the reasons behind educational, occupational, and family plans. The unemployment rate for women in rural areas is generally higher than that for men. Her work reveals that few jobs in rural areas require post-secondary education, which accounts for the 60 per cent of women and only 38 per cent of men in rural Nova Scotia stating that they plan to attend university. Also affecting educational decisions is the fact that rural women tend to marry and have their children earlier than their urban counterparts.

Looker (1993) focuses on the apparent social cost associated with the transition to work for women and for rural youth. The men and women surveyed seemed to share a commitment to occupational attainment, but more women than men emphasized the importance of marriage and children. Most women believed that the presence of children would affect their career plans. The pattern most youth understand and follow is to first finish school, then find employment, and finally get married and have children.

The idea of family and settling down affects occupational plans quite differently for males and females, but rural women are more likely to stress the importance of family relationships. The ties to community make the decision to leave particularly difficult for rural women. The rural family is more likely to uphold traditional gender roles and stress the importance of family, while also endorsing the gender stereotyping of occupations. The academic potential of both male and female students, as well as the expectations of parents, strongly depends on a number of personal, structural, and institutional factors. The expectations they have for themselves regarding educational attainment and occupational mobility are influenced by personal and social constructions of gender identities, roles, and responsibilities. Any decision to pursue post-secondary education or training will undoubtedly be shaped by the individual response to these factors.

PERSPECTIVE

Social inclusion has become a popular topic for discussion and research amongst policy-makers, academic researchers, and civil society generally in recent times and the concept has been discussed under many names, including social cohesion, social integration, and its inverse – social exclusion. Klasen asserts that the goal of an inclusive society is for "people to have equal access to basic capabilities such as the ability to be healthy, well-fed, housed, integrated into the community, participate in community and public life, and enjoy social bases of self-respect" (Klasen, 1998, 1). This implies that the inability to participate in mainstream society is a violation of a basic right that should be open to all citizens and thereby places a burden on society to ensure that it supports the participation and integration of all its members (Klasen, 1998, 2). Duncan asserts that "social inclusion generates increased social capital and social exclusion reduces social capital, reduces the levels of trust required for a vibrant economy and a well-functioning society" ((Duncan, 2003, 31). Parents in both urban and rural areas make genuine efforts to activate social, cultural, and financial capital resources in preparing their children for post-secondary education. Despite such efforts, we find significantly lower university expectations among rural children and suggest the need for specific strategies that can enhance the participation of rural children in Canada's knowledge-based economy.

METHODOLOGY

Working Sample and Analysis

The selection of academic vs vocational pathways by a majority of students in Canadian schools occurs by grade 8. Thus, in using SAEP data to examine educational planning among parents, we have selected a working sample of children aged 9–18, none of whom was attending a post-secondary institution. We first profile our working sample by region and gender, in terms of educational planning (e.g., level of post-secondary education), socio-economic status, family (e.g., household income), and child (e.g., attitude towards school) characteristics. The profile of our working sample is presented in Table 8.1.

Educational planning activities include: saving status – whether a parent is currently saving for a child's post-secondary education; the total amount saved to the present; and for those not saving, whether they intend to save at a future time for their child's post-secondary education. Table 8.1 indicates that about 40 per cent of parents in both rural and urban areas are currently saving for their child's post-secondary education. Of those who are not currently saving, about 50 per cent intend to save in the future. The proportion of parents currently saving or who intend to save in the future is quite similar for both males and females irrespective of their region of residence. The total amount saved does not differ significantly by gender in rural and urban areas. In rural areas, approximately 13 per cent of parents had saved more than $5,000 for their male children compared to about 15 per cent for their female children. In urban areas, the percentages were approximately 16 and 17 per cent for males and females respectively.

Table 8.1
A Profile of Rural and Urban Children Aged 9–18

	Rural		Urban	
	Male (N=556)	Female (N=501)	Male (N=2441)	Female (N=2292)
Savings				
Status				
Yes	38.3	40.9	40.7	42.8
No	61.7	59.1	59.3	57.2
Future savings				
Yes	46.8	49.8	52.9	53.6
No	53.2	50.2	47.1	46.4
Amount				
$5,000 or above	13.4	15.2	15.7	16.9
Below $5,000	14.8	14.8	13.9	15.8
Unknown	71.8	69.9	70.4	67.3
RESP*				
Yes	31.6	25.3	36.6	39.1
No	68.4	74.6	63.7	60.9
RRSP				
Yes	90.4	89.7	88.5	88.9
No	9.6	10.3	11.5	11.1
Expectation				
Academic*				
University	38.4	49.3	55.7	64.3
College	24.8	28.3	21.5	20.3
Below college	36.8	22.4	22.9	15.4
Stay away from home for post-secondary ed.*				
Yes	44.7	48.1	21.5	21.5
No	9.7	9.6	30.5	31.9
Other responses	45.6	42.3	48.2	46.2
Family Characteristics				
Household income*				
$60,000 or more	25.8	26.3	41.0	38.9
$30,00 to $60,000	51.8	48.5	39.4	40.6
Less than $30,000	22.3	25.2	19.7	20.5
Mother's education level*				
University	11.9	10.0	20.9	19.2
Some post-secondary below university	40.5	40.7	36.5	38.6
No post-secondary	47.7	49.3	42.6	42.3
Father's education level*				
University	10.1	10.4	24.1	21.5
Some post-secondary below university	39.0	34.5	30.2	33.7
No post-secondary	51.0	55.1	45.8	44.7

Table 8.1
A Profile of Rural and Urban Children Aged 9–18 (continued)

Child Characteristics				
Age				
9–13	56.3	53.1	54.1	54.3
14–18	43.7	46.9	45.9	45.7
Academic Performance*				
Above average	34.5	49.9	38.6	51.4
Average	52.9	44.1	49.5	42.5
Below average	12.8	6.0	11.8	6.0
Attitude Towards School*				
Like or like very much	56.6	80.6	62.5	79.8
Neutral	23.1	10.5	20.5	11.4
Dislike, or dislike very much	20.3	8.7	16.9	8.8

Source: SAEP (1999)

Note: * Indicates chi square test of cross-tab distribution is statistically significant at P<0.05

When we examine RESPs (Registered Education Savings Plans), we find that a higher percentage of rural parents tend to save for their males – 31.6 per cent for rural males compared to 25.3 per cent for rural females. In urban areas this is reversed, with a greater proportion of parents employing RESPs for their female children rather than their male children – 39.1 per cent for females in contrast with 36.3 per cent for males. The percentage of parents using RESP savings for their child's post-secondary education is relatively small (about 10 per cent) in both rural and urban areas. These findings suggest that, for a typical child, being either male or female, or living in a rural or urban area does not make a significant difference in terms of the total savings parents allocate to their children's post-secondary education. However, the low RESP savings allocated by parents to female children living in rural areas limit their chances of attending university.

Our next analysis pertains to parents' educational expectations for their children and whether they expect their child to move away from home to attend a post-secondary institution. With regard to the level of educational expectations held by parents, Table 8.1 indicates significant differences by region and gender. While a higher proportion of parents in urban areas expect their child to attend university, in both regions parents are more likely to hold such expectations for their female rather than their male children. Many more parents living in rural areas of Canada anticipate that their child will leave home to attend a post-secondary institution. Thus, over 40 per cent of rural parents compared with about 20 per cent of urban parents anticipate that their child will leave home to pursue a post-secondary education.

When we examine the social and economic background of parents, we find that parents in urban areas have attained higher levels of education and earn more than their counterparts in rural areas. About 40 per cent of urban parents earn $60,000 or more, and about 20 per cent have had a university education. In contrast, approximately 26 per cent of rural parents earn $60,000 or more, and only about 10 per cent have had a university education.

Table 8.1 also provides a contrast between males and females with regard to parents' perception of their children's academic performance and attitude towards school. The analysis indicates that, in both rural and urban areas, parents perceive their female children as haring a more positive attitude towards school and attaining higher grades than their male children. By way of illustration, in rural areas, about 50 per cent of female children as compared with about 35 per cent of male children have above average academic performance; approximately 81 per cent of female compared to 57 per cent of male children liked school, according to their parents.

HOW SOCIOECONOMIC STATUS AFFECTS POST-SECONDARY EXPECTATIONS

Table 8.1 reveals a clear difference between rural and urban parents with regard to post-secondary expectations for their children, with a significantly larger proportion of parents living in urban areas anticipating that their children will pursue a university level education. Given that such expectations are generally influenced by parents' educational experiences and financial means, we anticipate that variation in post-secondary expectation across rural and urban areas will relate closely to the parents' socioeconomic status (SES). To explore this hypothesis we first construct an SES index and then analyse differences in the post-secondary expectations of parents living in rural and urban areas.

We constructed a socio-economic status index (SESINDEX) from a composite score of variables describing parents' educational background and household income. Educational background is defined in terms of three distinct categories (0 = no post-secondary education; 1 = post-secondary education below university; 3 = university education). Household income was divided into three distinct categories (0 = less than $30,000; 1 = $30,000 to $60,000; 2 = $60,000 or more). Note that in the SESINDEX, 0 indicates parents with no post-secondary education and less than $30,000 in total income, while 6 denotes parents with a university education and more than $60,000 in total income. Index scores between 0 and 6 represent a child in a family with a number of combinations of measures of the SESINDEX.

Table 8.2 presents the distribution of children by SESINDEX. It shows that approximately 32 per cent of children are at the lower end of the SESINDEX (0 or 1), while only about 15 per cent of children are at the higher end (5 or 6). Most are located in the middle of the distribution. The variation in university expectation by the SESINDEX is shown in Figure 8.1.

The graph presents a number of findings. In general, parents of high SES backgrounds are more likely than those from low SES backgrounds to expect their child to attend university. However, the strength of this relationship differs by region and gender. The relationship is particularly steep for rural males, suggesting that, for this group, the SES background of parents is particularly crucial in determining their children's chances of attending a university. For females living in urban regions the relationship is less steep, indicating that, unlike the case of rural males, the chances of females living in urban areas attending university do not particularly hinge on their parents' SES background. Figure 8.1 also illustrates the differential impact of region and gender on university expectation within households characterized by identical SES. Thus, in high SES households, there is no variation in university expectation based on region and gender. Much of the variation in university expectation is located within middle and low SES households, where parents are more likely to anticipate that female rather than male children will attend university. This is particularly the case in rural middle and low SES households where parents have very low university expectations for their male children.

WHAT ACCOUNTS FOR DIFFERENCES IN UNIVERSITY EXPECTATIONS?

Thus far, our analysis has demonstrated that greater proportions of parents living in urban areas anticipate that their children will pursue a university education. Furthermore, within rural and urban areas alike, parents are more likely to expect their female children to enrol in university. The variation in university expectations was particularly pronounced in low and middle level SES households. The next and final stage of our analysis employs logistic regression models to further understand variations in university expectations. To accomplish this objective we generate three such models – one that applies to the entire working sample and two that are applied separately to households classified as low SES and middle SES on our SESINDEX. The variables of note in these logistic regressions are: region, gender, age, school performance and attitude towards school, savings status and total amount saved, use of RESPs and RRSPs, and whether parents anticipate that their children will move away from home to attend a post-secondary institution. Given that the variation in university expectations is highest within low and middle level SES households, the comparison of the

Table 8.2
Distribution of Children by SESINDEX

SESINDEX	Frequency	Percentage
0	703	12.1
1	1163	20.1
2	1236	21.3
3	1036	17.9
4	763	13.2
5	465	8.0
6	426	7.3

Source: SAEP (1999)

Figure 8.1
Variation in University Expectation by Region, Gender,
and Socio-Economic Status

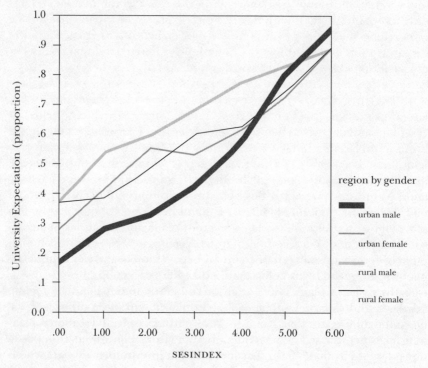

Source: SAEP (1999)

entire working sample model with the middle and low SES models provides important insights regarding the interplay of region and gender as these pertain to variation in university expectations.

The analysis presented in Table 8.3 involves the use of two main models with respect to the entire working sample and the low SES and middle SES groups. The first model includes dummies representing rural males and females, and urban males and females, with rural males as the reference group. In the second model, we add variables describing the age of children, their school performance, and their attitude toward school. The model also includes parents' financial planning for their child's post-secondary education, and whether they expect their child's post-secondary education to occur away from home.

The first model indicates that, compared to rural males, parents in urban areas are two to three times more likely to plan for their children to attend university. For low SES families in rural areas, parents are twice as likely to expect their female rather than their male children to attend a university. The difference in university expectations is not statistically significant for male and female children in middle SES households.

In the second model, the odds ratio for urban female children is reduced slightly, while the odds ratio for rural female children in the entire working sample is reduced to a statistically non-significant value. The ratio for the low SES group decreased from 2.0 to 1.5, suggesting that the model explains much of the variation in university expectations between males and females residing in rural areas. Table 8.3 further reveals that a child's school performance and attitude towards school make a difference to the level of parents' post-secondary expectations. The odds ratio for below average performance is 0.1 for the low SES group and 0.2 for the middle SES group. This finding indicates that, for children from low SES families, an increase in school performance from below average to above average is likely to increase their parents' university expectations ten times. Within middle SES families, parents' university expectations are likely to increase by a factor of 5. The odds ratio for "do not like school" is 0.6 for the low SES group and 0.3 for the middle SES group. This suggests that a change in a child's attitude towards school – from disliking school to liking school – is likely to raise their parents' university expectations by 70 per cent in the low SES group and by three times in the middle SES group.

As discussed in the previous analysis, compared to females, males in rural areas tend to have poor school performance and often dislike school. Our model indicates that, when we control for parents' educational planning, parents in rural areas tend to have comparable university expectations for their male and female children, presuming similar school performance and attitudes toward school. The immediate implication of this finding is that efforts to raise the chances of male children in rural

Table 8.3
The Effects of Child School Characteristics and Parents' Financial
and Other Educational Planning on University Expectation (Odds Ratio)

| | SESINDEX | | | | | |
| | (All-0, 1, 2, 3, 4, 5, 6) | | (0, 1, 2) | | (3, 4) | |
	I	II	I	II	I	II
Rural						
Male	–	–	–	–	–	–
Female	1.6*	1.2	2.0*	1.5*	1.4	1.00
Urban						
Male	2.0*	2.4*	1.9*	2.4*	1.7*	2.0*
Female	2.9*	2.6*	2.9*	2.7*	2.8*	2.4*
Child characteristics						
School performance						
Above average		–		–		–
Average		0.3*	–	0.4*		0.4*
Below average		0.1*		0.1*		0.2*
School attitude						
Like school		–		–		–
Neutral		0.6*		0.6*		0.6*
Do not like school		0.5*		0.6*		0.3*
Financial planning						
Status						
Yes		–		–		–
No		1.3		1.0		1.1
Amount						
$5,000 or above		–		–		–
Below $5,000		0.8*		0.8		0.9
Unknown		0.7*		0.7		0.9
RESP*						
Yes		–		–		–
No		0.6*		0.6*		0.6*
Other responses		0.8		1.4		0.4
RRSP						
Yes		–		–		–
No		1.1		1.0		1.1
Other responses		0.8		0.4*		1.5
Move from home for post-secondary education						
Yes		–		–		–
No		0.6*		0.5*		0.7*
Other responses		0.6*		0.6*		0.8
Age						
9–13		–		–		–
14–18		0.8*		0.8*		0.8*
R-square (percentage)	2.4	19.6	2.5	16.1	2.4	16.5

Source: SAEP (1999)
Note: * = p < .05

areas attending university should emphasize policies and processes that will not only raise their school performance but also develop a positive attitude towards school.

When we examine parents' educational planning, we find that, for low and middle SES families, RESP savings and an understanding that children may need to leave home to pursue post-secondary studies significantly contribute to the development of university expectations by parents. For the analysis of RESPs, the reference group is those who responded that they have RESP savings for their child. The odds ratio for those who responded "no" to RESP savings is 0.6, indicating that an RESP is likely to increase parents' university expectations by about 67 percent.

In analysing the influence of children leaving home to pursue their post-secondary studies, "move away from home" was designated as the reference group. The odds ratio, 0.5 for those in the low SES group who responded "no" to "move away from home," and 0.7 for those in the middle SES group, indicates that low SES parents who anticipate that their children will leave home are twice as likely to expect their child to attend university, while for middle SES parents, those expecting their children to leave home are 42 per cent more likely to anticipate that their children will enrol in university. These findings suggest that after controlling for school performance and school attitude, parents living in rural areas who invest in RESPs, and encourage their children to move away from home to attend a post-secondary institution, increase their children's chances of attending a university.

We included age as a dummy variable (0 = age 9–13, 1 = 14–19) in our model with the 9–13 age group as the reference group. The odds ratio of 0.8 indicates that parents' expectations that their children will enrol in university tend to decrease as their children grow older. This effect remains after controls for student performance and attitude to school are introduced, suggesting a need for further research to understand parents' lower university expectations for older children.

The R-squared indicated that our full model for low and middle SES group accounted for about 16 per cent of the total variation in parents' university expectations, suggesting that other explanations besides those offered by this model should be explored in further studies.

CONCLUSIONS AND POLICY IMPLICATIONS

Our analysis of regional variations in parents' educational plans is consistent with previous studies that document the greater likelihood of parents living in urban areas planning on a university education for their children. In rural and urban areas alike, parents anticipate that a greater proportion of their female children will attend university. These expectations are consistent with the higher academic performance and the more positive attitudes displayed by female children towards school.

After creating an SES index consisting of a composite measure of parental level of education and household income, we tested and confirmed a positive relationship between SES and the development of university expectations on the part of parents. Using a gradient analysis approach, we revealed that this basic relationship does differ by region and gender in ways that suggest policy considerations that could enhance university access. For those at the high end of the SES index, we see few gender or regional differences in the development of university expectations by parents. Such variations are quite marked when we inspect low and middle ranges of the SES and are strongly linked to gender. We also know from our regression analysis that parents within low and middle SES families respond to increases in children's school performance and positive attitude towards school. Thus, efforts within schools to enhance the school performance of low and middle SES children would yield substantive increases in university expectation levels. Such efforts need to be encouraged. Strategies for enhancing school performance and fostering more positive school attitudes among low and middle SES children should be developed. Given that male children in rural areas are least likely to be positive about their schooling and most likely to perform below average, special initiatives should target this group.

While there are no regional differences in savings status and the total amounts parents save for their child's post-secondary education, parents living in rural areas are less likely to invest in RESP savings than parents residing in urban areas of Canada. Within rural areas, male children are particularly advantaged with regard to their parents' use of RESPs as a post-secondary savings strategy. Regression analysis reveals that, for children from families of comparable SES backgrounds and with similar school outcomes, an investment by parents in RESPs increases the chances of their children attending university by 67 per cent. Bearing this in mind, efforts should be made within rural regions to encourage parents to increase the use of RESPs for their female children.

Many more parents living in rural communities anticipate that their child will need to leave home to pursue a post-secondary education and particularly a university education. More than twice as many rural parents indicated that their children would move away from the community to study at a post-secondary institution. Within both low and middle SES rural families, the indication that children will leave home proves to be a good marker of university expectations. However, the increased costs of higher education, ample evidence for which is provided in chapter 4, mean that this decision by rural parents will serve to increase their economic disadvantage in future years. Our analysis shows that rural families are no more likely to invest in post-secondary savings for their children than urban based families. The household income of rural families is significantly lower than that of urban families. If rural children are to develop the skills and abilities needed in a knowledge-based economy they will need the level of post-secondary education that their parents appear motivated to provide. Given the burgeoning costs of post-secondary education in Canada, strategies must be formulated to ensure that participation rate gaps based on region will decrease.

The findings in this chapter emphasize the need to improve social inclusion opportunities for children in rural areas of Canada through improved educational opportunities. This may be especially important for female children. We suggest a number of specific policy directions that could be considered to help achieve the goal of greater equity in post-secondary participation. If educational opportunities for children and their realization in the form of improved life chances are to be improved, new policy directions must be articulated at the level of the state, the community, the school, and the home. Efforts to alter only one level do not recognize the complexity of social inclusion and the need to implement change at all levels of our society if we are to witness marked improvements in the life chances of children. Efforts must recognize the importance of bridging forms of social capital for improving social inclusion of rural children (Kunz, 2003, 33).

Role of the State

- Different levels of government – federal, provincial, and municipal – should be informed of the regional and gender differences revealed by this chapter and a task force struck to consider specific recommendations for increasing the educational opportunities and life chances of children residing in rural areas.
- Strategies for enhancing the financial capital (savings and RESPs) available for children's educational future need to be developed at appropriate levels of government – in particular, affordable saving plans for parents with economically disadvantaged backgrounds.
- In addition to these strategies, information brochures should be prepared and circulated among rural households; these should inform parents of the value of and means available for investing in their children's post-secondary education – both male and female. Information packages detailing strategies for helping parents to realize these goals for their children should be made available and distributed.

Role of the Community

- Community programs geared to children and youth must also involve parents. Youth initiatives, generated by local communities and designed to enhance the active development of talents and skills among rural youth, should be supported. In addition to sports facilities and programs, investment in cultural activities is important.

• Community programs are required to provide children and youth with opportunities to explore their educational futures and job opportunities. Directed educational future planning through trips to post-secondary educational institutions and the provision of job-related information in print and media form should be explored. Public institutions such as community agencies can offer youth valuable service-work experiences.

• While the rural economy is not robust, those occupations that are available – often in the small manufacturing and high-tech sector – can provide valuable job experience. Local employers can help young people shape their occupational aspirations through such programs, especially when they are coordinated with schools.

Role of Schools

• Principals, teachers, and counsellors should be encouraged to play a more proactive role in rural communities with regard to the educational and career futures of children, working inclusively with family members and other agencies in the community.

• Schools should develop active and inclusive strategies to encourage the participation of parents in their children's schooling and permit educational planning by parents to respond more sensitively to children's performance outcomes.

• An adequate curriculum should be created to address the needs of all students, to ensure students' completion of high school and the pursuit of post-secondary education for those with the requisite competencies.

REFERENCES

Andres, L.P. and Looker, E.D. (2001). *Rurality and capital: Educational expectations and attainments of rural, urban/rural, and metropolitan youth. Canadian Journal of Higher Education, 31*(2), 1–46.

Frenette, M. (2002). *Too far to go? Distance to school and university participation.* Analytical Studies Research Paper, No. 191. Ottawa: Statistics Canada. Retrieved August 2004, from http://www.statcan.ca/cgi-bin/downpub/listpub.cgi?catno=11F0019MIE

Furlong, A. and Cartmel, F. (1997). *Young people and social change: Individualization and risk in late modernity.* Buckingham: Open University Press.

Gibbs, R. (2000). "The challenge ahead for rural schools." *Forum for Applied Research and Public Policy, 15*(2). Retrieved 4 August 2003, from http://web.utk.edu/~enr/spotlights/mccarthy.htm

Government of Canada (1999). *Rural solutions to rural concerns: National rural workshop, final report.* Ottawa: Government of Canada. Retrieved 6 August 2003, from http://www.rural.gc.ca/nrw/final_e.html

Haller, E. and Virkler, S. (1993). "Another look at rural-nonrural differences in students' educational aspirations." *Journal of Research in Rural Education, 9*(3), 170–8.

Hektner, J. (1995). "When moving up means moving out: Rural adolescent conflict in the transition to adulthood." *Journal of Research in Rural Education, 11*(1), 3–14.

Hossler, D., Schmitt, J., and Vesper, N. (1999). *How social, economic, and educational factors influence the decisions students make.* Baltimore: The Johns Hopkins Press.

HRDC (2002). *Knowledge matters: Skills and learning for Canadians.* Executive summary. Ottawa: Human Resources Development Canada.

Industry Canada (2000). "Rural Canada in the knowledge economy, policy analysis." Retrieved 20 August 2003, from http://strategis.ic.gc.ca/pics/ra/sp00q4_e.pdf

Jeffrey, F. (1996). *After high school: The first years. The first report of the high school leavers follow-up survey, 1995.* Human Resources Development Canada Catalogue No. LM-419-09-96. Ottawa: Minister of Public Works and Government Services Canada.

Klasen, S. (1998). *Social exclusion and children in OECD countries: Some conceptual issues.* Munich: Department of Economics, University of Munich.

Krahn, H. (1996). *School-work transitions: Changing patterns and research needs.* Ottawa: Applied Research Branch, Human Resources Development Canada.

Kunz, J. (2003). "Social capital: A key dimension of immigrant integration." *Canadian Issues.* Toronto: Immigration: Opportunities and Challenges, Metropolis Project.

Looker, D. (1993). "Interconnected transitions and their costs; gender and urban/rural differences in the transitions to work." In P. Anisef and P. Axelrod, eds. *Transitions: Schooling and employment in Canada.* Toronto: Thompson. 43–64.

– (2001). *Policy research issues for Canadian youth: An overview of human capital in rural and urban areas.* Ottawa: Applied Research Branch, Human Resource Development Canada.

Mackinnon, D. and Looker, D. (1999). *Under the influence: The role of significant other in youths' occupational and educational choices.* Paper presented to the Fourth National Congress on Rural Education, Saskatoon, SK.

Minister of Public Works and Government Services Canada (2000). *Working together in rural Canada: Annual report to parliament.* Retrieved 5 August 2003, from http://www.rural.gc.ca/annualreport/2000/charact_e.html

Sarigiani, P., Wilson, J., Petersen, A., and Vicary, J. (1990). "Self-image and educational plans of adolescents from two contrasting communities." *Journal of Early Adolescence, 10*(1), 37–55.

Schneider, J. (2000). "The increasing financial dependency of young people on their parents." *Journal of Youth Studies, 3,* 5–20.

9

Family Structure, Child Well-being, and Post-Secondary Saving: The Effect of Social Capital on the Child's Acquisition of Human Capital

JAMES M. WHITE, SHEILA MARSHALL,
AND JAMIE R. WOOD

Families play an important role in shaping children's educational and social adjustment and subsequent attainment. A source of variation between family environments that is frequently included in assessments of children's academic and social outcomes is family structure. This chapter focuses on the argument that family structure predicts children's academic and social adjustment and that parents of children who are doing well socially and academically are more likely to save for their children's post-secondary education. We employ Coleman's (1990) rational choice theory to develop a conceptual model and then test the proposed relationships with data from the Survey of Academic and Educational Planning (SAEP). Embedded in this work is a challenge to the assumption that family structure is of significant import to children's academic and social adjustment and future attainments.

To those interested in research on familial influences on child educational outcomes (e.g., Dunifon and Kowaleski-Jones, 2002), child adjustment (e.g., Carlson and Corcoran, 2001; Lipman, Offord, Dooley, and Boyle, 2002), and policy (e.g., Baker and Tippin, 1999), family structure is frequently viewed as quite important. The interest in family structure appears to emerge from the consistent statistically significant findings that children do not fare as well in single-parent families as in dual-parent families. Such consistency has led to the tendency for researchers to systematically use family structure as a control variable in multivariate models predicting child outcomes (e.g., Willms, 2002) or focus on structure as a context for children's adjustment (e.g., Bankston and Caldas, 1998). For those interested in the development and implementation of policy, the consistency of the research findings and the ability to focus on a portion of the population to reduce the vulnerability of children has been enticing. North American policy-makers have been interested in developing interventions to ensure that children in single-parent families can enjoy the same salutary outcomes as children in dual-parent families. Ideas about how to ameliorate the effects of living in single-parent families have ranged from getting single mothers on welfare in the United States to marry (*Vancouver Sun*, A4, 8 April 2002) to assisting Canadian single mothers to become self-sufficient through employment training (Mijanovich and Long, 1995).

We believe that the use of family structure to explain child adjustment is questionable on several fronts. The purpose of this chapter is to illuminate some central theoretical and conceptual problems associated with linking family structure to child outcomes such as educational attainment or achievement. In particular, we address the following: (a) whether family structure can be defined and whether there is an adequate theory to explain the effects of family structure on children's well-being; (b) whether family structure has a ubiquitous effect on all child outcomes and, if not, which child outcomes family structure should predict; and (c) what are the mechanisms by which family structure influences children, particularly children's academic and social adjustment. The discussion of these issues is followed by the development of a conceptual model to guide empirical research using the SAEP data. The analysis of the data is useful in discerning whether the issues we highlight are critical to future research on families and children's academic and social adjustment and of import to the development of social policy in Canada.

THE CONCEPT OF FAMILY STRUCTURE

Although some scholars (e.g., Coleman, 1990) approach family structure as a relatively unambiguous concept, we do not. The idea of family structure is not clearly defined in either the contemporary research or theoretical literature: the broad gamut of meanings span from simply being the "membership of the family" to "social roles in the family" to "conflict in the family" to "divorce in the family." Family structure first emerged as a key theoretical construct in the functional theory of the 1950s. Family structure was referred to as role structure and was theoretically tied to Freudian psychodynamics (Parsons and Bales, 1955). In these early developments the family with a full set of role relationships was viewed as complete, since it contained the full complement of role relationships by gender and power (father-son, father-daughter, mother-son, mother-daughter, husband-wife). This perspective on complete versus incomplete family role relationships gradually permeated the study of the family. Thus, it was not surprising to find Rodgers (1973) discussing families without the father-husband role as an example of families that are "deficit in structure" (1973, 196). Social demographers adopted a similar perspective, as suggested by the title of Andrew Cherlin's (1978) paper "Remarriage as an incomplete institution." With little doubt, the dominant perspective since the 1950s has been that the intact biological family represents not just the best but also the most "normal" situation for children.

Research in several areas has challenged this conception. One area of inquiry has been the effect of divorce on children. Certainly in the beginning, authors such as Heatherington, Cox, and Cox (1982) argued that divorce has a significant negative impact on children. However, as research has become more sophisticated, the study of these negative effects and their causes has brought into question the superficial view that children in non-intact or non-biological families are destined to have difficulties. For example, results from Amato, Loomis, and Booth (1995), Amato and Booth (1997), Hanson (1999), and Jekielek (1998) suggest that when there is high chronic marital conflict, youth might experience more salutary outcomes if divorce ends the conflict. Acock and Demo (1994) also point out that some negative effects attached to single-parent family structures are due to continued conflictual interactions with the previous spouse and may only subside when one parent finally remarries. This perspective clearly views causal efficacy as abiding in interactional processes rather than in the family structure. Indeed, certain types of interactional processes can continue through transitions to different family structures (e.g., intact to single parent) (Duncan and Brooks-Gunn, 1997; McLanahan, 1997; Cherlin et al., 1998).

Which Measure of Family Structure?

Empirical research on family structure itself challenges the prevailing perspective that family structure is unambiguous. The challenge comes from inconsistent operationalizations of the construct. Researchers investigating family structure have measured the construct in numerous ways. For example, Thomson et al. (2001) represent a minimalist approach by using "intact partnership" and "disrupted partnership." However, some researchers want to further distinguish whether the single-parent structure results from divorce or widowhood (Acock and Demo, 1994). Such analyses interject the criteria of types of life-course events or transition into the measure of structure. Additionally, multiple transitions or life-course events can be considered rather than assessing a single "state." For example, Carlson and Corcoran (2001) analyse transitions between two-parent and single-parent structures over time.

Although many researchers concerned with family structure consider the marital status of parents (never married, intact, or disrupted), others focus on the type of parent-child relationship (adopted or biological). For instance, Lansford et al. (2001) use a detailed measure of family structure that includes adoptive, two-parent biological, single-mother biological, stepfather, and stepmother families. Similarly, Biblarz and Gottainer (2000) use two biological parents, single mother divorced, single mother widowed, mother-stepfather due to divorce, and mother-stepfather due to death.

The diversity of measures should lead us to reflect on the definitional clarity and accuracy of the concept "family structure." While many researchers assume that family structure is a theoretically important construct few delve very deeply into the theoretical import of the concept. Two exceptions are found in the work by Biblarz and Gottainer (2000) and Lansford et al. (2001). Biblarz and Gottainer review five different theoretical models that provide distinct interpretations of the concept of family structure: family structure model, household economic model, evolutionary model, parental fitness model, and marital conflict model. Although Biblarz and Gottainer attempt to clarify thinking in this area, the links between their models and the extant theoretical schools (White & Klein, 2002; Boss et al., 1993) are ambiguous. Furthermore, their models do not portray structure as inherent in theory so much as being spuriously associated with other causal variables. For example, the household economics and evolutionary models focus on economic resources that are external to the notion of structure.

Lansford et al. attempt to divide influences on child outcomes into two-parent socialization, biological ties, and family processes. They conclude "we found the most support for the perspective suggesting that processes occurring in all types of families are more important than family structure in predicting well-being and relationship outcomes" (2001, 850). This builds on the work by Acock and Demo (1994) and Demo and Acock (1996) that suggests family structure, net of internal family process variables, accounts for small proportions of variation in child outcomes while the process variables account for more variance.

Which Child Outcomes Does Family Structure Predict?

Few scholars have directly addressed the issue of discerning the specific child outcomes that family structure predicts. If family structure or, for that matter, family processes have an effect on child outcomes, should we assume that the same family structure (intact) or family process (type of parenting) always has the same effect across all the various domains of child outcomes (e.g., behavioural, academic, physical, and psychological well-being)? We doubt that such a consistent outcome is likely. Our doubt is founded on the social domain perspective (Smetana, 1997) and research on changes in parenting strategies as children age. Parents and children generally do not view parents as having equal authority across all domains of children's lives or across ages of children (Collins and Luebker, 1994). Parents view their authority over their adolescent children as dependent on the conceptual domain or issue (e.g., personal safety or social conventions) (Smetana, 1995). The variance in beliefs about parenting by the conceptual domain stands to reason. Why would a parent use the same parenting strategies under all conditions (e.g., ensuring child safety versus learning to read)? Similarly, discipline strategies alter with the age of the child (Dunn and Munn, 1987; Kuczynski et al., 1987). Children tend to corroborate the variance in parenting strategies across domains and age. Children's views of the legitimacy of parental authority vary according to the social domain and the specific acts (Smetana, 1997).

On the surface it would seem unlikely that any one cause, such as family structure, would have robust and consistent positive or negative effects across domains of child outcomes at various ages and stages of development. As McLanahan (1997), among others, has argued, family structure might explain certain variables, while income-based resources might be associated with outcomes such as children's academic performance.

Finally, it is critically important to explain why family structure influences children's behaviour (e.g., school engagement) or mental processes (e.g., self-esteem). There is an empirical association but it could be spurious. Good empirical research and policy-making should rely on substantive explanations. Can we adequately explain the mechanisms by which family structure affects children's behaviour in specific domains? For example, can we articulate the mechanisms by which family structure differentially influences academic achievement and school-based social adjustment?

In summary, we believe that improved theoretical development regarding the concept of family structure is required. This development should address how family structure influences child outcomes and should identify the specific child outcomes that family structure can predict.

Which Theory?

Researchers have used a host of mini-theoretical models to inform their research hypotheses about the effects of family structure on children's adjustment. In this sense, the area is far from atheoretical, but this does not imply that it is theoretically or conceptually clear. As we have previously discussed, the models used by researchers vary greatly: for example, Biblarz and Gottainer (2000) employ a "parental fitness model" and a "marital conflict model"; Lansford et al. (2001), on the other hand, use "primacy of biological ties" and "two parents as optimal." Such perspectives often confuse various elements of role theory, functionalism, and socio-biological theory.

To test such competing models, clear operational distinctions need to be made between roles, biology, and resources.

For derivations about family structure to make sense, the concept of family structure should be contained within the theory. However, a careful review of the extant theories in the area of the family (Boss et al., 1993; White and Klein, 2002) reveals that most current family theories do not incorporate the notion of family structure.

Among the few theories that have incorporated a well-developed notion of family structure is "structural-functionalism," which detailed this concept almost fifty years ago in the work of Parsons and Bales (1955). Not only do Parsons and Bales develop the concept of family structure in some detail they also tie it to child outcomes. It seems clear, however, that most contemporary scholars do not consciously utilize the Parsons and Bales' perspective or the psychodynamic underpinnings of this perspective in their research.

The only other theory that deals directly with family structure is the approach offered by Coleman (1990) and other rational choice theorists (e.g., Becker, 1981). This theory not only incorporates the notion of family structure but also explains why it has an effect on children. Child outcomes are an expression of the child's human capital (knowledge and skills). Such human capital is more readily acquired when the child is part of a stable and intense social network with adults. Thus, parents and family structure are forms of social capital that lead directly to the child's acquisition of human capital and success. This is often viewed as a form of investment in the success of children.

INVESTING IN CHILDREN

The investment in children framework (Haveman and Wolfe, 1994) argues that the present cohort of adults should be concerned with the well-being and success of the current cohort of children, if for no other reason than the desire of adults to see their society continue to prosper as they enter old age and greater social dependency. The success of children as a cohort is closely tied to the continued prosperity of the society on which these adults will depend. Thus, adults should invest in the success of children as the succeeding generation (hence the double entendre of the title of Haveman & Wolfe's book *Succeeding Generations*).

The Haveman and Wolfe argument clearly invokes the economic self-interest of adults and as such it can be identified with a framework known variously as social exchange, rational choice, microeconomics, and utilitarianism (White and Klein, 2002). Some versions (notably Coleman, 1990, and Becker, 1981) have broadened the limited economic perspective of this theoretical framework by the addition of concepts of different forms of capital. The framework sees rational actors making economic and social choices favouring one form of capital acquisition rather than another. For example, Haveman and Wolfe state:

in our view the success of a child is determined by three primary factors: the *choices made by society*, primarily the government, regarding the opportunities to children and their parents (the social investment in children); the *choices made by the parents* regarding the resources to which their children will have access (the "parental investment in children"); and the *choices that the child makes* given the investments in and opportunities available to him or her (Haveman and Wolfe, 1994, 26).

Rational Choice and Types of Capital

A critical tenet of the investment framework is that actors behave rationally. That is, between various options, actors choose the option that they perceive as supplying the greatest rewards relative to costs. When there are only costs, actors seek to minimize costs. In classical economic theory, the ability to act rationally depends on unconstrained choices and information. As a result, two actors sharing identical values regarding rewards and given the same information and the same options would make identical choices. Thus, the differences between actors' choices are explained by differences in values, information, or external constraints such, as laws or regulations (White and Klein, 2002).

Capital refers to a broad category of resources. However, capital resources differ from general wealth in that capital is used to further production of wealth and resources. Physical capital is a familiar concept of lengthy heritage in economic theory and social theory. This form of capital refers to the physical objects that are the means by which one can produce marketable goods and services. Financial capital is also a well-known term that refers to the money or other medium of exchange one might possess. To these two forms of capital, the framework has added the newer concepts of human capital and social capital.

HUMAN CAPITAL
According to Coleman, "human capital is created by changing persons so as to give them skills and capabilities that make them able to act in new ways" (1990, 304). Common sources of human capital would be educational institutions and information media. However, the medium is not the capital. Human capital refers to the knowledge and skills acquired by the individual. For example, two individuals completing university degrees in the same area might have different degrees of human capital based on what they actually learned. It is not uncommon, however, to find that our

measures of human capital rely on assumptions about its acquisition as indicated by years of formal education or training.

SOCIAL CAPITAL

Social capital is created when the relations among persons change in ways that facilitate action (Coleman, 1990). Social capital is a much more abstract concept than the other types of capital because it refers to the network of relationships with others. Within this network reside the potential and actual exchanges that allow for the acquisition of the other, more concrete types of capital: human, physical, and financial. For example, if two groups have the same number of members, and are equal in regard to other forms of capital, the group with the greatest trust among its members should be able to achieve more than groups with less trust (Coleman, 1990).

An example using child outcomes might help to clarify the distinction. If we imagine a parent-child dyad where the relationship between them is diagrammed as a line and the individuals are points, human capital would reside in the points while social capital would be represented by the line. As Coleman suggests, social capital and human capital are often complementary. For example, if B is a child and A is the parent of B, then for A to further the cognitive development of B, there must be capital in both the node and link. Human capital must be held by A and social capital in the relation between A and B. (1990, 304).

Social capital clearly resides in the network of social relations. One particularly important corollary to this perspective is that the type of network has properties that either favour or disfavour the amount of social capital. In other words, the amount of social capital is not simply assigned by the number of members or nodes in the network but by other properties. Coleman (1990) lists three major properties among the many possible properties that might influence the strength of a group's social capital: closure, stability, and ideology. Closure is a property of a group that allows for the emergence of group norms and social control reinforced by all members. For a network to have the property of closure every member must be related to other members directly or indirectly. As we will see later, closure is especially important for understanding family structure. Stability of the network promotes trust and long term exchanges. The ideology of the group is important because, for example, groups with highly individualist ideology will manifest less social capital than more collectivist groups. All three properties have important implications for the social capital we find in families.

Family as Social Capital

For most children, the family is the single most important source of social capital. The social capital of the family provides the child with choices in acquiring human capital. However, the inverse of this proposition is even more important; that is, the social capital inherent in the strong relation between an adult and the child is important or necessary for the development of the child (Coleman, 1990).

The three properties of networks predict the amount or degree of social capital. A collectivist ideology would predict the concern and investment of other members in the child's well-being as part of the collective. The stability of the group is clearly important for the child's development of trust and feeling of security. Closure requires a more detailed analysis. Coleman describes the effects of network closure on children in the following passage: "Closure is present only when there is a relation between adults who themselves have a relation to the child. The adults are able to observe the child's actions in different circumstances, talk to each other about the child, compare notes, and establish norms. The closure of the network can provide the child with support and rewards from additional adults that reinforce those received from the first and can bring about norms and sanctions that could not be instituted by a single adult alone" (1990, 593).

Coleman also points out that adults can and need to reinforce each other with patterns of discipline and rewards to strengthen approval and disapproval of the child's behaviour. Closure becomes essential for the consistency and reinforcement of the child but also for the transmission of potential human capital to the child in the form of knowledge and skills.

Coleman (1990) sees the family as tied to an important dimension of social capital for children. He argues that social relations are composed of role-segmented relations such as doctor-patient and lawyer-client on the one hand and natural relations where one person relates to another as a whole person on the other. He argues that this whole person relation is found in *primordial* families and kinship, and constitutes a valuable and increasingly endangered form of social capital in modern social systems dedicated to role-segmented corporate actors. For example, the mother relates as a natural person to the whole child whereas the daycare worker, babysitter, and teacher relate to the child as role segments. Coleman uses the metaphor of "claiming the body" when someone dies to demonstrate the notion that these natural relations are qualitatively different from role-segmented relations. He argues that the role-segmented or corporate role structure in general fails to deal with the child as a whole person. However, regarding future social change, Coleman speculates: "There appear to be two general strategies that can be employed to ensure that in the society of the future the child will be attended to as a whole person. One is the nurturing or strengthening of the primordial relations of kinship, which have constituted the principal source of such attention and responsibility. The second is explicit creation of purposive organizations – that is, modern corporate actors – structured so that persons do give attention to and take responsibility for the whole child" (1990, 598).

Thus, family and kinship represent natural or primordial relations where the child is treated as a whole person rather than a role segment. As closure, ideology, and stability of the child's family increase so does the degree that the family network affords the child social capital. This social capital then is tied to the child's further acquisition of human, financial, and physical capital, all of which are associated with "success" in modern societies.

Coleman argues that the degree of social capital can be measured in several ways. For the current study, two of these measures are especially relevant. Coleman offers the following propositions:

When both parents are present, there will be, if all else is equal, a stronger parent-child relation than when only one parent is present.
and,
Other things being equal, parents who have an interest in their child's attending college are more interested in their child and concerned about the child's future than are parents who have no interest in their child's attending college. (1990, 595)

The notion of social capital in the family clearly leads to the deduction that both family structure and parent interest in post-secondary education for their child are associated with high social capital. Coleman is careful to point out that these measures are *net* (other things being equal, ceteris paribus) of effects for other forms of capital such as financial and physical capital. Of course, both financial and physical capital (money and resources) have long been viewed as having effects on child outcomes in the child poverty literature.

Families provide children with access to financial and physical capital through parental income, financial management, learning resources, and opportunities such as summer camps and home computers. These forms of economic capital can facilitate the acquisition of both human and social capital. The social capital may be gained by extending the number and types of adults passing on human capital and the number and types of peers sharing and reinforcing human capital. Although parents provide children with social capital through parental investments in time, energy, discipline, and normative culture, this social capital may not be associated with the transfer of human capital, such as skills and knowledge transferred to the child by teachers, media, and peers. Social integration in school, community, and with peers also functions as social capital. For example, Martin, White, and Perlman (2003) found that, above and beyond family, peers contributed important functions in religious socialization. Social integration with peers both within and outside school might provide further social capital and transference of human capital to the child.

Figure 9.1
Orienting Model

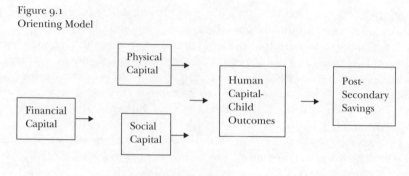

Orienting Model

At this point, it may help to take a step back and to develop a general orienting model to summarize and capture the argument thus far. To summarize, two types of social capital, family structure and parental encouragement, have been conceptualized as leading to the child's acquisition of human capital (social engagement and school engagement). These measures are independent of resources that the family makes available to the child. These resources (financial and physical capital), in addition to the social capital in the family, produce differential child outcomes. These child outcomes (social engagement and school engagement) then predict whether the parents will actually save for their child's post-secondary education. Once the target child has grown, the cycle will repeat itself with the transfer of capital to the next generation. The orienting model captures this process, as in Figure 9.1.

METHODS

Sampling

The SAEP was administered in October 1999 to a sub-sample of the dwellings in the Labour Force Survey (LFS) sample, and therefore its sample design is closely tied to that of the LFS. The LFS is a stratified, multi-stage monthly survey of Canadian households, excluding the territories, members of the armed forces, and members of Native reserves. The SAEP used five groups in the October 1999 LFS sample. Unlike the LFS, where information is collected for all eligible household members, the SAEP collected information from one household member about the children 18 years of age or younger in the household and/or about the savings activities of the household. Upon completion of the LFS interview, the interviewers asked to speak to the SAEP respondent. If there were no children 18 years of age or younger in the household, the SAEP respondent was the same as the LFS respondent. In households with children 18 years of age or younger, the SAEP respondent was the person most knowledgeable (PMK) about the children in the household and about any plans made for the children's post-secondary education. The SAEP was administered to one individual per household. The response rate for the rotations of the LFS was approximately 95 per cent and the response rate for the SAEP was approximately 79 per cent.

Measures

DEPENDENT VARIABLES
Post-secondary savings is a one item measure (Q20) asking about *current savings*. It is coded as no savings (0) or savings (1). Current savings has a mean of .44 and a standard deviation .49, indicating that about 43 per cent of the selected sample (10,793) are currently saving.

INDEPENDENT VARIABLES
Financial capital   is measured by the household income. Household income is a constructed variable derived from the LFS data. It is a categorical variable (10 categories) ranging from no income to a high of "$80,000 or more." The median category for income for the sub-sample was $40,000 – $49,999.

Physical capital   is measured by the PMK's report that books and at least one computer are available in the household for the child's use. This measure was coded as yes or no for each of these and summed to construct an index of the available physical capital for the child's learning, which ranged from no books or computer in the house (0) to having both available (2). The mean for the physical capital index is 1.62 with a standard deviation of .58.

Social capital   is measured by two distinct constructs. The first construct, *family structure,* is composed of two variables, the dual vs single structure of the family and the parental availability in the family. The second construct, *parental encouragement,* measures more directly the actual social capital the parents contribute through their parenting: praising the child, planning the child's schoolwork, and expecting that the child will "go far" in school. Each of these will be discussed below.

Family structure   is first measured in conformance with the Coleman (1990) concept of family as social capital, which he measured as whether the family has two parents or one. The second measure we use attempts to operationalize the availability of parents as a resource and hence as available social capital. The rationale for this measure is consistent with Coleman's argument, but clearly offers a different measure from whether the family has two parents or one.

The variable (intact) measuring whether the target child's family has two parents or one parent is constructed from the information available in the tabulation of families. All two-parent families were coded as "1" and single-parent and other types were coded as "0." The mean for this variable was .94 with a standard deviation of .24. This indicates that over 93 per cent of the target children in the selected sample reside with two parents.

The second measure, parental availability, is also constructed from the types of economic families. However, in this case the salient information was the number of earners in the family. The logic used for the construction of this variable is that if one parent is staying at home, the child would have more available social capital than if both parents are working. Note that if a single mother is at home and a mother in an intact family is at home, they would receive the same score on this variable since each child would have the same number of parents available to them. Parental availability ranged from where neither parent was available (0), such as dual-career families, to where one parent is available (1), to a high score where both parents were available (2). The mean is .34 with a standard deviation of .54.

Parental encouragement contains three measures: praise, planning, and expectations. A factor analysis confirmed two distinct components that we labelled *praise* (Q17a and Q17b) and another component labelled *planning* containing the remaining seven items. The alpha for the praise scale is .70. The planning scale had a relatively low alpha until the question regarding monitoring of TV was deleted. The subsequent scale of parental planning for their child's education has an alpha of .70. A parental expectation that the child will "go far" in school is composed of one item (Q3) that has a mean of 3.66 with a standard deviation of .69.

Human Capital is a measure of the current capital the child has attained at the time of the study. Human capital is measured in two domains: school engagement and social engagement outside school.

Social engagement is an index of social activity outside school. It is composed of four questions (Q15a-c and Q16). Each question is a four-point likert-type response. These four response codes were collapsed into response codes indicating that the target child is either involved or not involved in each of the four distinct activity areas, because of the skewed distributions for each item. These four questions, then, were summed to create an index of social activity outside school ranging from no activities (0) to activities in all four areas (4). The mean is 1.24 with a standard deviation of 1.12 on 10,793 cases selected for inclusion in analysis.

School engagement is composed of three items measuring achievement (Q10), enjoyment (Q11), and effort at school (Q18). A factor analysis

Figure 9.2
Research Model

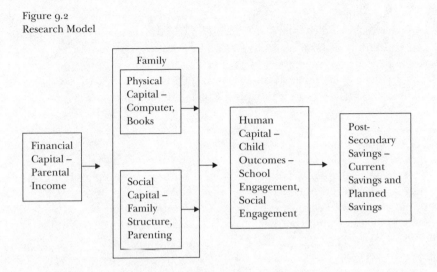

suggested that enjoyment and achievement in school (Q 10 and 11) formed a unidimensional indicator. The Cronbach's alpha for this two-item scale was judged as acceptable (.59). Amount of homework (effort) was excluded from the analysis.

The measures discussed above may be integrated into the research model in Figure 9.2 to assist in getting a picture of the consistency between theoretical concepts and our measures.

RESULTS

The sub-sample used for this study is drawn from the full sample of 18,805 cases in cycle 1 of the SAEP. The sub-sample is generated by excluding those children who have health problems that prevent normal participation in school or play, and restricting the sample to those currently in secondary school or primary school where the PMK is either an adoptive or a natural parent. The final sample for analysis included 10,793 cases with reports by the parent PMK on the target children currently in elementary or secondary school and their families. Table 9.1 contains the means and standard deviations for the variables used in the multivariate analyses of the research model.

Effects on Social Engagement

Both social engagement and school engagement represent indicators of child success. We first examine whether family structure has significant effects on social engagement as we follow the flow of the research model (Figure 9.2).

Table 9.1
Means and Standard Deviations for Variables

Variable	N	Mean	SD
Number of persons in household	10,793	4.28	1.09
Age of child	10,793	10.75	3.33
Sex of child	10,793	1.49	.50
Father's education	10,793	19.57	34.53
Mother's education	10,793	8.44	18.74
School engagement	9,445	6.28	1.42
Social engagement	10,793	1.24	1.12
Currently saving	10,793	0.44	.50
Income	9,671	7.21	2.14
Physical capital	10,490	1.62	.58
Two-parent family	9,370	0.94	.24
Parents at home	10,561	0.34	.54
Praise	9,418	5.07	.91
Expectations	10,448	3.66	.69
Planning	9,121	16.76	2.63

Source: SAEP (1999)

Note: male = 1, female = 2

Table 9.2 shows that model 5 explains the greatest proportion of the variation in social engagement. Clearly, in regard to parenting, financial capital, physical capital, and family social capital contribute in positive and significant ways to the child's acquisition of social capital in social activities. Both household income and physical capital (books and computers) are strongly related to social engagement. Having an intact two-parent family has no significant effect on the child's social engagement when control variables are entered (model 5, Table 9.2). Only having parent(s) at home is significantly related to the child's social engagement. This relationship is negative, however, suggesting that having a full-time parent or parents at home tends to dampen a child's social engagement. It might be that the children with a parent at home spend more time relating to the parent than relating to other children and engaging in social activities. Among the parenting variables, all three measures of parental encouragement have independent and significant effects on the child's social engagement. These effects are robust in that they remain when the control variables are added to the equation. However, with all of the variables in the equation (model 5), we account for only about 10 per cent of the variance in social engagement.

Table 9.2
Standardized Regression Coefficients for Model Blocks for Effects on Social Engagement

Blocks	Models				
	1	2	3	4	5
Financial Capital (Income)	.235***	.180***	.184***	.154***	.154***
Physical Capital		.137***	.136***	.108***	.105***
Social Capital					
Family Structure					
Two Parents			−.042***	−.039**	−.045
Parents at Home			−.032**	−.035**	−.036**
Parental Encouragement					
Praise				.063***	.055***
Expectation				.122***	.117***
Planning				−.058***	−.067***
Controls					
# in Household					.002
Age of Child					−.002
Sex of Child					.095***
Father's Education					−.014
Mother's Education					−.030**
R²	.055	.071	.073	.097	.107

Source: SAEP (1999)

Note: male = 1, female = 2; * p < .05 ** p < .01 *** p < .001

Effects on School Engagement

Table 9.3 shows an even stronger effect for parenting variables. Model 5 (Table 9.3) accounts for about 18.6 per cent of the variation in school engagement. Financial capital and physical capital are weakly related to the child's acquisition of human capital in terms of school engagement. Family social capital in regard to parenting (praise, expectation, and planning) contributes in positive and significant ways to the child's acquisition of human capital in the school environment. Contrary to Coleman's conjecture (1990), the family structure variables (two parents and parents at home) were weak and insignificantly related to the child's human capital acquisition. All of the parenting variables are strongly related. Again, these parenting effects are robust in that they remain when the control variables are added to the equation.

Effects on Currently Saving

We would expect that children's acquisition of human capital in the form of school engagement and social engagement would be strongly related to

Table 9.3

Standardized Regression Coefficients for Model Blocks for Effects on School Engagement

Blocks	Models				
	1	2	3	4	5
Financial Capital (Income)	.118***	.103***	.119***	.079***	.086***
Physical Capital		.037***	.039***	.047***	.069***
Social Capital					
Family Structure					
Two Parents			−.009	−.006	−.013
Parents at Home			.027*	.018	.016
Parental Encouragement					
Praise				.218***	.184***
Expectation				.184***	.163***
Planning				−.182***	.14***
Controls					
# in Household					.004
Age of Child					−.183***
Sex of Child					.199***
Father's Education					.016
Mother's Education					.008
R^2	.014	.015	.016	.115	.186

Source: SAEP (1999)

Note: male = 1, female = 2; * $p < .05$ ** $p < .01$ *** $p < .001$

whether or not the parents are saving for their children's post-secondary education. But children's school engagement is only modestly related to savings (= .077), especially when compared to children's social engagement (= .268, see Table 9.4). The provision of physical and financial capital is significantly associated with parents' current saving. The social capital of family structure is related to current saving; two-parent families and fewer parents at home are associated with current saving for post-secondary school. The emergence of the effect of two-parent families on savings is somewhat suspect since it only emerges in model 5 and seems to be due to a complex interaction with several of the control variables (age of child and number of individuals in the household). Although we do not go further with the examination of this "suppression" effect, we would speculate that much of the effect for two-parent families is tied to the fact that early savers are often still together because they are in the early years of their marriage and they have only their first-born child. The finding that having fewer parents at home (= −.291, model 5) is not related to the trade-off between at-home parents or greater resources, because this effect is net of

Table 9.4
Logistic Regression Coefficients for Model Blocks for Effects on Current Saving for Post-Secondary Education

Blocks	Models				
	1	2	3	4	5
Financial Capital (Income)	.343***	.290***	.256***	.211***	.208***
Physical Capital		.554***	.546***	.430***	.493***
Social Capital					
Family Structure					
Two Parents			.153	.236	.778***
Parents at Home			−.281***	−.290	−.291***
Parental Encouragement					
Praise				.027	.006
Expectation				.335***	.324***
Planning				−.026***	−.010***
Human Capital					
Social Engagement				.261***	.268***
School Engagement				.084***	.077***
Controls					
# in Household					−.267***
Age of Child					.031***
Sex of Child					−.063**
Father's Education					.010**
Mother's Education					.007*
R^2	.055	.071	.073	.097	.107

Source: SAEP (1999)

Note: male = 1, female = 2; * p < .05 ** p < .01 *** p < .001

physical and financial capital; rather, this finding suggests that parents in the labour force may place a higher value on post-secondary education. In addition, having both parents at home may have a negative effect on household organization and operation. This speculation is, however, beyond the focus of the present study. Most interesting is that the only parenting variable strongly related to saving for the child's post-secondary education was the expectation that the child would go to university.

DISCUSSION

Family Structure and Child Outcomes

The preceding analyses make it clear that family structure largely fails to predict child outcomes. In the case of the child's social engagement, being in a two-parent family is not significantly related to the outcome when control variables are in the equation. Similarly, neither of the family structure variables, parents at home or intact two-parent family, is significantly related to the child's school engagement. Both social and school engagement are much better predicted by the parenting processes of praise, assisting the child in planning for schoolwork, and high expectations net of family structure and control variables.

These findings suggest that regardless of family structure, family parenting processes predict child outcomes. Although correlation is not causation, it is the first step in attributing causal efficacy. In this light we might say that family structure is an unlikely cause of child outcomes whereas parenting processes are much more likely to contribute significantly to child outcomes.

The contributions of parenting processes, in contrast to family structure, can be better understood if we address the notion of transmission of social capital to the child. It is difficult to understand how family structure is transmitted. A child could have an intact two-parent family where the parenting strategies are negative (such as yelling and hitting). It is simply not clear how structure, independent of economic resources, was ever thought to automatically bring about the child's acquisition of human capital in the form of academic and social adjustment. On the other hand, parenting processes are more proximal to the child and therefore have a greater opportunity to influence the child. Parental praise and encouragement of children is much more likely to contribute to human capital (self-efficacy or skills) that the children can then transport to the academic and social domains.

Parenting processes do not have consistent influences on all child outcomes. The analyses in this study suggest that certain parenting processes account for more variance in specific child outcomes than do others. Thus, while we can suggest that parenting processes are associated with the accumulation of human capital, it is not correct to assume that interventions should target one or two aspects of parenting. Child "domains," where children use their human capital, require the acquisition of different skills. Thus parents need to provide the specific social resources required for a specific domain along with appropriate financial and physical resources.

Does this mean that social capital is less structural than Coleman's propositions indicated? We believe so. In these data, it seems that social capital resides more in the interpersonal processes and techniques that parents use with their children. This implies that a single parent mother that praises and encourages her child in school and sets high expectations for achievement might have more salutary outcomes for her child than an intact family where neither parent is involved with the child. Coleman's assumption that structure operationalizes a component of social capital might have been mistaken. We will discuss this theoretical ramification shortly.

Family Structure and Educational Savings

The data in Table 9.4 indicate that both measures of family structure, having two parents and having a parent at home, assist us in predicting which families are currently saving for their child's post-secondary education. There is a strong effect for two-parent families on savings net of other economic and parenting variables. Interestingly, having a parent at home is negatively related to current savings net of economic variables and we have speculated that the effect might well be curvilinear. This might also indicate that families where both parents are at work are more likely to be contributing to savings because of their higher disposable income. Furthermore, this might indicate a stronger value on post-secondary education for families where both partners are in the labour force.

Theoretical Implications

It is clear from these data that family structure fails to predict our measures of child outcomes. Coleman (1990) formulated fairly extensive propositions regarding why family structure is related to child outcomes using the concept of "closure," and he directly hypothesized that a relation should exist. Yet this research is quite consistent with other empirical research that finds either no relation or only a modest one (Acock and Demo, 1994; Amato, 2000; White, Marshall, and Wood, 2002). On the other hand, this study finds strong support for the proposition that parental interaction with the child has an effect on child outcomes. This finding echoes some of those from previous research (Acock and Demo, 1994; Lansford et al., 2001).

The anomaly in this general picture is that the theory provides a strong argument for expecting family structure to be related to the child's acquisition of social capital. Is the theory to be abandoned? This research raises several options in this regard. One is that the theory is simply wrong and some other competing theory focusing on parenting might be more adequate. A second option is that the theory incorrectly operationalizes the concept of social capital as family structure. Last, we could argue that the measures for family structure we use in this study do not adequately measure Coleman's concept.

The last option, that our measures of family structure do not measure Coleman's notion of family structure, is the easiest to dismiss. Coleman (1990) cites his own work in this area, which used only the number of parents in the household. That measure is virtually identical to the one used in this study. Coleman did not measure parental processes as others have and, therefore, lacked the data to make comparisons as to effect size. We do not believe that this option would explain the anomaly of these data and the theoretical expectations.

The first option is also possible, but when we ask "What are the competing theories?" we find few direct contenders. Few family theories (functionalism and rational choice) have paid much attention to predicting child outcomes in families or even to incorporating concepts that would readily link to child outcomes. Functionalism has largely fallen into abuse and disuse and would not be considered a viable theory by many scholars because it is seen as maintaining unwarranted assumptions. Only rational choice theory remains available for use.

The second option is that Coleman incorrectly operationalized the concept of social capital in regard to families. In this study we incorporated parental processes as a form of social capital even though Coleman did not directly indicate such inclusion. A reasonable case can be argued that parental processes are an even better measure of social capital than family structure.

Recall that social capital is defined by Coleman (1990) as not being the same as the network or structure but residing in the network or structure. Social capital is not the node but is the line between nodes, the relationship. If social capital resides within the family relationships it might be that parental encouragement processes such as praise and support better capture what Coleman called social capital than merely assuming the structure determines the social capital. Certainly the data in this study would support such a position.

Parents that assisted their child in organizing and planning for school, praised and rewarded the desired behaviour and outcomes, and held high expectations for their children had better outcomes in regard to both social engagement with peers and academic success in school (school engagement). Family structure made little difference. However, we believe that these parental encouragement measures are simply more accurate measures of the social capital in the parent-child relationship. Rather than argue that the concept of social capital is flawed, we contend that family structure is a poor operationalization of social capital.

Policy Implications

The idea that single families are inherently less able to successfully raise children than intact families has been an "opinion" supported by politicians and some researchers. Some early theorists such as Parsons (1943) and more recently Coleman (1990) have lent credibility to this view. However, as researchers partition out the effects of differential resources and economic advantages, it becomes increasingly clear that family structure accounts for very little in regard to child outcomes (Lansford et al., 2001).

This study indicates that the Canadian situation is similar to that found by Lansford et al. (2001) in the United States. Furthermore, we have tested the major extant theory in regard to family structure (social capital) and found little support for the original formulation. It is our contention that parental processes of support and encouragement are important forms of social capital in family relationships, exclusive of the structure of the family.

One implication of this contention is that policy and intervention might be better directed at parental education regarding the encouragement of children rather than focusing on finding a solution to single parenthood. We see no reason that with adequate economic and social supports, single parents would be inherently different in their encouragement and positive interaction with the child. We would suggest a focus on programs of parental education encouraging parenting.

Post-secondary Savings

It is interesting that in Table 9.4 so many of the independent variables are significant predictors of a family currently saving for their child's post secondary education. These include financial capital, physical capital, social capital including family structure, the child's school and social engagement, the number of people in the household, and both parents' education level. In reality there are few surprises here. Families with supportive, financially well-off, well-educated parents are more likely to save for their child's future education. The child contributes by being active socially and successfully engaged in school. It is of further interest that the parental encouragement variables that are so significant for child outcomes are at best only modest predictors of savings. This suggests that savings are largely a function of values related to education and ability to save rather than of the human capital of the child.

CONCLUSION

This study examined the relationship between family structure, child outcomes, and saving for post-secondary education. Although a clear linkage exists between parental encouragement and child outcomes, indications of a relationship between family structure and child outcomes were much more limited. The second part of the analysis hypothesized that child outcomes would predict parental saving for their child's post-secondary education. Although a modest relationship to current savings behaviour was found, most of the variance is accounted for by economic and structural variables, including family structure. However, family structure in this context might simply be measuring ability to save (two earners) rather than any interactional component. We were not able to specify models to explain parental plans to save.

Theoretically and practically this study supports the view that parental encouragement is a more important and useful measure of social capital than family structure. Theoretically, this suggests a critical "rethinking" of family structure as a measure of social capital in the family. The practical component of this is that interventions should address parenting skill rather than the structure of the family. We find little evidence to suggest that family structure accounts for much other than a lack of resources. It is not a proxy for a type of parenting. We must remember that although dual-earner parents may have more resources, they may not have any more quality parenting time with children than a single-parent family.

APPENDIX
SAEP QUESTIONS SELECTED FOR ANALYSIS

(Q3) How far do (child's) parents/guardians hope that he/she will go in school?

- Primary school
- Secondary or high school
- Community college, technical college or CEGEP
- University
- Learn a trade

(Q10) Based on your knowledge of (child's) schoolwork, including report cards, how did he/she do *overall* in school?

- Above average
- Average
- Below average

(Q11) How did (child) feel about his/her schoolwork?

- Liked it very much
- Liked it
- Neither liked nor disliked it
- Disliked it
- Disliked it very much

(Q15a-c) In a typical week during the last school year, how often did (child) participate in organized activities that were *not* run by the school such as:

a. Sports or physical activities like Little League, swim club or hockey league?

b. Social club activities like scouts, girl guides, boys and girls clubs or church groups?
c. Cultural activities like music lessons, art lessons, dance lessons or drama lessons?

- More than once a week
- About once a week
- Less than once a week
- Never

(Q16) In a typical week during the last school year, how often did (child) participate in organized activities that were run by the school *outside* of school hours? This includes any activity such as team sports, social clubs, music, band or school plays run by the school.

- More than once a week
- About once a week
- Less than once a week
- Never

(Q17a-g) How often did (child's) parents/guardians ...

a. Praise (child) if he/she did well in school?
b. Praise (child) for trying in school, even if he/she did not succeed?
c. Help (child) with homework when he/she did not understand?
d. Remind (child) to begin or complete homework?
e. Help (child) plan his/her time for getting homework done?
f. Decide how much television (child) could watch on school days?
g. Tell or remind (child) that he/shewas not working to his/her full potential or ability

- Very often
- Often
- Sometimes
- Never

(Q18) In general, how much time did (child) spend doing homework?

- A lot
- A fair amount
- Very little
- None at all

REFERENCES

Acock, A.C. and Demo, D.H. (1994). *Family diversity and well-being.* Thousand Oaks, CA: SAGE.

Amato, P.R. and Booth, A. (1997). *A generation at risk: Growing up in a generation of upheaval.* Cambridge, MA: Harvard University Press.

Amato, P.R., Loomis, L.S., and Booth, A. (1995). "Parental divorce, marital conflict, and offspring well-being in early adulthood." *Social Forces, 73,* 895–916.

Baker, M. and Tippin, D. (1999). *Poverty, social assistance, and the employability of mothers: Restructuring the welfare states.* Toronto, Ontario: University of Toronto Press.

Bankston, C.L. and Caldas, S.J. (1998). "Family structure, schoolmates, and racial inequalities in school achievement." *Journal of Marriage and the Family, 60,* 715–23.

Becker, G.S. (1981). *A treatise on the family.* Cambridge, MA: Belknap.

Biblarz, T.J. and Gottainer, G. (2000). "Family structure and children's success: A comparison of widowed and divorced single-mother families." *Journal of Marriage and the Family, 62,* 533–48.

Boss, P., Doherty, W., LaRossa, R., Schumm, W., and Steinmetz, S., eds. (1993). *Sourcebook of family theories and methods: A contextual approach.* New York: Plenum.

Carlson, M.J. and Corcoran, M.E. (2001). "Family structure and children's behavioral and cognitive outcomes." *Journal of Marriage and Family, 63,* 779–92.

Cherlin, A.J. (1978). "Remarriage as an incomplete institution." *American Journal of Sociology, 84,* 634–50.

Cherlin, A.J., Chase-Lansdale, P.L., and McRae, C. (1998). "Effects of parental divorce on mental health throughout the life course." *American Sociological Review, 63,* 239–49.

Coleman, J.S. (1990). *Foundations of social theory.* Cambridge, MA: Harvard University Press.

Collins, W.A. and Luebker, C. (1994). "Parent and adolescent expectancies: Individual and relational significance." In J.G. Smetana, ed. *New directions for child development,* vol. 66. San Francisco: Jossey-Bass. 65–80.

Demo, D.H. and Cox, M.J. (2000). "Families with young children: A review of research in the 1990's." *Journal of Marriage and the Family, 62,* 876–95.

Duncan, G.J. and Brooks-Gunn, J., eds. (1997). *Consequences of growing up poor.* NY: Russell Sage Foundation.

Dunifon, R. and Kowaleski-Jones, L. (2002). "Who's in the house? Race differences in cohabitation, single parenthood, and child development." *Child Development, 73,* 1249–64.

Dunn, J. and Munn, P. (1987). "The development of justifications in disputes." *Developmental Psychology, 23,* 781–98.

Hanson, T.L. (1999). "Does parental conflict explain why divorce is negatively associated with child welfare?" *Social Forces, 77,* 1283–316.

Haveman, R. and Wolfe, B. (1994). *Succeeding generations.* NY: Russell Sage Foundation.

E.M., Cox, M., and Cox, R. (1982). "Effects of divorce on parents and children." In M. Lamb, ed. *Nontraditional families: Parenting and child development.* Hilldale, NJ: Erlbaum. 233–85.

Jekielek, S.M. (1998). "Parental conflict, marital disruption and children's emotional well-being." *Social Forces, 76,* 905–35.

Kuczynski, L., Kochanska, G., Radke-Yarrow, M., and Girnius-Brown, O. (1987). "A developmental interpretation of young children's non-compliance." *Developmental Psychology, 23,* 799–806.

Lansford, J.E., Ceballo, R., Abbey, A., and Stewart, A.J. (2001). "Does family structure matter? A comparison of adoptive, two-parent biological, single-mother, stepfather, and stepmother households." *Journal of Marriage and Family, 63,* 840–51.

Lipman, E.L., Boyle, M.H., Dooley, M.D., and Offord, D.R. (2002). "Child well-being in single-mother families." *Journal of the American Academy of Child and Adolescent Psychiatry, 41,* 75–82.

Martin, T., White, J., and Perlman, D. (2003). "Religious socialization: A test of the channeling hypothesis of parental influence on adolescent faith maturity." *Journal of Adolescent Research, 18,* 15–26.

McLanahan, S. (1997). "Parent absence or poverty: Which matters more?" In G.J. Duncan and J. Brooks-Gunn, eds. *Consequences of growing up poor.* NY: Russell Sage Foundation. 35–48.

Mijanovich, R. and Long, D. (1995). "Creating an alternative to welfare: First year findings on the implementation of welfare impacts, and the costs of the self-sufficiency project." Ottawa, ON: Human Resources Development Canada (Applied Research Branch, R-96-11E).

Parsons, T. and Bales, R.F. (1955). *Family socialization and interaction process.* Glencoe, IL: Free Press.

Rodgers, R.H. (1973). *Family interaction and transaction: The developmental approach.* Englewood Cliffs, NJ: Prentice Hall.

Smetana, J. (1995). "Parenting styles and conceptions of parental authority during adolescence." *Child Development, 66,* 299–316.

– (1997). "Parenting and the development of social knowledge reconceptualized. Value socialization in a bidirectional context." In J.E. Grusec and L. Kuczynski, eds). *Parenting and the internalization of values: A handbook of contemporary theory.* Toronto: John Wiley & Sons. 162–92.

Thomson, E., Mosley, J., Hanson, T.L., and McLanahan, S. (2001). "Remarriage, cohabitation, and changes in mothering behavior." *Journal of Marriage and Family, 63,* 370–80.

van den Berghe, P. (1979). *Human family systems.* New York: Elsevier.

White, J.M. and Klein, D.M. (2002). *Family theories.* 2nd edition. Thousand Oaks, CA: SAGE.

White, J.M., Marshall, S.K., and Wood, J.R. (2002). *Confusing family structures: The role of family structure in relation to child well-being.* Paper presented at the Northwest Council on Family Relations, June, 2002, Vancouver, Canada.

Willms, J.D., ed. (2002). *Vulnerable Children.* Edmonton, Alberta: University of Alberta Press.

10

Parental Involvement in the Creation of Home-Learning Environments: Gender and Class Patterns

NANCY MANDELL AND ROBERT SWEET

Two trends have emerged in Canadian education in the past twenty years. The first is the greater value assigned to a post-secondary education (PSE). Almost half of the new jobs created in the next five years will require at least seventeen years of education. Canadians understand that some post-secondary education is essential to secure a "good" job (Duffy, Glenday, and Pupo, 1997). The increasing importance of further education and training is reflected in the rising educational aspirations of teenagers and their parents (Davies, this volume; Bibby, 2001). Along with rising aspirations, post-secondary participation rates are increasing (Bouchard and Zhao, 2000; de Broucker and Lavallee, 1998; Butlin, 1999).

A second trend is the changing gender composition of post-secondary aspirations and actual participation in college and university programs. Canada stands out as one of the few countries in which more women than men achieve a post-secondary level of education (de Broucker and Underwood, 1998; Trusty, 1998). Women are more likely than men to attend university (46 per cent vs 40 per cent) and college (50 per cent vs 46 per cent) (Knighton and Mirza, 2002). Throughout the system, girls have higher grades, are more involved in high school activities, and have higher educational aspirations then boys (Hossler and Stage, 1992). Recent gains in female school engagement and educational performance have given rise to the "masculinity" question – a growing concern with the relatively poor school performance of boys (Archer, Pratt, and Phillips, 2001; Connell, 2000; Epstein et al., 1998; Gilbert and Gilbert, 2000; Head, 1999).

However, if we look more closely at these two trends – rising PSE aspirations and increased numbers of women achieving higher education credentials – we see distinct class and gender divisions. While PSE is generally in demand by both young people and older adults, class patterns in achievement remain. Youth from middle-class families are more likely to attend university, while those from working-class families gravitate towards the community colleges. In short, education continues to promote class stratification. Moreover, while more women than men attend both university and college, it is primarily women from the middle-classes who are most likely to disrupt traditional gender tracking by obtaining professional degrees in what were once thought of as "male" fields of concentration. We do not see a corresponding movement of men into traditionally female occupations. This suggests that gender stereotypes have blurred more for women than for men.

Our study takes these two themes as its starting point and asks how the intransigence of class and the unevenness of gender are embedded in the learning environments of homes. We thus situate our investigation within the broad research question that asks how families affect children's success in school. An extensive literature in education investigates links between children's academic achievement and adult support of schooling in the home. In general, this literature takes either a structuralist or an interactionist perspective – studies either focus on larger social structures that predict student achievement or look inward at family processes. Few studies take both structure and process into account.

Using data from the 1999 Survey of Approaches to Educational Planning (SAEP), we look at the larger structural context that shapes families' involvement in their children's schooling. As well, we attempt to capture family processes by examining types of parental involvement in children's schooling. Specifically, we ask two research questions.

First, are there family social address features, such as income and parental education, that shape the ways in which parents become involved in their children's education? Family social status variables such as income, education, ethnicity, and marital status have been overwhelmingly linked to children's school achievement (Coleman, 1988; Hoover-Dempsey and Sandler, 1997; Kmec and Furstenberg, 2002; Knighton and Mirza, 2002), to parental child rearing practices (Chao and Willms, 2002; Darling and Steinberg, 199; Dornbusch and Wood, 1989; Deslandes et al., 1997; Herman et al., 1997), and to the resources – income, time, energy, and community contacts – parents bring to child-rearing (Cook and Willms, 2002; Fuligni, 1997). For our investigation, the power and significance of status variables lies in what family background allows parents to do with and for their children. What parents think, say, and do within the context of class provides the basis for their involvement with their children through various interaction processes such as modelling, reinforcement, and instruction.

Second, are parents involved with their children, in gendered ways, in construct-ing home-learning environments? Here we examine differences in parents' school-related interactions with their sons and daughters. Taken together, these two questions form the basis for developing an initial picture of the home-learning environments of a large sample of Canadian families.

BACKGROUND

In examining parents' role in fostering a positive home-learning environ-ment, families first are viewed in relation to the constraints (and opportuni-ties) imposed by social structure. Basic structural features of families include income, parents' level of education, and the provision of the material necessities of a home-learning environment. The gendered nature of the home-learning environment is then examined in relation to indicators of parenting style involving dimensions of monitoring and encouragement.

Families as Structure

Bourdieu (1986, 1997) describes the construction of class in families as a social reproduction process that sees the intergenerational transmission of various forms of social, cultural, and symbolic capital. Theories of cultural capital and family educational resources explain why and how background matters for educational achievement (Andres, 1994; Reay, 1998a; Roscigno and Ainsworth-Darnell, 2000). Privileged family backgrounds are conse-quential in part because of parents' ability to ensure access to schools that differ in type and quality, the resources they can provide their children (such as books, computers and newspapers), and the attitudes and dis-positions through which parental values, dreams, and goals are transmitted to children.

How does social class reproduction proceed such that inequalities are magnified? Families mobilize a range of social, economic, and cultural re-sources to ensure their continuing social advantage (Pallas, 2002). Of all the forms of capital, parental education is emerging as the most significant in the reproduction process. De Broucker and Lavallee (1998) used data from the Adult Literacy Survey to examine the role of the family in the acquisition of post-secondary education. They found that the intellectual climate of the family environment may lead to higher educational attainment through the intergenerational transfer of intellectual capital, the labour market experi-ences of parents and their transfer to children, and the impact of level of educational attainment on the educational investment strategies of parents in support of their children's education. More highly educated parents are more likely to have children who attain a post-secondary level of education

(Guppy and Pendakur, 1989; Parcel and Dufur, 2001). According to social reproduction theory, more highly educated parents are thought to possess greater amounts of social capital to transmit to their children in terms of values, dispositions, and aspirations. In the Canadian context, Knighton and Mirza (2002) confirm this theory, suggesting that in addition to the involvement of parents in their children's education, other important factors include aspirations, values, and motivations that facilitate educational attainment. Highly educated parents also possess the "know-how" to make social capital work effectively for their children. In other words, it is not sufficient to have money, material resources, education, or other forms of financial, cultural, and social capital if you do not know how to turn it into an advantage for your children. While some of this "working" of capital derives from personality or temperament (Reay, 1998c), the continual reproduction of social advantage in and through Canadian families suggests that the most important feature of advantage lies in its efficacious use (Lareau and Horvat, 1999).

INDICATORS

Two indicators of socio-economic status (SES) are widely used in the literature to describe the social address of families: total family income and mothers' education. Associated with these indicators are differences in the extent to which parents value education and, consequently, in the post-secondary aspirations they hold for their children.

Income Social class remains a powerful predictor of home-based involvement activities and children's school performance. Canadian studies reveal that post-secondary attainment increases with household income (Knighton and Mirza, 2002). Of those whose parents earn after-tax income in the highest quartile of income distribution, 70 per cent participate in PSE vs 56 per cent of those whose parents' income is in the lowest quartile (Knighton and Mirza, 2002). Children with parents in the highest income quartile were more than twice as likely as those with parents in the lowest quartile (39 vs 17 per cent) to choose university over college. College is the more typical route for those in the two lowest income quartiles, whereas university is favoured by those in the highest quartile (Bouchard and Zhao, 2000).

In Canada class differences appear early. Looking at grade 3 performance levels of Canadian children, Tremblay, Ross, and Berthelot (2001) found that a large variation in academic achievement is associated with classes and schools across the country. Moreover, initial inequalities are magnified over the life course (Pallas, 2002). Using data from the 1986 and 1994 General Social Surveys, Bouchard and Zhao (2000) found a widening gap in university participation by family socioeonomic status (SES).

While the university participation rates for young people from low and middle SES background were quite similar in 1986 – 13.7 and 14.5 per cent respectively – by 1994 a wide gap had opened between these two groups, with the rates standing at 18.3 and 25.3 per cent, respectively (Bouchard and Zhao, 2000).

Despite the general salience of SES in studies of social structure and educational outcomes, effective parental involvement is not strongly linked to income (Harris and Marmer, 1996). Recent work by Chao and Willms (2000) using Canadian data found only a weak link between SES and an authoritative parenting style. Cook and Willms (2002) similarly found relatively low correlations between SES and measures of parental affective engagement with their children.

Provision of the material resources required for a functioning home-learning environment is within the means of nearly all Canadian families. These include provision of a quiet place to study, the necessary books, and relevant reference material. However, SES differences exist in the ability of low-income parents to supply their children with a computer and the increasingly necessary internet connection (Corbett and Willms, 2002).

Mother's Education   Previous research shows us that mothers' more than fathers' level of education is predictive of parental involvement activities. We focus on the educational status of the mother as mothers constitute the majority of single parents and, in two-parent families, mothers are more involved than fathers in the day-to-day schooling activities of children. Stevenson and Baker (1987) found that the higher the educational status of the mother, the greater the degree of parental involvement in school activities. Such mothers are more likely to implement strategies for managing their child's transition to high school, are better informed about their children's school performance, have more contact with their children's teachers, and are more likely to select college preparatory classses for their children. The educational level of the mother seems to indicate the mother's experience and knowledge of how one can progress through the educational system and therefore a more educated mother's involvement in a child's school career may be more effective (Lareau, 1989; Reay, 1998b). Parents, particularly mothers, with more education tend to share in their children's intellectual pursuits, pass down skills and beliefs that are more conducive to achievement (De Broucker and Underwood, 1998), get more involved in their children's education, have higher educational expectations for academic success, and have greater familiarity with schools and teachers. The high value parents place on education and their knowledge of how to achieve educational goals can thus be transmitted when they actively provide their children with a home-learning environment that encourages educational attainment (Trusty et al., 2000; Wilson and Wilson, 1992).

Parents' Aspirations   Davies (this volume) notes the generally rising level of post-secondary aspirations most Canadian parents hold for their children. Nevertheless important SES differences are seen in the specific post-secondary destinations parents have in mind. Among middle-class parents, most hope that their children will gain access to a university, while a much smaller proportion feel the technical and vocational training offered by community colleges is preferable. Among lower-income parents the proportion favouring a college education for their children increases significantly. Very few parents – whatever their SES level – have no post-secondary ambitions for their children, although parents of younger children may not yet have formulated a particular post-secondary pathway, perhaps awaiting some further indication of the child's potential. Others will modify their expectations in the light of children's educational achievements and interests. Recent research on college and university participation patterns of 18 to 20-year-olds suggests that post-secondary aspirations are not always achieved (Bowlby and McMullen, 2003). Parents' aspirations for their children may nevertheless guide educational planning – a key element of which is the construction of an effective home-learning environment.

Families as Process

The family learning environment or home academic culture provides both the context and the processes in and through which capital is transmitted from parents to children. Recent Canadian research suggests that children's performance in school is directly affected by the interaction of formal schooling with a home environment that is supportive of learning (de Broucker and Lavallee, 1998). Furthermore, considerable evidence indicates that what happens at home is very significant in promoting the academic school performance of children (Bowen and Bowen, 1998; Milne, 1989; Ryan and Adams, 1995, 1999; Tremblay, Ross, and Berthelot, 2001; Wentzel, 1998).

But what do we know about parental involvement? First, parental involvement in children's education is associated with a range of positive outcomes for elementary school children, including fewer behavioural problems, lower dropout rates, higher student achievement, and less chance of male delinquency (Muller, 1993; Schneider and Coleman, 1993; Stevenson and Baker, 1987; Zellman and Waterman, 1998). Chao and Willms (2002) found that children do better in school when parents monitor their behaviour, are responsive to their needs, and encourage independence with a democratic approach.

Second, parental involvement has been conceptualized broadly to encompass a wide range of parent-child-school interactions. These include school-based involvement (PTO, driving on a field trip, volunteering at school, serving on a parent board, informal conversations) and home-based involvement (reviewing the child's work, monitoring the child's progress, helping with homework, discussing school events or course issues, providing enrichment activities pertinent to school success, talking by phone with the teacher).

Third, Canadian data reveal that parents understand the value of constructing a positive home-learning environment for children as a way to facilitate children's academic success. In an analysis of the 1994–95 National Longitudinal Survey of Children and Youth (NLSCY), Norris (1999) demonstrates that parental involvement was rated as highly by parents and children as it was by teachers. Moreover, Canadian parents are very involved in their children's education. Parents believe that through their involvement, they can exert a positive influence on children's educational outcomes (Hoover-Dempsey and Sandler, 1995, 1997). Using the NLSCY data, Ertl (1999) explored the relationship between parents and their children's academic achievement by examining the role of the parent in the child's learning environment. She, along with others (Steinberg et al., 1992) discovered that the impact of home practices is substantial. Such interactions as verbally stimulating conversations, reading sessions, educationally related resources (books and magazines), and parental warmth are educationally consequential parental practices because they directly stimulate intellectual development and engagement. Parents contribute to their children's academic achievement by monitoring school performance through such practices as establishing explicit or implicit rules regarding homework, establishing study routines, checking that homework is completed, checking on children's performance and behaviour in school, setting limits on TV watching, and setting limits on spending time with friends (Scott-Jones, 1995).

Parents who convey to their children explicit expectations about school-related activities such as studying and accompany these demands with emotional support and encouragement have been characterized as practicing an "authoritive" parenting style. Parental monitoring of children's home-based academic activities establishes clear educational expectations and the accompanying structure within which they can be accomplished and is most effective when it is accompanied by responsiveness and warmth toward the child. The combination of demands for homework diligence – accompanied by emotional support – promotes and enables children to eventually become autonomous, self-directed learners (Cooper et al., 1998). The authoritative parenting style has been associated with positive school outcomes and adjustment for children from a variety of family backgrounds and situations (Corak, 2001; Jones et al., 2002; Chao and Willms, 2000).

Fourth, parental involvement is used generically to refer to the actions of both mothers and fathers when we are really talking about the behaviour of mothers. Mothers have a different relationship from fathers to the generation of social advantage and disadvantage. While fathers are clearly significant, their role has been less studied (Hawkins et al., 2002) than that of mothers who, as the primary domestic labourers and emotional caretakers in families, become the primary agents of social reproduction. Mothers seem to be the ones who, through their day-to-day involvement in constructing and reproducing home learning environments, make cultural capital work for their children. In this perspective, class becomes much more than materiality and socio-economic status. Both class and gender are played out in mothers' activities in support of their children (Arnot, David, and Weiner, 1999; Baker and Stevenson, 1986; Mann, 1998; Reay, 1998a).

GENDERING THE HOME-LEARNING ENVIRONMENT

Gender is a powerful ideological and cultural device that structures and organizes the experiences of women and men. In turn, social structures shape the gendered behaviours and educational outcomes of individuals (Kmec and Furstenberg, 2002). Families, schools, and labour markets perpetuate gender segregated tasks, behaviours, and outcomes (Kmec and Furstenberg, 2002). Considerable Canadian evidence indicates that traditional gender socialization still assigns women to the private sphere, where they perform the bulk of domestic labour while men remain primarily responsible for paid labour (Luxton, 1990).

Children learn gender appropriate behaviour (rules, stereotypes, roles, and norms) at an early age and employ these gender designations in their day-to-day experiences and interactions with others (Thorne, 1993). A very large literature now exists on the ways in which gender shapes children's play, friendships, language, social networks, and intimate relations (Nelson and Robinson, 2002).

To the extent that parents respond differently to their male and female children these differences can be traced to societal gender scripts. For males motivational factors seem most important, while for females family factors appear most important. By family factors we refer to elements of family cohesion and interaction, such as feelings of support, togetherness, mutual monitoring, and openness in discussing problems. For both males and females though, family learning environments that advance supportiveness, togetherness, mutual monitoring, parent-child discussion of problems, open communication, and sharing of leisure time may be assumed to be associated with children's success in school. Yet few studies have explored the ways in which gender directly shapes parental involvement in regard to children's schooling. We assume, but actually have little empirical evidence, that parents treat daughters and sons differently in regard to their schooling (Lytton and Romney, 1991; Ruble and Martin, 1997).

Some researchers suggest that the relationship between parental involvement and achievement is similar for girls and boys but diminishes over the course of high school to the point that parental involvement has essentially no relationship to the gains in achievement made by seniors (Muller, 1998). Others suggest that parents are more likely to be involved in school activities with boys and in home activities with girls; on average though, parents tend to be more involved with girls. Parental involvement with boys is more likely to diminish as the children grow older but remains at a more constant level with girls (Stevenson and Baker, 1987). Still others suggest that parental involvement makes a difference in achievement in general and specifically in adolescents' math performance (Alexander, Entwistle, and Horsey, 1997; Muller, 1995; Epstein, 2001).

Indicators

Two indicators of parental involvement – encouragement and monitoring of children's behaviour – have been identified in the literature as important antecedents of children's school performance (Ryan and Adams, 1995, 1999; Weston, 1989; Willms, 2002). These parallel the basic dimensions of the authoritative parenting style discussed in this section in terms of their gendered application in families.

ENCOURAGEMENT

Generally, educational and social psychological research sees parents as both more restrictive and more nurturing with daughters. Daughters are encouraged to stay close to home, to be rule bound, obedient, docile, studious, meticulous, and careful. Sons, on the other hand, are more likely to be encouraged to be risk takers, rule makers and breakers, adventurous, free, independent, and to explore more widely outside the family (Nelson and Robinson, 2002; Thorne, 1993). In short, sons associate independence with lack of parental control while girls associate independence with fulfilling normative expectations. How then are these gendered messages translated into parent-child interactions around schooling activities in the home?

All parents want their children to succeed at school, but not all parents are successful in facilitating success. Most studies have found that when the overall volume and tenor of parent-child interactions are limited and negative, with many critical messages, that little support of a sense of educational efficacy is conveyed to the child. The child is less likely to want to please the parent by doing well (Dornbusch and Wood, 1989; Zellman and Waterman, 1998). In contrast, open communication at home and parent enthusiasm operates to energize the child and make her/him more eager to succeed (Darling and Steinberg, 1993; Ho and Willms, 1996). Emotionally supportive parents convey to children the value of academic achievement. They also tend to downplay the role of ability and emphasize the importance of effort and hard work in getting the best results.

Encouragement and an environment highly supportive of achievement are found in families where parents believe that education is the most significant way for children to improve their status in life. Parental encouragement and stated aspirations may be the most important ways that they can influence their children's lives (Fuligni, 1997). Adolescents with higher educational achievement are likely to have parents who are concurrently demanding (strict and in control) and responsive (supporting and involved) (Steinberg et al., 1992). Ho and Willms (1996) found that affective engagement is associated with academic achievement. It increases the likelihood that children will approach parents and peers for advice and information. Higher grades are consistently associated with joint decision-making involving both parents and adolescents, leading eventually to youth autonomy and independent decision-making as the child ages.

In general, high achievers receive more parental encouragement to attend college and to pursue their educational and career goals. Parents provide the most encouragement to the child with the highest academic ability (Cabrera and Nasa, 2001). In a study of Canadian science students, Hein and Lewko (1994) found that parental encouragement for science achievement was significantly higher among females than among males in the authoritative parenting group. For females, the more supportive family environment appeared to produce benefits, including more positive views of science and higher levels of curiosity and involvement in science-related activities.

MONITORING
Developing independent study skills in children and fostering their sense of agency is an essential goal of the home-learning environment. Although close surveillance can force students to do what immediately needs to be done, such a level of oversight cannot be sustained over the years; therefore, parents are aware of the need to promote children's intrinsic motivation (Dornbusch and Wood, 1989). The intensity of parental involvement in monitoring the home-study process gradually diminishes as children gain the necessary independent learning skills (Mandell and Sweet, 2004).

Parental involvement is context-specific, such that parents may respond to their adolescents' needs and adjust their involvement at home or at school accordingly (Muller, 1998). The contextual nature of involvement helps to explain the general disengagement of parents over time, but it also sheds light on why parents of more successful students may be more likely to disengage. When children are doing well at school, parents see less need to monitor their progress, have less motivation to engage actively in school-related activities, and have less reason to meet with teachers, whereas when students are having trouble in school, parents may be more likely to become involved (McNeal, 1999; Csikszentmihalyi and Schneider, 2000).

Whether parents' monitoring behaviour differs in relation to their child's gender has been examined in preliminary work by Campbell and Beaudry (1998) and Crosnoe (2001). The findings in these studies (as in others) are mixed. However, when achievement levels are considered in the analysis of parenting effects, girls are more likely to have involved parents if they are enrolled in a remedial program at school but are less likely to have involved parents if they are enrolled in an academic track (Crosnoe, 2001). The lower level of involvement by parents of girls enrolled in the academic track is, however, selective. Capable teenagers can manage such tasks as homework and course selection and there is little need to communicate with teachers about their academic progress. Parents still remain engaged in their children's sports activities and other extracurricular events.

Finding the correct balance between monitoring and intrusion can be difficult for parents. Parents who have strict rules about doing homework and limiting TV may also have more structured parenting practices and may more overtly monitor their children's behaviour. However, it is likely that monitoring or rule-setting at later ages is a reactive strategy inversely related to academic achievement. While too close surveillance can lead to dependence (or resistance), too little supervision also can have negative effects. Dornbusch and Wood (1989) note that the deleterious consequences of excessive permissiveness are greater for boys than for girls, whereas the risks of excessive control are greater for girls than for boys.

Summary

Parents approach the task of constructing a positive home-learning environment in various ways. While diverse, their activities can be characterized as: 1) providing the material resources needed for effective home study; and 2) socializing their children to the role of student. The latter requires that home-learning demands made by parents be accompanied by generous encouragement if children are to acquire the skills of independent study.

This chapter addresses the question of whether parents' rising aspiration levels for their children's PSE are matched by the necessary investment of resources and effective use of supportive strategies for studying in the home. Specifically, we want to examine factors that constrain or qualify parental involvement in their children's home learning across the elementary and secondary grades. Acknowledging the gradual lessening of parental involvement that occurs as children mature, we nevertheless anticipate that family SES and children's gender will influence the extent and nature of parental involvement. Given the findings of recent research, we are particularly interested in examining the impact of class and gender on the pattern of parental monitoring and encouragement that characterizes the home-learning environment.

ANALYSIS AND RESULTS

Data Source and Variables

The data used in the analysis were obtained from the 1999 Survey of Approaches to Educational Planning (SAEP). Questions about the home-learning environment and parents' involvement in their children's studying were examined for families with school-age children. The working sample was then limited to 11, 243 cases distributed over grades 1 to 12.

Indicators were constructed for the two dimensions (monitoring and encouragement) of parental involvement suggested in the literature as characterizing an authoritative parenting style. The monitoring indicator comprised three items that assessed parental interventions designed to help their children plan a homework schedule, maintain that schedule, and regulate the amount of television the children watched. Encouragement consisted of two items. The first assessed the frequency with which parents' praised their children for how well they performed in school. The second assessed the frequency with which they praised their children's efforts to do well in school. The monitoring and encouragement dimensions were identified through a principal components analysis, with orthogonal rotation to simple structure. The monitoring component accounted for 31 per cent of the variance and the encouragement dimension accounted for 41 per cent.

Among the antecedent variables selected for inclusion in the analysis, family income, mothers' educational level, and the presence of a computer in the home were used to index SES. Another dimension included in these indicators of family "social address" was the post-secondary aspirations parents held for their children.

Family income was a derived variable that captured all sources of family income. Mother's education level was selected as being a particularly appropriate indicator of class. Previous research has shown a relatively weak link between broad indicators of SES and parent involvement (Cook and Willms, 2002). However, because mothers retain primary responsibility for maintaining the home-learning environment, their level of education may be more sensitive to variations in the monitoring and encouragement practices. While material resources in the home are closely associated with family income, they do indicate an additional willingness to invest in the infrastructure needed for home study. Only a single item – indicating the presence or absence of a computer in the home – was used to determine the state of the physical resources available to assist the child's studying. Other indicators used to assess physical resources in previous studies – such as the availability of books or a place to study – were included in the SAEP survey but the data showed that virtually all children in the sample were provided with these basics. Parents' educational aspirations for their children distinguished college and university goals from no post-secondary ambitions.

The inclusion of grade and gender variables reflects previous findings on individual difference factors that affect the degree and nature of parental involvement. Parents gradually disengage from direct involvement with homework as children mature. After adjusting to the high school culture, most adolescents are able to manage their academic work schedules and routines. Significant differences nevertheless remain in children's acquisition of independent learning skills and these divide along gender lines. To the extent that gender differences exist in children's school performance and in their acquisition of academic study skills and personal autonomy, it is likely that parents' pattern of monitoring and encouragement will also vary by gender.

RESULTS

Table 10.1 shows the relationship between various indicators of parental involvement and the antecedents of SES and child's gender.

With the exception of family income, each of the SES indicators appeared to play a role in determining the extent of parents' monitoring of their children's study and learning activities. A computer in the home, mother's level of education, and parental expectations were positively related to monitoring activity. All three are more specific expressions of a family's general economic position. Having a computer in the home to facilitate the child's home learning represents parents' willingness to invest their financial resources. In this sense, family wealth is an essential substrate for the building and management of an adequately resourced home-learning environment. Mother's education is significant while the family income variable is not, indicating the particular importance of the mother's role in monitoring children's home-learning activities. The negative coefficient for parental expectations (-.05) likely indicates the greater success and smoother transitions that children with an academic orientation experience in the school system.

This pattern of gradual disengagement by parents is seen in the effect of the grade variable. Consistent with the findings of previous research, grade

Table 10.1
Structure and Process Antecedents of Parental Involvement[1]

Antecedents	Monitoring	Encouragement
Socio-economic Status		
Income	.02	.04*
Computer in Home	.04*	.06*
Mother's Education	.04*	.02*
Parents' Aspirations	−.05*	.08*
Individual Differences		
Grade	−.42*	−.18*
Female	−.14*	.06*
R²	.19	.05
N	11,243	11,243

Source: SAEP (1999)
Notes: [1] Standardized coefficients
* p < .01

effects are quite strong in this analysis. However, this literature demonstrates that the decline in involvement is evenly distributed over various indicators of class – including family income, mother's education, and father's occupation (Cook and Willms, 2002). Since it characterizes most parents' responses to the growing autonomy of their adolescent children, it is an important baseline for the examination of other individual differences among children, especially gender.

Of particular interest to this study is the significant finding for gender (−.14) net of all other effects, including school grade. This result indicates that girls are subject to significantly less parental control and supervision. The finding that boys' more than girls' home-learning behaviour requires greater attention and monitoring by parents lends support to the thesis that girls are better able to adjust to the demands of academic learning, not only in the classroom but also in the home.

In parallel with the analysis of parental monitoring, we analysed the relationship of social structural variables to the amount of encouragement parents gave to their children. We found the amount of praise (for effort and performance) increases across all indicators, while being strongly associated with parents' post-secondary aspirations (.08). Overall, the association between SES and encouragement is somewhat stronger and more consistent than for monitoring processes. It is possible that parents of higher SES are inclined to be more generous in their praise for achievement and effort.

The sign of the coefficient linking parental encouragement to the child's grade in school is similar to that of monitoring, although its value (−.18) suggests a rather gradual withdrawal of praise. While children

acquire independent learning skills they continue to need a measure of
encouragement from their parents (Kaplan and Davidson, 2002). The effect for gender is significant, with girls receiving more encouragement
than boys.

The results shown in Table 10.1 indicate a considerable difference in the
strength of the relationship between antecedent variables and the parental
involvement dimensions of monitoring and encouragement – the amount
of variance for which these factors could account amounted to 19 and 5
per cent, respectively. When we consider the profiles of monitoring and
encouragement together it becomes apparent that gender is important in
a direction that would seem to give greater parental attention to boys'
learning needs, but in fact favours girls' development of independence
and autonomy. Boys are subject to more monitoring than girls, but these
greater constraints and concerns are seemingly not compensated for by
higher levels of encouragement.

Analysis of the effects of various SES measures does not recommend any
particular indicator. However, given that mothers accept primary responsibility for managing their children's home learning, the mothers' education variable likely is of greatest relevance to the further analysis of class
and gender in the SAEP data.

Consistent with our interest in the role these factors play in shaping the
course of parental involvement, the relationship between monitoring and
mother's education is traced separately for boys and girls. Figure 10.1
shows the relationship between monitoring and mother's education for
males and females, adjusted for grade. Monitoring behaviour is converted
to a standardized form.

From the results shown in Figure 10.1, parental monitoring is clearly associated with class, but in a limited sense. While there is some variation in
the degree of monitoring engaged in by parents with educational levels beyond high school graduation, the most distinct difference in monitoring
behaviour occurs with mothers with less than high school graduation. The
latter group is significantly less involved in their children's home learning.
This degree of disengagement among mothers who possess a minimal education themselves may result from their not valuing education, not appre-
ciating the value of home study, or not possessing the skills needed to
effectively monitor their children's home learning.

Gender differences in monitoring are marked at all levels of mothers'
education. Males consistently receive much higher levels of direct parental
assistance in managing their home-learning behaviour. This is not, however, evenly distributed over class levels (mother's education). The most
obvious differences occur between mothers with less than high school education and those who have high school graduation or some form of post-
secondary education. Boys receive less supervision in families where the

Figure 10.1
Parental Monitoring by Mother's Education and Child's Gender

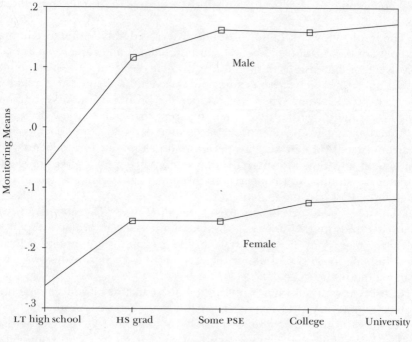

Source: SAEP (1999)

mother has less than high school education. Despite much less overall involvement, mothers in this group respond as do mothers with higher levels of education in giving greater attention to the home-study needs of their boys. Again, this may be due to the greater needs of boys as compared to girls.

Figure 10.2 shows the relationship between parental encouragement and mother's education for males and females. Parents with less than high school education provide relatively little encouragement – to either male or female children. Parents with higher levels of education are more inclined to encourage their children. However, obvious gender differences occur in the pattern of encouragement displayed by these parents. For males, encouragement declines as the level of parental education increases. This trend is reversed for female children.

The analysis of parents' involvement in constructing home-learning environments with their children's future in mind suggests the presence of class differences. These are, however, most obvious when parents with less than

Figure 10.2
Parental Encouragement by Mother's Education and Child's Gender

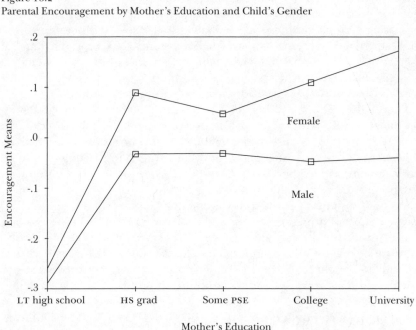

Source: SAEP (1999)

high school education are contrasted with parents who possess higher levels of formal education. Differences in monitoring and affective engagement are not pronounced among parents with high school graduation or some form of post-secondary education. However, marked gender differences are found in both monitoring and affective engagement. Boys appear to require more guidance and help in dealing with the planning and persistence demands of becoming an autonomous learner. At the same time they receive less praise and encouragement from their parents. Where gender intersects with class to create a pattern of more intensive regulation and less encouragement for boys, the form of gendered parenting that emerges is rather different from that typically found in the literature (Connell, 2000).

CONCLUSIONS

The rise in educational aspirations for both sexes, but especially for girls, has meant that Canada has joined the "great credential race." Raising the achievement bar has meant that we raise the minimum level of entry-level credentials for jobs. For example, having a basic post-secondary degree is required for many jobs that two decades ago did not have this requirement. In preparing their children for this new labour market (and other domains of life) advantaged parents can no longer assume class reproduction but increasingly have to work to make it happen. Parental involvement in home- and school-based activities is one of the most important ways in which parents can ensure that social advantage accrues to their children.

Our findings in this study reveal that class intersects with gender to produce specific patterns of parental involvement. Social reproduction processes operate in and through home- and school-based parental involvement practices (Lynch and O'Riordan, 1998). In the home-learning environment, as in other facets of the domestic sphere, class differences persist, proving remarkably intransigent.

We also found that parental involvement differs by child's gender. The pattern of monitoring and encouragement appears to reflect the growing concern with boys' relatively poor school performance. Where girls outperform boys and to the extent that parents respond to the latter's relative inability to benefit from the schooling process, gender contributes less to established male privilege and social stratification than class (Volman and Ten Dam, 1998). These Canadian patterns fit into a broader American trend in which researchers predict that gender is becoming less significant than class and other social constructions as a stratification mechanism (Mandell, 2002). Data on job earnings substantiates the consequences of girls' realization that education is a key to social mobility and improved life chances. Increasing numbers of women have entered post-secondary education and subsequently have been successful in negotiating their credentials in the labour market. Women have made substantial economic gains. The average earnings of male graduates of the more recent cohorts have either held steady or shown small to moderate declines relative to earlier groups, while women's earnings have risen (Finnie, 2000).

In Canada we are at the beginning of a wave of emergent research investigating the "boy" question (Matthews, 2003; Mandell, 2002). As middle-class females take up more of the traditional professions, middle-class males will be able to maintain their class positions only by taking up traditional female careers (men as househusbands, teachers, social workers, and health care professionals) and, in the process, elevating the social status of these careers. Research into masculinity has already begun to expand gender role definitions for boys so that it will become ideologically and culturally more acceptable for boys to take up traditionally female jobs, in much the same way that a similar process took place for women thirty years ago. As we de-gender occupational stereotyping, it may well be that for many professional jobs academic requirements like high grades, which are seen to favour many girls, will alter to other criteria that reflect the breadth and variety of male and female achievement.

REFERENCES

Alexander, K., Entwistle, D.R., and Horsey, Carrie S. (1997). "From first grade forward: Early foundations of high school dropout." *Sociology of Education, 70*, 87–107.

Andres, L. (1994). "Capital, habitus, field and practice: An introduction to the work of Pierre Bourdieu." In L. Erwin, and D. MacLennan, eds. *Sociology of education in Canada: Critical perspectives on theory, research, & practice.* Toronto: Copp-Clark, Longman. 120–36.

Archer, L., Pratt, S.D., and Phillips, D. (2001). "Working-class men's constructions of masculinity and negotiations of (non) participation in higher education." *Gender and Education, 13*, 431–49.

Arnot, M., David, M., and Weiner, G. (1999). *Closing the gender gap: Postwar education and social change.* London: Polity Press.

Baker, D.P. and Stevenson, D.L. (1986). "Mothers' strategies for children's school achievement: managing the transition to high school." *Sociology of Education, 59*, 156–66.

Bibby, R.W. (2001). *Canada's teens.* Toronto: Stoddart.

Bouchard, B. and Zhao, J. (2000). "University education: Recent trends in participation, accessibility and returns." *Education Quarterly Review, 6*(4), 24–32.

Bourdieu, P. (1986). "The forms of capital." In J.C. Richardson, ed. *Handbook of theory and research in the sociology of education.* New York: Greenwood. 241–57.

– (1997). "Cultural reproduction and social reproduction." In J. Karabel and A. Halsey, eds. *Power and ideology in education.* New York: Oxford University Press.

Bowen, N.K. and Bowen, G.L. (1998). "The mediating role of educational meaning in the relationship between home academic culture and academic performance." *Family Relations, 47*, 45–51.

Bowlby, J.W. and McMullen, K. (2002). *At a crossroads: First results for the 18-20-year-old cohort of the youth in transition survey.* Ottawa: Human Resources Development Canada.

Butlin, G. (1999). "Determinants of postsecondary participation." *Education Quarterly Review 5*(3), 9–35.

Cabrera, A.F. and La Nasa, S.M. (2001). "On the path to college: Three critical tasks facing America's disadvantaged." *Research in Higher Education, 42*(2), 119–49.

Campbell, J. and Beaudry, J.S. (1998). "Gender gap linked to differential socialization for high-achieving senior mathematics students." *Journal of Educational Research, 91*(3), (January/February), 140–7.

Chao, R. and Willms, D. (2000). *Family income, parenting practices, and childhood vulnerability: A challenge to the "Culture of Poverty" thesis.* Policy brief. Fredericton, NB: The Canadian Research Institute for Social Policy.

– (2002). "The effects of parenting practices on children's outcomes." In D. Willms, ed. *Vulnerable children*. Edmonton: The University of Alberta Press. 149–65.

Coleman, J. (1988). "Social capital in the creation of human capital." *American Journal of Sociology, 94*, Supplement: S95-S120.

Connell, R.W. (2000). *The men and the boys*. Berkeley and Los Angeles: University of California Press.

Cook, C. and Willms, D. (2002). "Balancing work and family life." In D. Willms, ed. *Vulnerable children*. Edmonton: The University of Alberta Press. 183–97.

Corak, M. (2001). *Are the kids all right? Intergenerational mobility and child well-being in Canada*. Paper prepared for Family and Labour Studies, No. 171. Ottawa: Statistics Canada.

Cooper, H., Lindsay, J., Nye, B., and Greathouse, S. (1998). "Relationships between amount of homework assigned and completed, and student achievement." *Journal of Educational Psychology, 90*(1), 70–83.

Corbett, B.A. and Willms, J.D. (2002). "Information and communication technology: Access and use." *Education Review Quarterly, 8*(4), 8–14.

Crosnoe, R. (2001). "Academic orientation and parental involvement in education during high school." *Sociology of Education, 74*, 210–30.

Csikszentmihalyi, M. and Schneider, B. (2000). *Becoming adult: How teenagers prepare for the world of work*. New York: Basic Books.

Darling, N. and Steinberg, L. (1993). "Parenting style as context: An integrative model." *Psychological Bulletin, 113*(3), 487–96.

Davies, S. (this volume). "A Revolution of Expectations? Three Key Trends in the SAEP Data."

de Broucker, P. and Lavallee, L. (1998). "Getting ahead in life: Does your parents' education count?" *Education Quarterly Review, 5*(1), 22–8.

de Broucker, P. and Underwood, K. (1998). "Intergenerational education equity: An international comparison with a focus on postsecondary education." *Education Quarterly Review, 5*(2), 30–51.

Deslandes, R., Royer, E., Turcotte, D., and Bertrand, R. (1997). "School achievement at the secondary level: Influence of parenting style and parent involvement in schooling." *McGill Journal of Education, 32*(3), 191–207.

Dornbusch, S.M. and Wood, K.D. (1989). "Family processes and educational achievement." In W. Weston, ed. *Education and the American family: A research synthesis*. New York and London: New York University Press. 66–95.

Duffy, A., Glenday, D., and Pupo, N. (1997). *Good jobs, bad jobs, no jobs*. Toronto: Harcourt Brace.

Epstein, D., Elwood, J., Hey, V., and Maw, J., eds. (1998). *Failing boys? Issues in gender and achievement*. London: Open University Press.

Epstein, J. (2001). *School, family, and community partnerships: preparing educators and improving schools*. Boulder, CO: Westview.

Ertl, H. (1999). "Parental involvement and children's academic achievement in the National Longitudinal Survey of Children and Youth, 1994–1995." *Education Quarterly Review,* 6(2), 35–57.

Finnie, R. (2000). "Holding their own: Employment and earnings of postsecondary graduates." *Education Quarterly Review,* 7(1), 21–37.

Fuligni, A.J. (1997). "The academic achievement of adolescents from immigrant families: The roles of family background, attitudes, and behaviour." *Child Development,* 68(2), 351–63.

Gilbert, R. and Gilbert, P. (2000). *Masculinity goes to school.* London: Routledge.

Guppy, N. and Pendakur, K. (1989). "The effects of gender and parental education on participation within post-secondary education in the 1970's and 1980's." *The Canadian Journal of Higher Education,* 19(1), 49–62.

Harris, K. and Marmer, J. (1996). "Poverty, parental involvement, and adolescent well-being." *Journal of Family Issues,* 17(5), 614–40.

Hawkins, A.J., Bradford, K.P., Palkovitz, R., and Christiansen, S.L. (2002). "The inventory of father involvement: A pilot study of a new measure of father involvement." *The Journal of Men's Studies,* 10(2), 83–196.

Head, J. (1999). *Understanding the boys: Issues of behaviour and achievement.* London: Palmer Press.

Hein, C. and Lewko, J.H. (1994). "Gender differences in factors related to parenting style: A study of high performing science students." *Journal of Adolescent Research,* 9(2), 262–81.

Herman, M.R., Dornbusch, S.M., Herron, M.C., and Herting, J.R. (1997). "The influence of family regulation, connection and psychological autonomy on six measures of adolescent functioning." *Journal of Adolescent Research,* 12(1), 34–67.

Ho, E. and Willms, J.D. (1996). "Effects of parental involvement on eighth-grade achievement." *Sociology of Education,* 69, 126–41.

Hoover-Dempsey, K.V. and Sandler, H.M. (1995). "Parental involvement in children's education: Why does it make a difference?" *Teachers College Record,* 97(2), 310–31.

Hoover-Dempsey, K.V. and Sandler, H.M. (1997). "Why do parents get involved in their children's education?" *Review of Educational Research,* 67(1), 3–42.

Hossler, D. and Stage, F.K. (1992). "Family and high school experience influences on the postsecondary education plans of ninth-grade students." *American Educational Research Journal,* 29(2), 425–51.

Jones, C., Clark, L., Grusec, J., Hart, R., Plickert, G., and Tepperman, L. (2002). *Poverty, Social Capital, Parenting and Child Outcomes in Canada.* Report to Human Resources Development Canada, Ottawa, Ont.

Kaplan, E. and Davidson, C. (2002). *Scheduling, worrying, and stepping up: working parents' strategies for providing care to middle-school children.* Working Paper No. 52, Sloan Foundation, USA.

Kmec, J.A. and Furstenberg, F.F. (2002). "Racial and gender differences in the transition to adulthood: A longitudinal study of Philadelphia youth." *Advances in Life Course Research*, 7, 435–70.

Knighton, T. and Mirza, S. (2002). "Postsecondary participation: The effects of parents' education and household income." *Education Quarterly Review*, 8(3), 25–32.

Kralovec, E. and Buell, J. (2000). *The end of homework: how homework disrupts families, overburdens children, and limits learning*. Boston: Beacon Press.

– (2001). "End homework now." *Educational Leadership*, 58(7), 39–42.

Lam, S.F. (1997). *How the family influences children's academic achievement*. New York & London: Garland Publishing, Inc.

Lareau, A. (1989). *Home advantage: Social class and parental intervention in elementary education*. London: The Falmer Press.

Lareau, A. and Horvat, E. (1999). "Moments of social inclusion and exclusion: Race, class and cultural capital in family-school relations." *Sociology of Education*, 72, 37–53.

Luxton, M. (1990). "Two hands for the clock: Changing patterns in the gendered division of labour in the home." In M. Luxton, H. Rosenberg, and S. Arat-Kov, eds. *Through the kitchen window: The politics of home and family*. Toronto: Garamond.

Lynch K. and O'Riordan, C. (1998). "Inequality in higher education: A study of class barriers." *British Journal of Sociology of Education*, 19(4), 445–78.

Lytton, H. and Romney, D. (1991). "Parents' differential socialization of boys and girls: A meta-analysis." *Psychological Bulletin*, 109, 267–96.

Mandell, N. (2002). *Male underachievement in school performance*. Paper presented to the Canadian Policy Research Networks "Access to Post-Secondary Education in Canada: Facts and Gaps" Conference sponsored by the Canada Millennium Scholarships Foundation, Ottawa, April 5–6.

Mandell, N. and Sweet, R. (2004). "Homework as home work: Mothers' unpaid educational labour." *Atlantis*, 28(2), 7–18.

Mann, C. (1998). "The impact of working class mothers on the educational success of their adolescent daughters at a time of social change." *British Journal of Sociology of Education*, 19(2), 211–25.

Matthews, F. (2003). "The forgotten child: The declining status of boys in Canada." *Transition*, Spring, 3–6.

McNeal, R.B. (1999). "Parental involvement as social capital differential effectiveness on science achievement, truancy, and dropping out." *Social Forces*, 78(1), 117–44.

Milne, A.M. (1989). "Family structure and the achievement of children." In W. Weston, ed. *Education and the American family*. New York: New York University Press. 32–65.

Muller, C. (1993). "Parent involvement and academic achievement: An analysis of family resources available to the child." In B. Schneider and J. Coleman, eds. *Parents, their children and schools*. San Francisco: Westview Press. 77–113.

– (1995). "Maternal employment, parent involvement, and mathematics achievement among adolescents." *Journal of Marriage and the Family,* 57, 85–100.

– (1998). "Gender differences in parental involvement and adolescents' mathematics achievement." *Sociology of Education, 71,* 336–56.

Nelson, A. and Robinson, B.W. (2002). *Gender in Canada.* 2nd ed. Toronto: Prentice Hall.

Norris, C. (1999). "Parents and schools: The involvement, participation, and expectations of parents in the education of their children." *Education Quarterly Review,* 5(4), 61–80.

Otto, L.B. and Atkinson, M.P. (1997). "Parental involvement and adolescent development." *Journal of Adolescent Research, 12*(1), 68–89.

Pallas, A.M. (2002). "Educational participation across the life course: Do the rich get richer?" *Advances in Life Course Research,* 7, 327–54.

Parcel, T.L. and Dufur, M.J. (2001). "Capital at home and at school: Effects on student achievement." *Social Forces, 79*(3), 881–911.

Reay, D. (1998a). *Class work: Mothers' involvement in their children's primary schooling.* London: UCL Press.

– (1998b). "Engendering: Social Reproduction: Mothers in the educational marketplace." *British Journal of Sociology of Education, 19*(2), 195–209.

– (1998c). "Classifying feminist research: exploring the psychological impact of social class on mothers' involvement in children's schooling." *Feminism and Psychology, 8*(2), 155–71.

Roscigno, V.J. and Ainsworth-Darnell. (2000). "Race, cultural capital, and educational, resources: Persistent inequalities and achievement returns." *Sociology of Education 73,* 158–78.

Ruble, D. and Martin, C. (1997). "Gender development." In W. Damm and N. Eisenberg, eds. *Handbook of Child Psychology.* 5th edition. Vol. 3: Social, Emotional, and Personality Development. New York: Wiley. 933–1016.

Ryan, B.A., and Adams, G.R. (1995). "The family-school relationships model." In B. Ryan and G. Adams, eds. *The family-school connection: theory, research, and practice.* Thousand Oaks, CA: SAGE. 3–27.

– (1999). "How do families affect children's success in school?" *Education Quarterly Review,* 6(1), 24–30.

Schneider, B. and Coleman J.S. (1993). *Parents, their children and schools.* Boulder, CO: Westview Press.

Scott-Jones, D. (1995). "Parent-child interaction and school achievement." In B. Ryan, G. Adams, T. Gullotta, R. Weissberg, and R. Hampton, eds. *The Family-School Connection: Theory, Research and Practice.* Thousand Oaks, CA: SAGE. 75–105.

Steinberg, L., Lamborn, S., Dornbusch, S., and Darling, N. (1992). "Impact of parenting practices on adolescent achievement: Authoritative parenting, school involvement, and encouragement to succeed." *Child Development, 63,* 1266–81.

Stevenson, D.L. and Baker, D.P. (1987). "The family-school relation and the child's school performance." *Child Development, 58,* 1348–57.

Thorne, B. (1993). *Gender play: Girls and boys in school.* New Jersey: Rutgers University Press.

Tremblay, S., Ross, N., and Berthelot, J. (2001). "Factors affecting Grade 3 student performance in Ontario: A multilevel analysis." *Education Quarterly Review,* 7(4), 25–36.

Trusty, J. (1998). "Family influences on educational expectations of late adolescents." *The Journal of Educational Research, 91*(5), 260–70.

Trusty, J., Robinson, C.R., Plata, M., and Muming, K. (2000). "Effects of gender, socioeconomic status, and early academic performance on postsecondary choice." *Journal of Counseling and Development, 78,* 463–72.

Volman, M. and Ten Dam, G. (1998). "Equal but different: Contradictions in the development of gender identity in the 1990's." *British Journal of Sociology of Education, 19*(4), 529–45.

Wentzel, K. (1998). "Parents' aspirations for children's educational attainments: Relations to parental beliefs and social address variables." *Merrill-Palmer Quarterly,* 44, 20–37.

Weston, W.J., ed. (1989). *Education and the American family: A research synthesis.* New York and London: New York University Press.

Willms, D., ed. (2002). *Vulnerable children.* Edmonton: The University of Alberta Press.

Wilson, P.M. and Wilson, J.R. (1992). "Environmental influences on adolescent educational aspirations: A logistic transform model." *Youth & Society, 24*(1), 52–70.

Zellman, G. and Waterman, J.M. (1998). "Understanding the impact of parent school involvement on children's educational outcomes." *The Journal of Educational Research, 91*(6), 370–80.

11

Exploring Limits to Parents' Involvement in Homework

ROBERT SWEET AND NANCY MANDELL

The period during which children move from elementary to middle school is critical to their educational futures. A smooth transition from the neighbourhood elementary school to the larger middle or high school can be difficult: classes typically are larger, the curriculum is more diverse and challenging, and there are heightened expectations regarding personal autonomy and self-regulated study behaviour. Parents, particularly mothers, play an important role in facilitating their children's adjustment to these changed conditions. During this period many establish closer ties with the school, become more knowledgeable about their children's educational progress, and become more directly involved in their homework assignments (Epstein and Lee, 1995).

Parents' links to the school and their involvement in the home-learning activities of their children are complementary activities. School policies encourage parents to become engaged through volunteering and increased parent-teacher contact. Although relatively few parents become directly involved in the daily activities of the school, most maintain some communication with their child's teacher. School contact is an important means of personalizing the relationship between parents and teachers. Its more immediate purpose, however, may be to better inform parents as to how they can complement the work of the teacher by becoming more active in guiding, supervising, or directly helping their children with their homework (Cooper, 1994; Weston, 1989). From this perspective, homework represents an opportunity for parents to become informed about what the school is teaching and actively involved in their children's academic development.

In such a partnership, the parental role with respect to homework is varied and complex. Parents may, for example, initially regulate or monitor their children's homework in an attempt to instill a sense of commitment towards academic effort and develop the child's ability to regulate homework time. Where children don't comprehend details of the homework task, parents may provide explanation and guidance. And where homework assignments prove too difficult, parents may undertake to teach the child. These various regulatory and instructional activities are generally represented in the literature as defining the major "monitoring" and "helping" dimensions of parents' involvement in the homework process (Eilam, 2001; Hoover-Dempsey, Bassler, and Burrow, 1995).

Contact with the school and involvement in homework represent key elements in the set of management strategies parents employ to help their children navigate the middle school years. Parental engagement in homework is often a response to difficulties faced by children who are struggling with their schoolwork or having difficulty adapting to the changed demands of the middle school (Baker and Stevenson, 1986; Ho and Willms, 1996). However, a more general imperative underlies parental involvement. Post-secondary credentials are increasingly seen as essential to success in the knowledge-based economy, and access to college or university depends on high school achievement and the acquisition of the necessary disposition to study and learn (Gladieux and Swail, 2000). School is now seen as both more important and more competitive. Children's academic success then requires greater involvement and closer monitoring by parents. This addition to the traditional role of parents has given rise to the characterization of childcare as increasingly a process of "intensive" parenting – an expanded set of activities designed to ensure that children successfully establish themselves in the school system.

While we speak of intensive parenting as involving both parents, it is mothers who assume primary responsibility for "educational work" in the family. Griffith and Smith (1990) were among the first in Canada to deconstruct the concept of the "genderless" parent by showing how, discursively, this usage denies the range of responsibilities women assume as domestic labourers. This analysis applies particularly to mothers' attempts to marshal the necessary material and intellectual resources to facilitate children's home study and learning (Mandell, 2001; Reay, 1998; Mandell and Sweet, 2004). An expansion of mothers' domestic responsibilities occurs at a time when women are entering the labour market in unprecedented numbers and finding it difficult to balance the time demands of work and family life (Duxbury and Higgins, 1994) Being a full partner with the school in nurturing children's learning also assumes an educational background that parents do not always possess. Mothers vary in their own level of education and in their understanding of the norms governing classrooms and the larger school system (Lareau, 1989/2000). For reasons of both time availability and personal resources, some parents may find it difficult to become fully and effectively engaged in the homework process.

THE HOMEWORK DEBATE

An established practice of teachers, widely supported by parents, homework nevertheless remains a controversial topic in discussions of home-school relations. Currently, three issues are being debated in the academic literature and popular media: homework's relationship to achievement; the assumption that all parents have the time and the skills to effectively guide their children's home study; and the effect homework has on family harmony and well-being (Gill and Schlossman, 2003).

Proponents of homework claim it enhances older children's achievement and engenders in younger children a positive attitude towards formal learning. It also provides a means by which parents can become involved with the school in the education of their children; and assigned in moderation, it offers the opportunity for developing positive communication between parent and child (Cooper, 1989; 2001). Opponents assert that (more) homework has little demonstrable impact on achievement. It disadvantages children whose parents lack the time, ability, or resources to be meaningfully involved in the home-study process. And, finally, it disrupts families by displacing time that might be better spent in leisure activities (Kralovec and Buell, 2000).

Kralovec and Buell's critique emphasizes the likelihood that children of parents who lack sufficient time or personal resources to become involved in homework will be placed at risk of failure and discouragement. There are, however, important qualifications to this analysis. First, recent evidence indicates that the majority of u.s. high school students (seniors) spend less than one hour per day on homework. And this modest level of engagement has been constant for over twenty-five years (Gill and Schlossman, 2003). Recent analyses of Canadian data indicate a similar pattern among 16-year-olds. (Sweet, 2003). Second, parental involvement is particularly intense during the primary grades but declines through the intermediate and secondary grades as children mature and acquire the self-regulating skills of the autonomous learner (Steinberg et al., 1992; Mandell and Sweet, 2004).

Constraints on Parents' Involvement

Kralovec and Buell (2000) argue that homework and the expectation that parents will supervise the child's home study make unreasonable demands on already busy family schedules. Homework also reinforces existing class differences. Homework then disadvantages children whose parents lack the time or the intellectual and cultural resources to become meaningfully involved.

MOTHERS' EMPLOYMENT STATUS

Several factors limit the available time parents have to engage in their children's schooling. These include family structure and size. Single parents are usually female and many work in sectors of the labour market that are poorly paid and have inflexible work schedules (Duxbury and Higgins, 1994). The number of children in a family imposes further limits on available family time. Each sibling means a further partitioning of the time parents have available to spend with their individual children (Eccles et al., 1993). However, the principal constraint on parents' available time appears to be mothers' work status (Cook and Willms, 2002). As the critics of homework have pointed out, the majority of Canadian women have taken up careers or simply acquired a job to meet the financial needs of their families. After meeting the demands of work, community, and domestic maintenance, parents typically find they have little time to interact with their children about school matters.

Educational work emerged in the early 1900s as a key component of domesticity. The image of the "domestic angel" in the household (Lewis, 1986) expanded to include new definitions of mothering as middle-class women were removed from paid labour after both World Wars and shunted back into the home. Intensive parenting, associated with women's relegation to the private sphere, placed new educational obligations on mothers to aid in the cognitive as well as the emotional development of their children. Norms of "social adjustment" increasingly incorporated ideas of educational achievement. "Good" children became conflated with notions of socially well adjusted and scholastically accomplished children.

Intensive parenting makes mothers primarily responsible for children's academic performance. Definitions of mothers' educational work have expanded slowly from narrow ideas of exacting obedience from children to explicit behavioural demands of schools, to broader definitions in which mothers are expected to anticipate and address children's perceived educational needs. This shift from mothers as "domestic caretakers" to mothers as "social and cognitive developers" meant that, by the 1950s, mothers not only had to ensure their children were dressed, fed, and arrived on time at school but also had to take on explicit teaching tasks through the organization and regulation of homework (Kealey, 1979; Strong-Boag and Fellman, 1991; Trofimenkoff and Prentice, 1977; Weston, 1989).

SOCIOECONOMIC STATUS

Class has long been a marker of educational opportunity and success. As Davies (this volume) indicates, working and middle-class youth do not participate equally in post-secondary education. Distinctions between working-class and middle-class families typically are decided by measures of socio-economic status (SES). Among other things, SES describes major social divisions in the possession of resources that can be applied to educational participation and success. Typical indicators of an aggregate measure of SES include family income, father's occupation, and mother's education. These vary in their relevance to educational development in the home and school settings, with mother's education being particularly sensitive to involvement in planning and preparing for the child's educational future (Cook and Willms, 2002).

Lareau (2003) has outlined basic differences in the child-rearing logics of U.S. middle-class and working-class families. In her analysis, middle-class parents see themselves as obliged to direct or steer the development of their children, largely through organized leisure and skill-building activities. This pattern describes a process of "concerted cultivation" that is similar to other accounts in the literature of intensive parenting by the middle class. The parents of working-class children do not consider the concerted development of children as an essential aspect of good parenting. Working-class children have more control over their leisure time and activities, with is a notable absence of adult-organized activities. In this manner, their parents pursue the logic of "accomplishment of natural growth."

According to Lareau (2003, 2), the significant time and effort committed to cultivating middle-class children's talents and interests leads to a sense of entitlement that helps them adapt well in institutions like schools, which are run by adults and also pursue a concerted cultivation logic. The different experiences of the working-class child are not then compatible with the standards of conduct promoted in schools. As a consequence, a sense of distance and distrust emerges, as well as a constraint in their relations with the school.

Connell (2003) examined class barriers to educational participation in a recent analysis of the relationship between Australian working-class families and the school system. Connell specifically compared educational planning in working-class and middle-class families. This involved families undertaking a series of "projects" – coherent and persisting patterns of action that link the present with some imagined future. Connell found that while no evidence indicated that working class families were not concerned with and interested in education, their focus was primarily on the most direct route to acquiring a vocational credential and gaining entry to the labour market. Middle-class family projects focused more on post-school pathways with considerable attention given to choice of subjects and to maximizing marks.

Connell's research on educational planning also indicated class divisions in the perceived functions of home and school. Class differences in the understanding of appropriate roles for family and school in promoting children's development are of particular importance to an examination of parents' involvement in homework. Reay (2001) and Crozier (1999) studied families in the U.K. and found that while middle-class parents were involved in their children's academic progress and actively communicated with the school, working-class parents tended to rely on a tacit division of labour between school and home in which schools were responsible for teaching and academic advising.

Similar class differences in the relationship between educational participation and the possession of social and cultural capital have been studied in Canada. Using Bourdieu's (1986) analyses of social exclusion processes, Looker (1994) viewed parents as "active capital" in studying the formation and attainment of post-secondary aspirations among high-school students. They found middle-class children better able to navigate the institutional pathways to higher education. In many instances their parents or older brothers and sisters had attended a post-secondary institution and could give sound advice at crucial decision points. A second and related reason was that those parents, siblings, or even friends who had completed higher education were able to dispel the myth that one has to be especially clever to succeed in university. The post-secondary system is less familiar to many working-class parents and the notion that university is "not for me" can deter working-class youth with strong grade point averages from enrolling in university.

PARENTS' RESPONSIVENESS

Despite time constraints, varying educational backgrounds, and differences in the possession and availability of academically relevant resources, parents attempt to respond to their children's schooling needs (Statistics Canada, 2000). As children move through the grades they gradually acquire essential independent learning skills. The progression to autonomy is, however, uneven for many children. Significant numbers of children remain vulnerable to continued low achievement, disenchantment with their school experience, and, in some cases, eventual disengagement and dropout (Audas and Willms, 2001). Recent estimates based on the NLSCY indicate some 17 to 20 per cent of students are lagging in their cognitive, attitudinal, or emotional development (Willms, 2002). These figures are reinforced by recent analyses of the time to high-school graduation in Ontario following major curriculum changes and a move to more rigorous performance standards (King, 2003). Children who are having difficulty adapting to the demands of the school system require considerable parental involvement and support. Even those who are progressing normally through adolescence and the middle school period require time-consuming care and attention (Kaplan and Davidson, 2002).

To the extent that parental involvement is a response to children's school performance, it more likely will be greatest in families with academically vulnerable children. High achieving and motivated students, on the other hand, will be less closely monitored by their parents. The effect of children's individual differences in achievement and attitude is qualified by other factors, notably gender. Evidence indicates that girls' academic aspirations have steadily risen over the last two decades with a corresponding increase in academic achievement and engagement in school activities. Recent gender comparisons indicate the progress of girls in the core curricular areas of math and science, and their continued superiority in composition (Andres et al., 1999; Lauzon, 2002; CMEC, 2003).

PURPOSE

This chapter has two purposes. The first is to examine the contention that homework represents an additional burden to families where the mother is employed or lacks the educational background needed to become effectively involved. The second is to assess parents' ability to respond to individual differences in their children's homework needs. These needs are indicated by parents' perception of children's school achievement and their attitudes toward schoolwork. In examining parents' response to achievement and attitude differences we take into account not only time and resource constraints but also the child's gender. The following questions address time and resource issues and guide our analysis of parents' response to their children's homework needs:

1 To what extent does mothers' employment status constrain parents' involvement in their children's homework?
2 To what extent does mothers' educational level constrain parents' involvement in their children's homework?
3 Given time and resource constraints on mothers' ability to become involved in the homework process, how responsive are parents to their children's individual differences in school performance (achievement and attitude)?

METHOD

Sample and Data

The working sample was drawn from the 1999 Survey of Approaches to Educational Planning (SAEP). The sample was restricted to 2,525 respondents with children enrolled in grades 7 through 9. These grades represent the time following elementary school during which students must establish themselves in a new environment that makes quite different demands on their ability to establish new interpersonal relationships and take greater responsibility for their own learning. In some school districts "middle schools" that comprise grades 7, 8, and 9 have been established as distinct institutions (Kohut, 1988). More important than grade boundaries is recognition that ages 12 to 14 represent the entry into adolescence, a period that can be trying for many youngsters. Whether associated with a middle school or a junior-senior high school, the early adolescent years are a time of adaptation and adjustment that many maintain requires more, not less, parental guidance and support (Steinberg, 1996; Kaplan and Davidson, 2002).

The employment status variable used in examining the constraining effects of mothers' time availability differentiated mothers who were employed in waged work and those who were engaged in domestic labour. The former comprised 75 per cent of the sample. In general, parents with higher levels of education were more likely to be employed – some 85 per cent of those with a university degree held jobs while only 48 per cent of those with less than high school were employed. Mothers' educational backgrounds were defined as attainment and sample proportions were distributed across the levels as follows: less than high school (16 per cent), high school graduation (25 per cent), some post-secondary experience (19 per cent), community college graduates (22 per cent), and university graduates (17 per cent). Where mothers' level of educational attainment includes a post-secondary credential this signifies not only a personal valuing of further education but also a greater awareness of the linkages between current school performance and post-secondary participation. Among mothers with post-secondary experience, distinct vocational and academic orientations may also exist. However, there is no evidence that mothers with trades training or community college diplomas and those with university degrees differ in the importance they assign to their children's school performance (Mandell and Sweet, 2004).

Like other Statistics Canada household surveys, information for the SAEP was obtained from the Person Most Knowledgeable (PMK) with respect to the children in the family. In nearly all cases the PMK was the (target) child's mother, but given the structure of the SAEP it was not possible to isolate and identify them as the respondent in the interview. So, although we employ mothers' work and education as the contextual variables of interest, we nevertheless have to speak of "parents' involvement" rather than "mothers' involvement."

To assess parents' involvement in their children's homework, a Homework Involvement Index was constructed from three items. These included "remind the child to begin or complete homework," "help plan his/her time for getting homework done," and "help with homework when he/she did not understand." In describing the "educational work" of parents in this way it is important to distinguish between those tasks that are part of the general regulation of the child's behaviour, such as setting limits on the amount of TV watched per week, and those that require the presence of the adult or take significant amounts of time (for example, reminding the child to begin his or her homework or actually sitting down with the child and assisting him or her in solving a math problem). A principal components analysis was performed with these variables that accounted for 68 per cent of the total variance in the set. Based on this analysis the index was constructed. The reliability of the scale was .77 (Cronbach's Alpha).

In examining parents' homework involvement as a response to variations in a particular child's academic or attitudinal performance, we constructed an index of school performance that combined achievement and attitude on the assumption that parents respond to both aspects of performance and also that attitude towards schoolwork is correlated with achievement (Renninger, Hidi, and Krapp, 1992). Achievement and attitude indicators were first dichotomized (median splits) and then combined to produce three categories of performance: high achievement and high attitude; low achievement and low attitude; and combinations of both (high-low and low-high).

ANALYSIS AND RESULTS

Table 11.1 describes the pattern of parental involvement in their children's homework in relation to mothers' employment status and educational level. The overall relationship (R^2 = .04) between parental involvement and the structural features of mothers' education and employment status (adjusted for the child's gender) is modest but not unexpected when the range of grade levels is restricted (Willms, 2002). The more specific relationship between mothers' work and parents' involvement in their children's schooling is indicated in the row totals of Table 11.1. Here it can be seen that levels of homework involvement among employed parents are significantly greater than those of at-home parents (b = .028, p < .05). It appears families in which the mother works are prepared to commit more time to monitoring and helping with their children's homework. One would expect that at-home mothers would make use of their greater available time. However, as Gill and Schlossman (2003) point out, comparisons of parental involvement activities depend on the time of day (or night) these typically take place. Homework monitoring and help likely occurs during the evening when most working parents are at home.

The column totals in Table 11.1 indicate a significant, positive association between involvement and increasing levels of education (b = .180, p < .05). This appears consistent with previous accounts of the value of

Table 11.1
Parental Involvement by Education Level and Work Status

Work Status	Level of Education					
	Less Than High School	High School Graduate	Some PSE	College Degree	University Degree	Total
Employed	2.27 (.79)	2.33 (.88)	2.41 (.83)	2.43 (.83)	2.45 (.84)	2.39 (.84)
At Home	2.05 (.82)	2.37 (.86)	2.30 (.82)	2.12 (.83)	2.11 (.68)	2.19 (.83)
Total	2.15 (.81)	2.35 (.87)	2.39 (.84)	2.36 (.84)	2.39 (.83)	2.34 (.84)

Sources: SAEP (1999)

Notes:

a) Cell entries are means and (standard deviations).

b) Total N = 2615

c) $R^2 = .04$

d) Unstandardized coefficients (b) and standard errors (se), controlling for child's sex:

Education (b = .028, se = .084, p < .05)

Work Status (b = .180, se = .038, p < .05)

personal parental experience with the PSE system. However, the relationship does not mark a simple distinction between those with and those without post-secondary experience: parental involvement is lower in families where the mother has not graduated from high school; however, the level of involvement in families where the mother is a high school graduate does not appear to differ from those with PSE experience.

Mothers' educational background then is associated with parental involvement in homework, but this is much qualified by mothers' work status. Although homework interactions may occur in the evening, most working mothers retain additional responsibilities for general domestic labour and consequently have less available discretionary time than at-home mothers. Families with working mothers nevertheless commit more time to their children's homework requirements than do parents with at-home mothers. It is possible that families with working mothers invest more time in homework because they feel the need to compensate for the mother's "absence" (Kaplan and Davidson, 2002). It is more likely, however, that working mothers' higher levels of education account for the greater concern and involvement with homework in these families. Although one might expect the association between parent involvement and mothers' education to hold equally for those engaged in domestic labour, this is not the case: mothers' education seems not to be associated with greater parental involvement where the mother is at home. One can only speculate as to why more at-home mothers with post-secondary experience are less involved than either working mothers with comparable education levels or at-home colleagues who are high school graduates. It is possible parents in families where the at-home mother has a college or university credential invested more time and effort (or did so more effectively) when their children were in primary and intermediate grades so that their children are now more autonomous and better able to make the transition to the middle school (Mandell and Sweet, 2004). Other explanations are possible. Many parents recognize the value of social as well as academic engagement for their adolescent children's school success (Fredricks, Blumenfeld, and Paris, 2004). At-home mothers may be investing more time than working mothers in ensuring that their children are active participants in social, cultural, and athletic activities.

Despite differences in time and educational resources, parents must remain sensitive to their children's school performance. Children who encounter difficulty with the school curriculum or who have developed a negative attitude toward their schoolwork are assumed (by most parents) to be in need of additional homework monitoring and help (Cooper, 1994). To determine whether parents with a range of time commitments and with diverse educational backgrounds can remain responsive to children's needs, we examine in Figure 11.1 how their level of homework involvement is distributed in relation to children's school performance differences. The school performance indicator combines children's achievement and attitude towards schoolwork, as perceived by their parents. The level of parental involvement is adjusted for mothers' work status and educational background, and for the child's gender. Involvement is plotted across the three years that define the middle school period.

The trend lines presented in Figure 11.1 indicate that parents do allocate more time to those children most in need of monitoring and help with their homework. Children who have both low achievement and negative attitudes receive considerably more attention than those who have a mix of achievement and attitude levels; and certainly more than those who are high achievers and possess positive attitudes towards their schoolwork. Parents then are very aware of the more vulnerable children and assign them needed time and attention. Greater involvement with these vulnerable children occurs despite time constraints and resource differences among mothers. And this relatively greater involvement is sustained across the middle school years, although involvement with all groups reflects the general disengagement of parents that begins after the primary grades (Mandell and Sweet, 2004).

CONCLUSION

In this chapter we have examined two of the principal dimensions of parental involvement in their children's homework – mothers' work status and educational background. These were initially presented as constraints

Figure 11.1
Parent's Homework Involvement in Response to Children's
School Performance

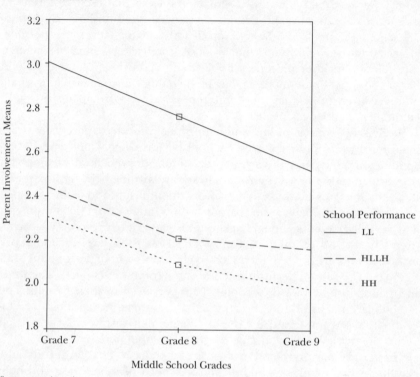

Source: SAEP (1999)

that disadvantaged children in families where the mother worked or lacked familiarity with the post-secondary system. In fact, higher levels of parental involvement were found in families with employed mothers. Higher levels of education were associated with greater parental involvement, but only when the mother was employed. Among families with at-home mothers, the highest level of involvement was provided when the mother had a high school graduation certificate. Mothers' work status and educational background then were associated with complex patterns of parental involvement. Despite mothers' employment obligations and diverse educational backgrounds, parents remain actively involved in their children's homework when this attention is required. Children whose academic performance or whose attitude toward schoolwork is unsatisfactory are more closely monitored and provided with homework help.

Although limited to the middle school years, our results do not support the critics' concern that homework disadvantages children whose parents lack sufficient time to become involved. We examined mothers' employment status as the most relevant indicator of discretionary time in families and because mothers are most directly involved in homework activities through the middle school grades. At-home mothers presumably had more available time. However, parents were more engaged in homework activities in families where mothers were employed. Class differences – indexed by mothers' level of education – were apparent in the pattern of parental involvement within families with working mothers. These were not replicated in the at-home group where a simple association between mothers' level of education and parental involvement was not found. Involvement peaked in families with at-home mothers who had no post-secondary experience, suggesting that interest and commitment to the home-learning environment is not directly determined by the greater familiarity with the post-secondary system that mothers with college or university experience presumably possess.

Several factors are undoubtedly associated with parents' involvement in their children's homework. As Hoover-Dempsey and Sandler (1997) point out, the reasons that parents become involved in their children's schooling are varied and complex. Mothers' employment and education nevertheless are essential dimensions in all accounts and models of parental involvement. Discretionary and leisure time may be less in families with employed mothers. But at certain periods in the child's educational career – school entry and the transition to middle school – priority may be given to homework activities and the necessary time allocated to that activity, especially for academically vulnerable children.

To determine whether these investments are more effectively made by parents with sufficient time and resources requires further work and a data set that contains an objective measure of student achievement (Cook and Willms, 2002). Parental involvement may mediate time and resource differences and, to the extent that it does, the established relationship between parents' social address and children's achievement may be challenged. In the meantime, it appears that, despite time and resource differences, Canadian parents have assigned high priority to involvement in their children's homework.

REFERENCES

Andres, L., Anisef, P., Krahn, H., Looker, D., and Thiessen, V. (1999). "The persistence of social structure: Class and gender effects on the occupational aspirations of Canadian youth." *Journal of Youth Studies*, 2, 261–82.

Audas R. and Willms, D. (2001). *Engagement and dropping out of school: A life-course perspective*. Ottawa: Applied Research Branch, Strategic Policy, Human Resources and Development Canada.

Baker, D.P. and Stevenson, D.L. (1986). "Mothers' strategies for children's school achievement: managing the transition to high school." *Sociology of Education*, 59(3), 156–66.

Bourdieu, Pierre. (1986). "The forms of capital." In J.C. Richardson, ed. *Handbook of theory and research in the sociology of education*. New York: Greenwood. 241–57.

CMEC (2003). *Mathematics learning: The Canadian context. School achievement indicators program (Mathematics III-2001)*. Toronto: Council of Ministers of Education, Canada.

Connell, R. (2003). "Working class families and the new secondary education." *Australian Journal of Education, 47*, 235–50.

Cook, C. and Willms, D. (2002). "Balancing work and family life." In D. Willms, ed. *Vulnerable Children*. Edmonton: The University of Alberta Press. 183–97.

Cooper, H. (1989). *Homework*. New York: Longman.

– (1994). *The battle over homework: An administrator's guide to setting sound and effective policies*. Thousand Oaks, CA: Corwin Press.

– (2001). *The battle over homework*. Thousand Oaks, CA: Corwin Press.

Crozier, G. (1999). "Is it a case of 'we know when we're not wanted'? The parents' perspective on parent-teacher roles and relationships." *Educational Research, 41(3)*, 315–28.

Davies, S. (this volume). A revolution of expectations? Three key trends in the SAEP data.

Duxbury, L. and Higgins, C. (1994). "Families and the economy." in M. Baker, ed. *Canada's changing families: Challenges to public policy*. Ottawa: Vanier Institute of the Family.

Eccles, J.S., Midgley, C., Wigfield, A., Buchanan, C.M., Reuman, D., Flanagan, C., and MacIver, D. (1993). "Development during adolescence: The impact of stage-environment fit on young adolescents' experiences in schools and in families." *American Psychologist, 48(2)*, 90–101.

Eilam, B. (2001). "Primary strategies for promoting homework performance." *American Educational Research Journal, 38(3)*, 691–725.

Epstein, J. and Lee, S. (1995). "National patterns of school and family connections in the middle grades." In B. Ryan, G. Adams, T. Gullotta, R. Weissberg, and R. Hampton, eds. *The family-school connection: Theory, research and practice*. Thousand Oaks, CA: SAGE. 108–54

Fredricks, J., Blumenfeld, P., and Paris, A. (2004). "School engagement: Potential of the concept, state of the evidence." *Review of Educational Research, 74*, 59–109.

Gill, B. and Schlossman, S. (2003). "A nation at rest: The American way of homework." *Educational Evaluation and Policy Analysis, 25(3)*, 319–37.

Gladieux, L. and Swail, S. (2000). "Beyond access: Improving the odds of college success." *Phi Delta Kappan, 81*: 688–92.

Griffith, A. & Smith, D. (1990). What did you do in school today?: mothering, schooling and social class. *Perspectives on Social Problems, 2*, 3–24.

Ho, E. and Willms, D. (1996). "Effects of parental involvement on eighth-grade achievement." *Sociology of Education, 69*, 126–41.

Hoover-Dempsey, K.V., Bassler, O.C., and Burrow, R. (1995). "Parents' reported involvement in students' homework: Strategies and practices." *The Elementary School Journal*, 95(5), 435–50.

Hoover-Dempsey, K. and Sandler, H. (1997). "Why do parents become involved in their children's education?" *Review of Educational Research*, 67, 3–42.

Kaplan, E. and Davidson, C. (2002). *Scheduling, worrying, and stepping up: Working parents' strategies for providing care to middle-school children*. Working Paper No. 52, Sloan Foundation, USA.

Kealey, L., ed. (1979). *A Not unreasonable claim: Women and reform in Canada, 1880s-1920s*. Toronto: Women's Educational Press.

King, A. (2003). *Double cohort study: Phase 3 report*. Toronto: Ontario Ministry of Education.

Kohut, S. (1988). *The middle school: A bridge between elementary and high schools*. 2nd edition. Washington, DC: National Education Association.

Kralovec, E. and Buell, J. (2000). *The end of homework: How homework disrupts families, overburdens children, and limits learning*. Boston: Beacon Press.

Lareau, A. (1989/2000). *Home advantage: Social class and parental intervention in elementary education*. 2nd edition. London: The Falmer Press.

– (2003). *Unequal childhoods: Class, race, and family life*. Los Angeles: University of California Press.

Lauzon, D. (2002). "Gender differences in large-scale, quantitative assessments of mathematics and science achievement." In P. de Broucker and A. Sweetman, eds. *Towards evidence-based policy for Canadian education*. Montreal: McGill-Queens University Press. 355–72.

Lewis, J., ed. (1986). *Labour and love: Women's experiences of home and family, 1850–1940*. London: Basil Blackwell.

Looker, D. (1994). "Active capital: The impact of parents on youth's educational performance and plans." In L. Erwin and D. MacLennan, eds. *Sociology of education in Canada*. Toronto: Copp-Clark Longman. 164–87.

Mandell, N. (2001). "Women, families and intimate relations." In N. Mandell, ed. *Feminist issues: Race, class and sexuality*. 3rd edition. Toronto: Prentice-Hall. 193–218.

Mandell, N. and Sweet, R. (2004). "Homework as home work: Mother's unpaid educational labour." *Atlantis*, 22(2), 7–18.

Reay, D. (1998). "Engendering social reproduction: Mothers in the educational marketplace." *British Journal of Sociology of Education*, 19(2), 195–209.

– (2001). "Finding or losing yourself? Working-class relationships to education." *Journal of Education Policy*, 16(4), 333–46.

Renninger, K., Hidi, S., and Krapp, A., eds. (1992). *The role of interest in learning and development*. New Jersey: Erlbaum.

Statistics Canada (2000). *Growing up in Canada – 1994–95*. Ottawa: Statistics Canada.

Steinberg, L. (1996). *Beyond the classroom*. New York: Simon & Schuster.

Steinberg, L., Lamborn, S.D., Dornbusch, S.M., and Darling, N. (1992). "Impact of parenting practices on adolescent achievement: Authoritative parenting, school involvement, and encouragement to succeed." *Child Development, 63,* 1266–81.

Stevenson, David L. and Baker, David P.(1987). "The family-school relation and the child's school performance." *Child Development, 58,* 1348–57.

Strong-Boag, V. and Fellman, A., eds. (1991). *Rethinking Canada: The promise of women's history.* Toronto: Copp Clark Pitman.

Sweet, R. (2003). *Adolescent school engagement: Immigrant and non-immigrant comparisons.* Proceedings of Ninth Annual Ritsumeikan-UBC Seminar. Ritsumeikan University, Kyoto, Japan.

Trofimenkoff, S. and Prentice, A., eds. (1977). *The neglected majority.* Vol. 1. Toronto: McClelland and Stewart.

Weston, W.J., ed. (1989). *Education and the American family: A research synthesis.* New York and London: New York University Press.

Willms, D., ed. (2002). *Vulnerable children.* Edmonton: The University of Alberta Press.

Willms, D. & Flanagan, P. (2003). *Ready or not? Literacy skills and post-secondary education.* Report to Canada Millennium Scholarship Foundation. Montreal, QC.

12

Educational Planning in Families: Issues and Future Research Directions

PAUL ANISEF AND ROBERT SWEET

Important economic, social, and cultural changes in post-industrial and knowledge-based societies necessitate a better understanding of the role played by parents in planning and preparing their children for post-secondary education. Most Canadian parents now assume that their children must acquire a post-secondary education if they are to achieve some measure of success in their lives. Certainly the link between higher levels of education and meaningful, well-remunerated employment is generally acknowledged. But parents have also come to understand that the route to post-secondary education is a great deal more uncertain than it was in the past. This uncertainty results from a combination of factors, primarily the increased competition for limited spaces within universities and community colleges, and rapidly rising tuition fees. Careful planning and preparation by parents is now essential to ensure the post-secondary education prospects of their children. Parents appear to have assumed responsibility for preparing their children to "make the grade" and new partnerships with the state and with the schools have redefined the nature and scope of their parenting role. In this volume the authors have examined changes in the social and institutional environments within which parents must undertake the educational planning task. They also have begun to examine the planning processes engaged in by Canadian parents and their children.

The assessments of changing government policies towards student support in Part 1 of this volume are necessarily selective and limited in providing a cross-sectional picture of a constantly changing situation. The first objective of this chapter then is to identify some of the emerging contextual elements that should be taken into account in future analyses of the social and economic context of the educational planning environment. A second objective is to synthesize findings from the analyses of educational planning in Part 2. In the light of this overview, we identify some of the research directions to be followed if we are to fill important gaps in our knowledge and to develop a better conceptual understanding of the educational planning process.

THE CHANGING CONTEXT
OF EDUCATIONAL PLANNING
AND PREPARATION

Key social and economic changes have occurred or are occurring and these form a new context for planning and preparation by Canadian families. These changes challenge established structural certainties and introduce a note of risk and uncertainty among families that plan and prepare for their children's post-secondary education. Bell and Anisef in chapter 3 and Bell and Jones in chapter 4 have highlighted, from both a Canadian and an international perspective, some of the fundamental problems surrounding issues of access and the equitable financing of post-secondary education. In this section, we address additional on-going changes to the relationship between family and state that have an impact on parents' financial ability to ensure post-secondary accessibility for their children. We also indicate important demographic shifts and ethnic differences in the youth population that will influence demand for greater post-secondary access. These factors require further research to accurately gauge institutional capacity.

Increasing Population Size and Demand for Post-Secondary Education

The 19 to 24-years-old population, currently approximately 2.5 million, is expected to peak between 2011 and 2016 at nearly 2.7 million and to subsequently decline between 2016 and 2021 when it should stabilize at 2.3 million (CMEC, 2003, 6). Coupled with rising post-secondary educational expectations, population growth serves to increase demand for spaces within a post-secondary system that is no longer expanding. The dramatic growth in Canada's post-secondary system witnessed in the 1960s was not duplicated in the 1990s. The resulting shortage of post-secondary capacity exacerbates competition among equally well-qualified youth. Restrictions on accessibility have been noted by parents who are now more inclined to invest in the preparation of their children for a competitive entry to the post-secondary phase of their schooling.

Growing Cultural Diversity

Since 1990 an average of 225,000 immigrants of all ages have been arriving in Canada each year and, with the decline in the birth rate, more than half of the demographic growth is attributed to immigration. A vast majority of immigrants come to Canada from non-Western countries such as Asia, the Caribbean, Latin America, and Africa (CMEC, 2003, 11). As a result, the proportion of visible minorities among the school-age population has increased measurably since the 1991 census. In Toronto and Vancouver visible minorities account for over 40 per cent of youth (aged 5 to 24). These changes in cultural diversity have a strong impact on teaching, support services, and school dynamics, and require adaptations in the home-school learning environment to meet the needs of immigrant students (Anisef and Kilbride, 2003). Increases in poverty levels among recent immigrants, indicated by results from the 2001 census (Picot and Hou, 2003) suggest that some immigrant families will have additional difficulties finding the required financial capital to support their children's post-secondary plans.

The situation of Aboriginals in Canada, particularly in some provinces and territories, contributes to the challenges faced by parents of Aboriginal youth. Because the birth rate among the Aboriginal population is higher than that of non-Aboriginals, the proportion of the school-age population with Aboriginal ancestry is significant and is growing in Census Metropolitan Areas (CMAs) and areas outside CMAs in some provinces and territories. By way of illustration, in Manitoba, 30 per cent of the school-age population outside of the Winnipeg CMA claimed Aboriginal ancestry in 2001; the equivalent proportion for Saskatchewan was 26 per cent outside CMAs. The non-CMA parts of Alberta, British Columbia, and Newfoundland and Labrador, as well as the CMAs of Thunder Bay and Sudbury are other areas of the country with a high and growing proportion of the school-age population with Aboriginal identity in 2001 (CMEC, 2003, 14).

Continuing Increases in Private Expenditures on Education

Public expenditures in Canada altered in the 1990s as governments made it a priority to eliminate deficits. As a consequence, governments' capacity to increase expenditure for education has been limited insofar as the needs of this sector have been compared directly with those of other public priorities, including health. Thus, public expenditure on education declined slightly to $62.8 billion in 2001, from above $64 billion between 1993 and 1995 (CMEC, 2003, 35). Conversely, the expenditure on health increased to $72.8 billion in 2001. Note that until 2000 governments in

Canada, as a whole, spent more money on education than on health. In contrast, private expenditure on education rose from $9 billion in 1997–98 to $10.5 billion in 2001–02, a 16 per cent increase; of this increase fully $7.4 billion was spent at the post-secondary level. In addition, rising student debt levels among post-secondary graduates and the significant gap in participation between people from low versus middle and high income backgrounds raise concerns about post-secondary student access, especially at the university level (CMEC, 2003, 37, 45). These changes in expenditures on education illustrate the continuing shifts in government spending priorities and the increased reliance on individuals and families to shoulder the costs of post-secondary education. It also suggests a more precarious situation for parents, who must help their children finance post-secondary study costs.

VULNERABILITY IN FAMILIES: INCOME AND TIME LIMITATIONS

Social science amply documents that family income exerts a significant influence on children's academic performance and that living in a low-income environment often impedes school readiness among pre-school children and decreases the likelihood of these children eventually attending university. Though some evidence indicates a modest decline in recent years in the proportion of the school-age population (ages 5 to 24) living in low-income families (based on after-tax low-income cut-offs), the proportion in 2000 was only somewhat lower than 15 per cent. However, this proportion varies widely by family type and by region. By way of illustration, in 2000, 7 per cent of all children living in two-parent families were found to be in low-income circumstances. Among children living in single-parent families the proportion was 25 per cent and for those children not living with their parents, most of whom were between 19 and 24, the proportion was 35 per cent. Among specific groups the rates of child poverty are much higher. Some 34 per cent of visible-minority children, 41 per cent of Aboriginal identity children, and 42 per cent of immigrant children live below Statistics Canada's low income cut-off limit (Campaign 2000, 2003).

Fundamental changes in the Canadian labour market have directly affected the ability of families to increase their incomes and negotiate their way out of poverty. The introduction of technology into the workplace and the reorganization and restructuring of work has favoured workers with higher levels of education. Those with a high school credential (or less) have been relegated to a growing segment of the labour market characterized by what Vosko (2002) terms "precarious work." Employment in this sector has seen the gendering of jobs, continuing income polarization, and occupational sex-segregation. For those in the lower tier of an increasingly polarized work force, priorities in domestic expenditures are necessarily given to the more immediate needs of food, shelter, and transportation. Little is left over for the intellectual and social development of children through activities such as field-trips, musical instruction, or participation in cultural and social activities, all considered to contribute to the academic engagement of children. Nor are funds available for long-range planning initiatives like RESPs.

Time is another casualty of the greater economic pressures being placed on families. In approximately 54 per cent of employed Canadian families, both mother and father are working (Duxbury and Higgins, 2002). Many are working at minimum wage, frequently with two or more employers. Research on work-life balance in families indicates the increases in family stress levels imposed by low-waged work and multiple jobs (Campaign 2000, 2003).

STRUCTURES AND PROCESSES IN EDUCATIONAL PLANNING

Preparation for post-secondary education has two aims – access and completion (Gladieux and Swail, 2000). The planning and preparation in which parents engage while children are of pre-school and school age involve fostering in them the attitudes, dispositions, and achievement levels necessary for access to the post-secondary system. These qualities also must be sufficient to ensure continued academic success and, ultimately, post-secondary graduation.

We have indicated some of the markers of an increasingly competitive "planning and preparation" environment for parents as they attempt to facilitate their children's entry into and progression through the school system. The ability to respond to calls for greater involvement and investment in their children's education clearly differs among families. Difficulties in adapting to this more competitive environment are more apparent for families with certain characteristics, or combinations of characteristics.

Social structural factors such as region, family structure, gender, disability, ethnicity, immigrant status, and socio-economic status (SES) exert an influence on children's achievement. All either directly describe or are embedded in the family and are experienced and expressed in that context. To the extent that these place limits on resources, the family and its members become more vulnerable. Current research on the notion of vulnerability in children focuses on family SES and its consequences for school adjustment and performance (Willms, 2002).

Structural limitations frequently combine to make the task of preparing children for school success more complex. For example, the sole provider in about 90 per cent of single-parent families is a female, typically employed in a low-paying job. Low income then combines with other resource limitations of single parenthood to limit the opportunities of children in these families. Although they adopt complex configurations, these structural features of individuals and families serve to distinguish those that are more or less able to meet the demands of educational planning. Families constrained by structural factors are less capable of responding to the requirements of a changed and increasingly competitive planning environment. They are more vulnerable in being denied the necessary resources with which to invest in their children's schooling. The consequence is a reduction in the likelihood of their children being able to participate successfully in post-secondary education.

The position of structurally vulnerable families may be further compromised by the intentions and behaviours of parents. The processes involved in planning – principally the transfer or activation of social and cultural forms of capital – differ among families and may be more effectively undertaken by parents with better education and more responsible jobs. Parents with higher levels of education and more experience and knowledge of the school system and the world of work are in a better position to advise their children on the pathways they should follow to a post-secondary entry. They also possess and are able to develop in their children the attitudes and dispositions needed to succeed in the classroom, an essential antecedent to gaining entry to the post-secondary system. To the extent that these capacities are associated with "class" distinctions, low-SES families become more vulnerable and existing structural differences are further reinforced.

As indicated, the relationship between families and government with respect to financing children's post-secondary education is continually changing. Governments at both the federal and provincial level are attempting to reduce their fiscal commitments. Reductions in public education expenditures mean that vulnerable groups are less able to gain access to colleges and universities. Evidence of inequalities affecting low-income, single-parent, visible minority, and immigrant families is emerging but requires further research. This should be undertaken within a complex framework, as suggested by Finnie in chapter 2. Specific programs such as the Millennium Scholarship Foundation and the Canadian Educational Savings Grants should be scrutinized and their efficacy determined. Are they demonstrably broadening the social base of access or further narrowing the opportunities of vulnerable families? Proposed innovations like the Independent Learning Accounts scheme also require careful consideration based on comparative study of their usefulness in other countries. Monitoring the financial partnership between families and governments is essential to defining and understanding the context within which educational planning takes place in families.

Research Gaps and Priorities in Educational Planning

In this section we consider the findings and research implications of the chapters in Part 2. The discussion will be organized under three main headings: (1) post-secondary institutions and students; (2) family structure, social structure, and dynamics of education planning and preparation; and (3) parental involvement in children's schooling.

Post-Secondary Institutions and Students

Scott Davies in chapter 6 argues that Canadian parents now have very high educational expectations for their offspring, with the vast majority expecting their children to attend a post-secondary institution, especially university. He finds, however, that while the new economy is greatly altering the level of parental expectations, it is not diminishing class differences among parents. Canadian families, Davies predicts, will likely remain educationally stratified, albeit at higher levels, with some of the most disadvantaged and low-achieving students aspiring to enter community colleges. Davies discusses three implications or hypotheses that warrant further research study. He suggests, first, that universal expectations are likely to bring more institutional stratification in higher education; second, that the new era of post-secondary attendance is not likely to be any more equitable than in the past – that is, school expansion does not ensure equity; and third, that as more ill-prepared students enter higher education, particularly community colleges, we should expect to see a rise in student attrition and disappointment.

The analysis conducted by Davies raises additional questions that require research elaboration. For example, we need to delve more deeply into why parents have generally "bought into" the need for post-secondary education. What are their reasons? To what extent are parents pushing a post-secondary education on children who lack the academic background or motivation to persist through three or four years of university or community college? If, as Davies suggests, we are moving towards universal access and our colleges are taking on disproportionately more students that subsequently require remedial education or, even with remedial education, experience difficulty completing their program of study, what are the labour market consequences for them and for the larger Canadian society? What are the implications for the knowledge-based economy when the internal stratification bar of our post-secondary educational system is raised ever higher? Are the potential and talents of our youth being wisely employed? Or are increasing numbers of young people being channelled in the wrong directions? Though the value of trade-vocational programs in Canada is generally recognized, enrolments tend to either remain stable or decline (CMEC, 2003, 11). As Schuetze reveals in chapter 5, Individual Learning Accounts could be an innovative response, consistent with a life-long learning approach, to some of the thorny problems concerning participation by under-educated adults in post-secondary education or training. Yet without a change in the attitudes and values that emphasize university over other forms of post-secondary education, youth will continue to restrict their educational choices. Their parents, convinced that a university or community college education is the only pathway to success in the labour market, may choose to ignore or downplay the important achievement markers in their children's school performance record. Increasing the intake of students who are not academically prepared also has important research and policy implications, particularly for community colleges.

Family Structure, Social Structure, and Dynamics of Education Planning and Preparation

A key assumption underlying the analysis of different facets of educational planning and preparation by various authors in this collection is that structural factors (and their complex interrelationships) are important for more completely understanding the dynamics of educational planning and preparation as they occur in Canadian families. In chapter 8 Anisef, Frempong, and Sweet illustrate this in their analysis of regional variations in post-secondary expectations, revealing first that in rural and urban areas alike, parents anticipate that a greater proportion of their female children will attend university. The authors then employ gradient analysis to demonstrate that for those at the high end of SES, few gender or regional differences in the development of university expectations by parents can be observed. Such variations are quite marked when the low and middle ranges of the SES are examined closely and these are strongly linked to gender. The analysis further reveals that parents within low and middle SES families appear responsive to increases in school performance and positive attitudes towards school and suggests that such efforts may yield substantial increases in university expectation levels. Demonstration projects within rural areas that build on these findings and particularly target male children should be encouraged. Strong efforts to partner with schools and parents in developing effective strategies for enhancing positive attitudes towards school and school performance should be developed and researched.

Anisef, Frempong, and Sweet indicate the value of viewing various post-secondary outcomes in terms of the intersection of different structural antecedents – in this instance, socio-economic status, gender, and region. They demonstrate that, in conjunction with region and gender, class matters with regard to understanding variations in post-secondary expectations. In high SES households, no variation in university expectations based on region and gender was found; however considerable variation was found in low and middle SES households. These findings emphasize the importance of examining intersections among various structural and social-psychological factors in an effort to more finely tune models of educational planning and preparation. At the policy level, the development of models that incorporate intersections may serve to better identify the groups that require more aggressive forms of intervention and the substance of interventions that could produce positive outcomes.

In conducting such action research, better efforts should be made to elaborate the crude definition of "rural" employed in this chapter. Additional and more detailed analysis would employ postal code information available through the Data Liberation Initiative (DLI) to link census and postal code information to better specify common and more sophisticated dimensions of "rural" across diverse regions of Canada. We also suggest a re-analysis of SAEP data with respect to the new dimensions of "rural" that are generated. While the authors find that parents' indication that children will leave home to study is a good marker of university expectations, the DLI also allows us to calculate the distance that children would need to travel to access the nearest university or community college (Frenette, 2002).

The authors reveal one finding that has policy significance and also requires additional research. They report that within rural areas male children are particularly advantaged with regard to their parents employing RESPs as a post-secondary savings strategy. Regression analysis then revealed that, for children from families of comparable SES backgrounds and with similar school outcomes, an investment by parents in RESPs increased the chances of children attending university by 67 per cent. Future research studies should follow through on these findings. Why do rural parents privilege the post-secondary futures of their male children by investing in RESPs for them? Why do rural parents remain resistant to making similar financial investments in their female children, despite clear evidence that females are strongly motivated in school and also perform well?

The analyses conducted by Thiessen and Looker in chapter 7 and White, Marshall, and Wood in chapter 9 explored the strength of effects that family organization and structure exert on the educational planning dynamics within families. Thiessen and Looker pose the following question: Are educational savings divided equally between siblings or are savings more likely for children with certain characteristics, thereby diminishing post-secondary educational opportunities for those who do not possess these characteristics? The authors' findings indicate that equity is the paramount feature of parental educational investments. They report that between 80 and 90 per cent of the total variation in Canadian parents' educational savings are due to differences between families in their educational savings behaviour, rather than differential treatment of siblings within the family. Furthermore, the authors reveal that unequal savings for children are primarily a function of two intertwined family life-course factors: the age of the parent and the age of a given child. Thus, as attendance at a post-secondary institution becomes imminent for the first-born child, parents make savings for this child their priority. In the face of inadequate resources to meet all educational needs, parents dynamically balance current needs with anticipated future resources, rather than deciding to invest more in one child than another. These findings are reassuring from a equity perspective. They suggest that parents, rather than employing particularistic criteria in making financial investments in their children's post-secondary education, employ equitable standards in allocating resources.

Thiessen and Looker also point out that, in the small number of cases where parents hold different expectations for individual children, this is reflected in their savings patterns. What remains unclear is the basis for these differential expectations. Whether one child does better in school or seems to like school more is certainly a factor, but it is a surprisingly small factor. Perhaps parents have distinct careers in mind for their children, and base their savings decisions primarily on the educational requirements of these careers, discounting to some extent the child's current academic performance. This discussion (and that of Davies) indicates that we know very little about the bases for parent's aspirations and expectations.

The analysis conducted by White, Marshall, and Wood reveals that the role of family structure in accounting for child outcomes is relatively minor. This modest relationship of structure to current savings behaviour may simply reflect the greater financial resources of two-parent families. The authors argue that their analysis supports the view that parental encouragement is a more important and useful measure of social capital than is family structure. Theoretically, this suggests a critical "rethinking" of family structure as a measure of social capital in the family. The analysis by White et al. offers insights that are complementary to those revealed by Thiessen and Looker, emphasizing that family structure per se may be of less importance to educational planning and preparation than family engagement and parental encouragement. From a policy research perspective, it may be more productive to address variations in parental skills when transmitting cultural and social capital to their children and in their ability to activate cultural and social capital.

Parental Involvement in Children's Schooling

In chapters 10 and 11, Mandell and Sweet and Sweet and Mandell address issues related to the growing involvement of parents in their children's schooling. Involvement in this context is seen as an aspect of "intensive parenting." Reflective of parents' growing concern about their children's futures, intensive parenting requires a degree of involvement that taxes the time and resources of many parents, especially mothers. Parents perform at least two roles in facilitating their children's school performance: first, establishing contact with the school administration and the child's classroom teacher; second, developing a home-learning environment that complements the work of the school.

Mandell and Sweet are primarily concerned with the home as a site where parents may invest the time and effort needed to realize the aspirations they hold for their children's educational futures. In examining the home-learning environment, they focus on parental monitoring of children's home learning and encouragement of their academic efforts. Together, monitoring and encouragement strategies are consistent with an authoritative parenting style aimed at developing in children the self-regulating and autonomous behaviours needed for academic success. Mandell and Sweet explore parental involvement style in relation to class and gender. They raise the question of whether parents with fewer personal resources are disinclined to devote time to monitoring and encouraging their children's academic efforts. The authors also explore the extent to which parent-child interactions are gendered; that is, do parents interact differently with sons and daughters on school matters? Mandell and Sweet thus attempt to assess the extent to which social structure constrains important processes of involvement.

The authors conclude that class differences are present in the behaviours of parents to some extent but differences in involvement are quite marked – boys appear to require more guidance in managing their homework. This finding is not necessarily at odds with Thiessen and Looker's finding of equity in the distribution of family resources. In responding to the greater need of boys for help and guidance in becoming effective students, parents may be pursuing general equity by compensating for the imbalance in their sons' and daughters' performance.

The finding that parental involvement varies most obviously across gender lines – with boys requiring greater attention – has important research implications. While one can conclude that gender has receded as a marker of female stratification, it has emerged as a distinct indicator of boy's underachievement. This has become a recognized issue among educators, but has received less attention in the research literature on parenting.

Sweet and Mandell approach the issue of parental involvement in children's schooling from a somewhat different perspective. They first observe that parental engagement in nearly all cases involves mothers. And while mothers' involvement in their children's schooling peaks in the primary grades it nevertheless continues into early adolescence and is critical in

helping children navigate the transition from elementary school to middle
and high school. The assumption that mothers are primarily responsible
for the school performance of children is then linked to assertions by critics of homework that parents have too little time and others lack the necessary resources to be effective in helping their children. The results in this
chapter indicate that despite time and resource limitations, parents remain
engaged in the homework process where the child's academic performance indicates that this is needed.

While mothers' "educational work" has not been recognized in the
work-family balance literature, it represents a significant part of their domestic time commitment and is constrained by waged employment. The
findings in these two chapters are consistent with other research on the relationship between SES and parental engagement in children's schooling.
But they do not resolve the issue of whether parental involvement mediates
the relationship between SES and children's achievement. That remains a
task for future research.

SUMMARY AND CONCLUSIONS

We are entering a new era of social policy, one that is beginning to acknowledge the complexities inherent in living within a global and knowledge-based
society, which must contend with constant and often unpredictable change.
Higher education and advanced training are now recognized by individuals
as necessary for social mobility and by governments as essential for economic
productivity. Government policies have, however, shifted to families the
greater part of the financial burden for post-secondary education. This may
be borne by the middle class but makes lower-income families particularly
vulnerable to exclusion from post-secondary education. Federal and provincial governments not only are insisting on a new partnership with potential
students and their parents in respect of post-secondary study costs but also
are altering policies towards lower-income families. Instead of relying solely
on direct poverty alleviation measures, new policies of social inclusion are
proposed (Jensen, 2004; Klasen, 1998). Social inclusion goals include ad-
dressing problems of poverty and the conditions that make families vulnerable. However, they rely more on providing opportunities for individuals to
participate in public and community life and in this way develop the competencies to realize their personal goals. Among the critical societal institutions
of social mobility is the post-secondary education system. Making available
the necessary educational tools for personal and social advancement, however, requires that educational institutions be accessible. They may not be accessible to all and the financial support policies of governments will have to
undergo significant modification if the most vulnerable are to access and,
equally important, complete a university or college program of study.

There is compelling evidence, found within this book and provided by other researchers, that access to post-secondary education depends to some considerable extent on social capital – the relationships and networks that exist among people, organizations, and communities. Children's successful learning experiences from kindergarten to high school graduation depend on the availability in families of sufficient resources in the form of relevant cultural capital. Despite distinctions in social position and capital resources, parents now have primary responsibility for planning and preparing for their children's future education. This volume has only begun to examine the processes of educational planning that occur in families. Much remains to be done.

REFERENCES

Anisef, P. and Kilbride, K., eds. (2003). *Managing two worlds: The experiences and concerns of immigrant youth in Ontario.* Toronto: Canadian Scholars Press.

Campaign 2000 (2003). *Honouring our promises: meeting the challenge to end child and family poverty.* Retrieved August 2004 from www.campaign2000.org

Council of Ministers of Education Canada (2003). *Education indicators in Canada: Report of the pan-Canadian education indicators program.* Toronto: CMEC.

Duxbury, L. and Higgins, C. (2002). *The 2001 national work-life conflict study: Report one.* Ottawa: Health Canada.

Gladieux, L. and Swail, S. (2000). "Beyond Access: Improving the odds of college success." *Phi Delta Kappan, 81,* 688–92.

Jensen, J. (2004). *Catching up to reality: Building the case for a new social model.* Family Network Research Report F-35. Ottawa: Canadian Policy Research Networks.

Klasen, S. 1998. *Social exclusion and children in OECD countries: Some conceptual issues.* Munich: Department of Economics, University of Munich.

Picot, G. and Hou, F. (2003). *The rise in low-income rates among immigrants in Canada.* Analytical Studies Branch Research Paper Series (11 F0019 MIE-198). Retrieved August 2004 from http://www.statcan.qc.ca

Vosko, L. (2002). *Rethinking feminization: Gendered precariousness in the Canadian labour market and the crisis in social reproduction.* Robarts Canada Research Chairholder's Series. Retrieved August 2004 from www.Yorku.ca

Willms, D., ed. (2002). *Vulnerable children.* Edmonton: The University of Alberta Press.

Index

access, post-secondary, 94, 99, 103, 107, 117; capacity, 79; demand-supply, 20–2; equilibrium, 23–5; equity, 18; parents' view of, 166; social basis of, 45, 76; and tuition fee increases, 59

adjustment, children's: school attitude, 279; school engagement, 237; social engagement, 226, 235

aspirations. *See* expectations

Bourdieu, Pierre, 251, 278

Canada Student Loan Program: administration, 64; calculating student need, 60–2; changes, 63; number and distribution of loans, 64–6

capital
– cultural, 251, 255
– human, 80, 131, 171, 228
– social: dimensions of, 233; in families, 154, 229; and peers, 157

Coleman, James, 223, 227

college: expectations for, 157; "for all," 161; and remedial education, 161

debt: and access, 292; aversion to, 4; direct and indirect components, 94; level, 63, 95; and Millennium Scholarships, 4; negative consequences, 73; in the Netherlands, 99; repayment, 94, 98–9, 103, 106, 110, 114; in Sweden, 112; and work-study programs, 78

education
– parent: as cultural capital, 278; instruction for parents, 243; level, 79–82
– post-secondary: institutional stratification, 160; mass and universal, 150; participation, 38, 43, 79, 91–3; returns on investment, 157
– rural: system, 207. *See also* region, geographic

employment, mother's: family-work conflict, 276

environment, home-learning: as cultural capital, 157; gendered, 256–7, 266; physical, 253

exclusion, social, 56, 278

expectations: among minorities, 152–3; antecedents, 213; and aspirations, 162, 205; gender differences in, 153–4; parental, 150; rural, 151; and social stratification, 152

families
– disadvantaged. *See* families, vulnerable, *and* status, socio-economic
– vulnerable: low income, 292; precarious work, 292–4. *See also* status, socioeconomic

family
– financial capacity, 94; income, 71; loan default, 72–4; loan repayment, 66–71

– financial resources: household expenditures, 76; intergenerational transfers, 168; student contribution to costs, 77–8
– interactions, 224; time spent with children, 185, 187
– resource allocation factors: academic merit, 173, 187; affective closeness, 173, 186; birth order, 172, 184; effort, 174, 190; equality, 169, 182; gender, 170, 184; parental expectations, 176, 195; student need, 175, 192
– structure, 223, 252–4; measurement, 224; as process, 251; research importance, 224
– theories: investment in children, 227; rational choice, 228, 230–1, 241–2
fees, tuition: and demand, 22; deregulation, 87; increases, 3, 93; international comparisons, 118; and supply, 25
funding, post-secondary: by government, 58–60

gender: and course selection, 250; masculinity crisis, 266; and parenting, 170, 257; and participation, 40, 71, 91, 249; and rural effects, 208, 211; and school achievement, 261, 279; stereotypes, 250

homework: debate, 275; and parental involvement, 278

inclusion, social, 208, 300; school, community, and state, 219–20
individual learning accounts, 137; in Canada, 141–2; financing models, 134–6; and privatization, 132, 142; in Sweden, 139; in U.K., 137; in U.S., 140
institutions, post-secondary: capacity, 18, 22, 34, 45, 290; hierarchy, 157, 176; leave home to attend, 211; proximity, 203

learning
– lifelong, 127; models, 130–2
– life-wide, 128; formal, non-formal, informal, 129, 132–3; learner-centred, 129

parenting
– intensive: class differences, 277; mother's role, 274, 276, 281; school involvement, 273
– style: authoritative, 254; encouragement, 232, 234, 257; monitoring, 258
partnerships: families and government, 4, 294; parents and school, 5, 274

performance, academic: achievement, 212; attitude, 212; children's, 225, 278, 283–4
planning
– educational, 204–6; dimensions, 5, 6; research gaps, 295–8; and social class, 277; and social context, 290–1
– financial: and family size, 182; parents' intentions and behaviours, 238–9; relationship to parental expectations, 215–17; savings instruments, 211; savings intentions, 238–9; savings strategies, 179, 189, 211
policy
– student support: assumptions, 89; debt relief, 74; implementation, 101, 105, 111–12, 115; in Australia, 105; in Denmark, 108; in the Netherlands, 96, 97; in Sweden, 111; in the U.K., 100; loans, 211; public-private study costs, 88, 94; savings, 211; transparency, 119; voucher system, 109
– tuition, effects of: on access, 59; on family savings, 28–9; on fees, 30–3; on increase in student aid, 25–8; on institutional capacity, 34–5; on low-income families, 76
programs, student support: Canada Education Savings Grant (CESG), 4, 77, 93; Canada Student Loans Program (CSLP), 3, 60; Canada Millennium Scholarship Foundation, 4, 17; direct costs, 115; grants versus loans, 112; maintenance-living costs, 116

region, geographic: community social structures, 206, 219–20; rural-urban definitions, 206

status, socio-economic (SES), 276–7; and aspirations, 254; and family income, 252–3, 82; and institutional choice, 94; and mother's education, 253; and post-secondary expectations, 212–13; reproduction of, 266
surveys
– related: Post-secondary Education Participation Survey (PEPS), 40; School Leavers Survey (SLS), 43; Youth in Transition Survey (YITS), 40, 43
– Survey of Approaches to Educational Planning (SAEP): data anomalies, 178; project history, 6

transitions, school, 283

university: preferences for, 151, 157